Policy Analysts
in the Bureaucracy

To Russ

Policy Analysts

in the Bureaucracy

Arnold J. Meltsner

UNIVERSITY OF CALIFORNIA PRESS

BERKELEY   LOS ANGELES   LONDON

University of California Press
Berkeley and Los Angeles, California
University of California Press, Ltd.
London, England
Copyright © 1976, by
The Regents of the University of California
ISBN 0-520-02948-8
Library of Congress Catalog Card Number: 74-30529
Printed in the United States of America

4 5 6 7 8 9 0

Contents

Preface

This is a book about policy analysts in the federal government in Washington. I had three reasons for writing it: to improve the effectiveness of analytical activities by exploring the political and bureaucratic dimensions of the policy analyst at work; to extend our knowledge about bureaucracy; to develop teaching material for schools of public policy and public administration, such as my own, which are educating future policy analysts and public administrators.

While writing the book I had several different types of readers in mind. I wrote for students, who are never quite sure that policy analysts actually exist. I also had in mind those teachers of public policy analysis who, while well trained in their disciplines, have not had the benefit of bureaucratic experience. Then there are the practitioners and academicians who are trying to understand and improve the current process of policy analysis and the formulation of public policy. Given these various sorts of potential readers, I made no attempt to write a pure book for a single audience. Precise texts and focused studies will be written as policy analysis continues to evolve. Meanwhile, I have taken my snapshot of policy analysts and their work at this point in time.

The reader no doubt will be frustrated by my frequent use of examples and words such as "some," "many," "most." But analytical behavior, such as it is, has not converged to the point where there is always a central case to work with, an average analyst from whom one can assess deviations. We are dealing with an emerging profession—one that is just beginning the process of self-identification and standardization—and therefore it is essential to record the variances in behavior.

One caveat: at various places throughout the book I describe examples of bureaucratic skill or tactics. For the most part I report on the perceptions of the current generation of analysts concerning which bureaucratic devices are efficacious and work. This is not to say that I am recommending these devices, without reservations, for most would-be analysts. There are policy analysts who have no intention of working in the federal bureaucracy, and there are always some who will work there but will not care about being influential. More important, for many of these devices I have no way of knowing that they do work or at least of determining, in a scientific sense, the conditions under which they do. The point is that this study deals with the perspective of today's bureaucratic analyst, and that perspective surely is incomplete.

Much of the literature on analysis is utopian. In contrast, this is an empirical and inductive study—it is about what policy analysts say they do. Sometimes, for purposes of clarification or illustration, I interject my own experience as an analyst. Sometimes I cannot refrain from a critical or normative comment, but I try to delay most of this until the last chapter. What I am trying to do is to paint a realistic portrait of analysts in the federal bureaucracy. Reviewers of the manuscript have felt that the portrait is accurate, but some of them are worried that I may be throwing out the baby with the bathwater. Despite an occasional tone of pessimism, or perhaps cynicism, I am quite sanguine about the utility and future of policy analysis. I feel that we are better off because of the efforts of policy analysts in the bureaucracy.

By looking at what policy analysts say they do, we can enhance our understanding of policy analysis. If we do not like the picture, we will at least know where we can start to change it. If we do like it, then we can spread the word.

Acknowledgments

Many people have helped me write this book. I want very much to thank the policy analysts who sat with me and educated me about the current state of policy analysis; I am sure some of them were wondering about the costs and benefits of my interviews. Then I want to thank the policy analysts and social scientists who read the manuscript and gave me examples of analytical practice, raised important questions, and prevented misinterpretation, particularly Edward B. Berman, Guy Benveniste, William A. Carlson, John Fedkiw, Gene H. Fisher, Edward Friedland, Joseph Froomkin, Paul Y. Hammond, Herbert Kaufman, Martin H. Krieger, Frank Levy, Laurence E. Lynn, Jr., Robert H. McManus, Donald B. Rice, Michael B. Teitz, William A. Vogely, Jeffrey Weiss, Michael J. White, Richard W. White, Jr., and Walter Williams.

My colleagues in the Graduate School of Public Policy at the University of California, Berkeley, have my great appreciation. Our school provides a uniquely nourishing and stimulating environment in which to do research on questions of public policy, and the continual encouragement and comments from such people as Allan P. Sindler and Aaron Wildavsky have been extremely helpful. So too have been the interest and advice of Eugene Bardach, Robert Biller, Judith Blake Davis, Lee Friedman, David Kirp, and William A. Niskanen, Jr., and of Steve H. Hanke, a visiting professor at our school. A number of students have not only given me critical comments but have tracked down footnotes and helped me organize my material, and for this I thank Christopher Bellavita, Bonnie McKellar, James Marver, Lynn Miller, and Lois Robertson. Richard Winne was most helpful in commenting on the manuscript and in conducting sensitive and perceptive interviews in Washington, D.C. William J. McClung, of the University of California Press, deserves credit for helping me find a suitable title for the book and for his general interest in my work.

Among the most critical resources for any analyst are a good editor and a good secretary; without the capable assistance of Barbara Phillips and Shirley Thatcher, my manuscript would never have achieved what clarity and cogency it has.

I want to thank the Ford Foundation for its support of the Graduate School of Public Policy. From time to time this support made it possible for me to conduct parts of my research. Similar acknowledgment is due the University of California Committee on Research, whose grants also facilitated my research and the production of the manuscript.

Finally, I am most grateful to William Gorham and Worth Bateman of the Urban Institute for providing me with an office and facilities so that I could have a place to hang my hat in Washington. They were generous not only with space but also with their own time.

Although the merits of the manuscript are due in large part to this long list of people, I must claim for myself the blame for its deficiencies.

Introduction

Nobody can live in America without experts. They fix our cars, remove our warts, and help us pay our taxes. Our public bureaucracies also rely on experts, on professionals and specialists. We have a bureaucracy filled with scientists, engineers, physicians, and accountants—professional people with specialized technical knowledge. Bureaucracies have usually been good at dividing up the work and encouraging specialization, but today the specialist is also likely to be a professional. We have double experts; for example, the chemical engineer trying to prevent air pollution or the internist developing programs to help alcoholics. Among this army of bureaucratic experts there marches another expert. He is a professional—sometimes a specialist, sometimes a generalist. He helps formulate solutions to problems of public policy. He is a policy analyst in the bureaucracy and this book is about him.

Many people are unfamiliar with the term "policy analyst." But what the analyst does is quite familiar. Consider that the policy analyst provides information about the consequences of choosing different policies. Getting information to make policy decisions is nothing new. As certain as the winter solstice occurs every year, public bureaucracies continue to seek out information; and the latest in such intelligence gathering is policy analysis.[1] Only a few

1. Undoubtedly the terms "policy analysis" and "policy analyst" have a long history, but they began to be used by practitioners and academicians with greater

years ago it was systems analysis.[2] Working for a melange of nonprofit research corporations, the systems analyst made a splash in the operations of the federal bureaucracy. Perhaps the splash was not as big as President Johnson would have liked when he spread the program-budgeting gospel throughout the federal establishment in 1965. Nevertheless, today there are a number of offices that analyze, review, coordinate, and evaluate federal programs. The people in these offices are known by a variety of civil service titles: economist, budget administrator, program analyst, operations researcher, and management analyst. Some of these public servants merely shuffle paper and are not analysts. Many, however, not having any of their own programs to operate, are filling staff advisory roles. In this analytical residue from the days of program budgeting, and in a number of old and new policy analysis offices, we find the emerging roles of policy analysts.[3]

Attempts at defining policy analysis are usually unsatisfying. Here, for example, is Walter Williams' definition: "Policy analysis is a means of synthesizing information including research results to produce a format for policy decisions (the laying out of alternative

---

frequency in the late sixties. For example, see Yehezkel Dror, "Policy Analysts: A New Professional Role in Government Service," *Public Administration Review* 27 (September 1967): 197–203; and the various papers in U.S. Congress, Joint Economic Committee, *The Analysis and Evaluation of Public Expenditures: The PPB System*, vol. 3, 91st Cong., 1st sess., 1969. Yehezkel Dror was kind enough to share his notes on this subject with me and believes that Charles E. Lindblom was the first to use the term "policy analysis," in Charles E. Lindblom, "Policy Analysis," *American Economic Review* 48 (June 1958): 298–312. As to the term "policy analyst," he stated in a letter to me: "My subjective image is that I invented that term, but I may be wrong, in the sense that someone else may have used it before without my being aware of it, or even in the sense that I may have picked it up somewhere without remembering doing so." He first used the term in the above-cited article.

2. For a discussion of the confusion over the differences between systems analysis and policy analysis, see Steven E. Rhoads, *Policy Analysis in the Federal Aviation Administration* (Lexington, Mass.: Lexington Books, D. C. Heath and Co., 1974), pp. 1–5.

3. Program budgeting at the federal level was known as PPB or PPBS, standing for Planning-Programming-Budgeting System. In 1971, the Office of Management and Budget discarded much of the formal reporting requirements of PPB, but its analytical component was retained. See Allen Schick, "A Death in the Bureaucracy: The Demise of Federal PPB," *Public Administration Review* 33 (March-April 1973): 146–56; and John A. Worthley, "PPB: Dead or Alive?" *Public Administration Review* 34 (July-August 1974): 392–94.

choices) and of determining future needs for policy-relevant information."[4] Given its generality, most practitioners and students of policy analysis would agree with this definition. But when we get down to specifics, agreement on what policy is evaporates. Is decision making about policy a choice between alternative national health insurance schemes or between bedpans? Is policy what we aspire to rather than what we are doing now? Nor would one find agreement on the notion of alternative choices. Sometimes analysts feel it is important to define the problem and change the understanding of policymakers without cluttering up the discussion with options and alternatives. For myself, a policy analysis would be incomplete without alternatives. Then, again, what information is relevant for policy purposes? For many public policy problems, a little economic reasoning coupled with a little political sensitivity will go a long way. But there are policy problems for which merely a little political sensitivity is insufficient—as in reforming national electoral campaign practices—and there are policy problems that require specialized technical information. In short, I do not think it worthwhile to define policy analysis in general. Instead, the approach of this book is to illustrate the current state of policy analysis by examining the political and bureaucratic aspects of policy analysts at work.

A ROUGH GUIDE

Let us assume that four central factors are influential in the production of analysis: the analyst, the client, the organizational situation, and the policy area. Imagine these as a set of concentric circles of influence. The analyst occupies the innermost circle, which is bounded by the next largest one, that of the analyst's immediate client. The third circle, enclosing the first two, is the organizational situation in which both analyst and client work, and the final circle is the policy area, which encloses the other three. Placing the analyst at the center indicates the subject matter of this book but not necessarily the analyst's centrality in the making of public policy. Generally, the circles closer to the analyst probably

4. Walter Williams, *Social Policy Research and Analysis: The Experience in the Federal Social Agencies* (New York: American Elsevier Publishing Co., 1971), p. xi.

exert a greater influence on him and his behavior than do the circles farther away. The distant circles contain much of the substance of policymaking as we know it.

ANALYSTS

Each factor in the production of analysis is an umbrella concept which can be broken down into a number of variables. Analysts, for example, as discussed in chapter 1, differ from each other by their expectations, which stem from the norms of their professional training, their formal education, their beliefs about reality, and their motivations to make an impact on policymaking. No single analytical type exists, and at least three general types can be distinguished: the technician, the politician, and the entrepreneur. Because there are different types of analysts, what is a successful analysis for one will be a failure for another.

In part, the policy analyst sets his own expectations. Technicians feel that they have been a success when their peers like their work. Politicians are happy when their immediate boss or client is happy. Entrepreneurs are not happy unless their efforts change the allocation of resources and people's lives for the better. Intellectually, analysts in general perceive that the output of analysis should be measured in terms of implementation or actual social and behavioral change. But given their distance from the executors of policy, many are satisfied with peer approval or when the client accepts their recommendations and acts on them, regardless of the ultimate fate of their advice.

Because of self-imposed and situational constraints, the policy analyst in the bureaucracy is not at present a Lasswellian policy scientist. He does not always have the knowledge or opportunity to work on the critical and long-range problems of public policy which one might hope policy scientists would address.[5] The pressures of

5. Lasswell's expectations were for work on "fundamental problems of man in society, rather than upon the topical issues of the moment." See Daniel Lerner and Harold D. Lasswell, eds., *The Policy Sciences: Recent Developments in Scope and Method* (Stanford, Calif.: Stanford University Press, 1951), p. 8; more recently, in Harold D. Lasswell, *A Pre-View of Policy Sciences* (New York: American Elsevier Publishing Co., 1971), he restated his high expectations: "We provisionally define the policy sciences as concerned with knowledge *of* and *in* the decision process. As a professional man, the policy scientist is concerned with mastering the skills appropriate to enlightened decision in the context of public and civic order. As a professional man who shares the scientist's disciplined

time and the need for legislative ideas push the analyst into the role of an operating official who makes use of the state of the art of scientific understanding. He is more likely to compile information about a particular policy than to develop a theory of the process of policymaking. So the bureaucratic policy analyst is more a bureaucrat than a policy scientist. And, like other bureaucrats, he sets his own standard of performance and has his own private objectives. He has superiors or clients he wishes to please. He wants to be useful and used, and in order to do so he competes with other bureaucratic experts.[6]

CLIENTS

Clients differ on why they want analysis. Some need information to help make decisions to reduce or hedge against uncertainty. A few want analysis because it is fashionable. Others want analysts to explain or justify decisions that have already been made. Clients also differ in their capacity to listen to analysts and to clarify problems. The diverse backgrounds, education, and experience of clients result in particular styles: some adopt an executive, managerial posture; others are more reflective and intellectual. As we shall see in chapter 6, to talk about a client is to talk about a relationship between the analyst and client. Over his career the analyst will enter into many of these relationships. Sometimes he will be unaware of his ultimate client. Sometimes he will wish he did not know his client. He will find that the productive relationships are those in which there is informed trust and confidence rather than the inclination for one party to make a victim of the other.

Whether he knows it or not, every analyst needs a client. Without a supportive client, his work will not be used—which is an anathema even to a cerebral pen-and-pencil bureaucrat. As Department of Defense analysts Enthoven and Smith explain,

The most effective motivating factor for Systems Analysis studies was the knowledge that they would be seriously considered in the real decision-making process, not merely referred to in the after-decision advocacy

concern for the empirical, he is searching for an optimum synthesis of the diverse skills that contribute to a dependable theory and practice of problem solving in the public interest" (p. 13).

6. For an analysis of bureaus and bureaucrats, see Anthony Downs, *Inside Bureaucracy* (Boston: Little, Brown and Co., 1967), particularly pp. 49–111.

phase. Good systems analysts were willing to work for McNamara and Clifford because they knew that when they did good work it would be acted upon and would influence decisions.[7]

This motivation to have his advice used puts the policy analyst in the company of centuries of experts. "Few experts," Kelly tells us, "wish to prevail, to *become* the power—indeed their temperament and inclination are usually otherwise—but their function demands that they should wish their ideas to prevail."[8] Moreover,

Power attracts advice. Where a measure of centralized power exists, there, too, is the expert, sometimes more in sun, sometimes more in shade; in harmony with the rationale of power or working to change it; sometimes the "lion beneath the throne," sometimes the god Thoth handing the sacred letters to the temporal ruler and adding to his divinity. Leader of a priestly cult or sponsor of a busy corps of technocrats, the expert stands with a foot in knowledge and a foot in power, and prepares the arcane for practical use.[9]

How firmly the analyst is anchored in power or knowledge is an open question. The client partially answers the question because it is he who may determine the context, the organizational situation, in which the policy analyst works.

ORGANIZATIONAL SITUATION

Within the organizational situation both clients and analysts assume positions and titles. The analyst may be called an economist, for example, and his client an assistant secretary. In many cases there will be a number of analysts working for a collective client. A critical aspect of the situation is the distance between client and analyst. Propinquity or the lack of it can be expressed in terms of hierarchical levels between client and analyst, for example, or in terms of whether the analyst is an inside advisor or an outside consultant; but however it is measured it significantly affects the ease of communication between client and analyst. Besides propinquity or distance, the organizational situation provides a view or vantage point which orders and makes

7. Alain C. Enthoven and K. Wayne Smith, *How Much Is Enough? Shaping the Defense Program, 1961–1969* (New York: Harper & Row, 1971), p. 323.
8. George A. Kelly, "The Expert as Historical Actor," *Daedalus* 92, no. 3 (summer 1963): 543.
9. *Ibid.*, p. 533.

salient various policy problems and solutions. Finally, the activities of the particular organization and the degree of support it gets from its environment can also affect the production of analysis.

Policy analysis goes on in a variety of organizational situations. There are policy analysts working in profit and nonprofit consulting and research firms and in universities as faculty or members of campus research institutes. Each of these situations has certain characteristics that influence the analyst and his work. For illustrative and comparative purposes, consider a faculty member of a university who is doing policy analysis. Despite his reliance on external financial support, he can determine more than his bureaucratic counterpart can his own study agenda. He can look at a broad range of policy alternatives, some of which may have been suppressed in the bureaucracy. His time perspective for conducting his work is more open; he is likely to think that he has years rather than overnight. He may work by himself or with a few colleagues and research assistants. His work has a built-in quality control which is maintained by colleagues, peers, and the standards of his profession. Like other scientists, he works hard to develop his reputation.[10] Whether his work makes an impact on policy depends on his client, or on his own promotional efforts, or on the persuasiveness of his ideas. In any event, he is quite distant from the policy process and is not likely to see himself as powerful.

In the bureaucratic context, our main focus throughout the book and particularly in chapter 5, the analyst's study agenda is more often determined by other people. He looks at a fairly narrow range of alternatives, most of which have been discussed in the literature and the newspapers; he has a short span of time in which to do a study and generally works on only a fraction of it, on a small piece of a group effort. Because of the pressure of time and the lack of information, the level of technical competence for the study may not be elegant. However, the analyst compensates for his misgiv-

10. Most bureaucratic analysts are also concerned about their reputations, but unlike scientists they usually remain anonymous so the client can get the credit. In contrast, Merton observes that, for scientists, "Eponymy, not anonymity is the standard. And . . . outstanding scientists, in turn, labor hard to have their names inscribed in the golden book of firsts." Robert K. Merton, *The Sociology of Science: Theoretical and Empirical Investigations*, ed. Norman W. Storer (Chicago and London: University of Chicago Press, 1973), p. 302.

ings about quality by having a strong sense of personal power because of his immediate relationship to the policy and budgeting process of the federal government.

This is not to say that all the elegant work goes on in universities or that scholars or intellectuals have an atrophied sense of personal power in policymaking because of ivory-tower seclusion. No doubt each situation contains a considerable range of characteristics; and as the analyst and his work move toward proximity to government, such characteristics merge. The distinction between the outside, independent advice of the intellectual and the inside expertise of the policy analyst blurs in the situation of bureaucratic policymaking. If the outsider wants to be listened to, he has to put on the clothes of the insider. Robert Merton encapsulates the dilemma:

he who innovates is not heard; he who is heard does not innovate. If the intellectual is to play an effective role in putting his knowledge to work, it is increasingly necessary that he become a part of a bureaucratic power-structure. This, however, often requires him to abdicate his privilege of exploring policy-possibilities which he regards as significant. If, on the other hand, he remains unattached in order to preserve full opportunity of choice, he characteristically has neither the resources to carry through his investigations on an appropriate scale nor any strong likelihood of having his findings accepted by policy-makers as a basis for action.[11]

Once inside the encrusted and dark bureaucracy, the policy analyst sees himself as an intellectual with a flashlight of innovation. He thinks he is free to reflect and be a force for change. But the bureaucratic context does not allow the analyst to act like other intellectuals. Analysis, the gathering of advice, is a serious business; it has little of the playfulness that is often associated with intellectuals. In Lewis Coser's opinion, the intellectual "delights in the pleasures of sheer intellectual activity. Just as with the artist, the beauty of a set of formulas or a pattern of words may, for the intellectual, outweigh its practical application or immediate usefulness. Ideas, to him, have far more than mere instrumental value: they have terminal value."[12] In this sense, and without being pejorative, most analysts are not intellectuals. They see ideas as having instrumental value, as this analyst makes clear:

11. Robert K. Merton, *Social Theory and Social Structure* (Glencoe, Ill.: The Free Press, 1957), p. 217.
12. Lewis A. Coser, *Men of Ideas: A Sociologist's View* (New York: The Free Press, 1965), p. ix.

The more effective policy analysts really masquerade as bureaucrats. They're committed to an idea which they translate into a program, and spend much of their time making sure that the program is accepted by their department, by the Budget Bureau and, later, Congress. Some policy analysts, like myself, . . . set themselves a more modest course affecting the level of programs and lobbying in the agency, department, and the Budget Bureau to make sure their opinions are finally translated in the request for appropriation.

Not all the energy of the analyst goes into pushing ideas. Because there is a certain amount of pathology in the bureaucracy, expressed as an exaggerated concern for turf and personal aggrandizement, the policy analyst, like other bureaucrats, engages in a struggle for recognition, for status, and for reward. The bureaucratic context denies him a monopoly on knowledge. His is not the only voice whispering in the client's ear. Indeed, there is conflict over knowledge in a bureaucracy manned by professionals. Take analysis in the field of health: a physician relying on his own skills and values can urge a particular health measure; the analyst (usually not a physician) finds it difficult to argue against the suggestion on substantive grounds and thus falls back to his typical question, At what price? Often he is an expert in explaining the consequences of the preferences of other experts.

POLICY AREA

Finally, the policy area provides the analyst with a selected group of policy problems and their accompanying knowledge base and politics. Sometimes the politics of a policy area are open and conflict ridden; sometimes they are closed, involving technical issues and technical men. Some policy problems have a dimension of crisis to them. Others are more chronic; they never seem to go away and are subject to incremental solutions. Independent of the need to cope with problems is the available base of knowledge from which to derive solutions. We know more about building a highway, for example, than about educating children. And even when we know a great deal, the politics of the policy area may be so intractable as to require the assembling of unwieldy coalitions and the creation of public consensus.

The policy area is an important factor in the production of analysis, but we can treat it only tangentially in this book. We shall look at many different policy problems—from those of housing to outer space—but our focus will be on the analyst and on how he works across policy areas. Our net is not fine enough to distinguish precisely how the character of that work changes with the policy area. [13]

ANALYTICAL PROCESSES

When analyst, client, organizational situation, and policy area are combined, the result is an analytical process. Depending on how the factors are defined, we can easily see the possibility of a number of different kinds of processes. An analytical process involving a physicist working for a scientist on a presidential advisory committee on the pollution of space by experiments and probes should be quite different from one involving a city planner working for the city manager with a group of citizens on trying to prevent further deterioration of housing. But all analytical processes result in something we commonly call "advice." Policy analysis, I argue in chapter 2, is a form of advice.

Advice as a product can be characterized by a series of typical questions. Was the advice of sufficient quality and scope to meet the requirements of policymakers? Did it arrive in sufficient time to be used by policymakers and to mesh with other political forces to enhance acceptance? Did the advice help to make or support decisions? In short, was the advice congruent with the imperatives of policymaking? In addition, was it parsimonious, was it one-time or frequent, and was it robust enough to survive the many hurdles of policy adoption and implementation?

THE POLICY ANALYST AS POLITICAL ACTOR

Like the bureaucrat, the policy analyst is a political actor. This may sound strange to many practitioners of the craft who perceive

13. I feel comfortable with this approach, because fine works on American politics and the policy process have already been published. Furthermore, a comparative study of the interaction between policymaking and policy analysis would be a major undertaking in itself. For an excellent introduction to the policy process, see Charles E. Lindblom, *The Policy-Making Process* (Englewood Cliffs, N.J.: Prentice-Hall, 1968); Charles O. Jones, *An Introduction to the Study of Public Policy* (Belmont, Calif.: Wadsworth Publishing Co., 1970); and Graham T. Allison, *Essence of Decision: Explaining the Cuban Missile Crisis* (Boston, Mass.: Little, Brown and Co., 1971).

themselves and their work as "objective." Bureaucrats for many years have claimed, from conviction and as a matter of tactics, that administration is politically neutral. For both bureaucrat and policy analyst, an image of neutrality and objectivity is important. The counterimage might undermine the basis of their expertise and influence.

Now it is true that only a handful of policy analysts are aggressively and openly political. Not many of them run around assembling coalitions and working for partisan causes. Consider the story of the chief analyst of a large shop or office who was asked by his political superiors to make a contribution to a political campaign; he refused on the grounds that he was already sacrificing income by working for the government. Most analysts leave politics to their clients, but this does not mean they are not political. If they are not political in a grand way, they are certainly so in a small way. Whether they know it or not, they make a number of political decisions.

First, they decide to work in the bureaucracy rather than someplace else. While they have a number of reasons for doing so, making an impact on policy is a prevailing incentive. Second, they choose a client for whom to work. Even novice analysts have some measure of choice, and they want to make sure that they will have a supportive client, one who will push their ideas. Third, anticipating policy payoffs and the informational needs of their client, they select certain problems for analysis. Selecting some problems means leaving others out. Fourth, they define the selected problem and get closure on it. They choose assumptions and the ends to be accomplished. Their analyses state what is desirable and what can be ignored. Finally, they communicate the results of their work in such a way that clients will be receptive to analytical preferences.

In the following pages we will see that the problems besetting policy analysts and their varied behaviors are almost entirely predictable and understandable in light of what we know about the bureaucracy and its effect on its inhabitants. Why should this be so? Although there are important exceptions and reservations, I suggest that the following characteristics of bureaucratic policy analysts explain their susceptibility to bureaucratic influences: (1) they are members of an emerging profession without enforceable standards and sanctions;[14] (2) they lack an adequate base of knowledge and associated theoretical paradigms; [15] (3) they have tenuous communication networks;[16] and (4) they are low resource, low status political actors.[17] All of these characteristics add up to a lack of social and political support from outside of the bureaucracy. Therefore, it is not surprising that analysts succumb to bureaucratic forces, folkways, and incentives. Nor is it surprising to find such a variety of analytical behavior and roles, because the bureaucratic context has sufficient discretion or slack to allow the mutual expectations of both client and analyst to operate. The irony is that the analyst starts off expecting to influence the bureaucracy, but it is the bureaucracy that influences him. By working in it he takes on

14. Students of professions have suggested a number of essential attributes of a profession. Wilensky, for example, points out that there is a sequence or a process of professionalization: "There is a typical process by which the established professions have arrived: men begin doing the work full time and stake out a jurisdiction; the early masters of the technique or adherents . . . set up a training school . . .; the teachers and activists then achieve success in promoting more effective organization, first local, then national . . . Toward the end, legal protection of the monopoly of skill appears; at the end, a formal code of ethics is adopted." Harold L. Wilensky, "The Professionalization of Everyone?" *American Journal of Sociology* 70 (September 1964): 145–46. While we do not have to accept the notion of a sequence, it is still clear that policy analysis is not an established profession. Its practitioners work at it full-time, and there are a number of schools. The profession, however, lacks an organization to cover its various activities and has no monopoly of skill and no formal code of ethics.

15. Of course, this characteristic does not apply to situations where the policy analyst's education is congruent with his work in a policy area (e.g., an economist trained in public finance working for the Treasury Department). For many policy areas, however, such as in social policy, there is no such thing as a paradigm that can force a convergence of behavior. Ideology is just as likely to influence outcomes as the analyst's inadequate knowledge.

16. Work on income maintenance comes to mind as an exception, because analysts in a number of agencies kept in touch with each others' efforts. Some analysts had a "Thursday club" for sharing ideas; see Vincent J. Burke and Vee Burke, *Nixon's Good Deed: Welfare Reform* (New York and London: Columbia University Press, 1974), p. 55. Despite the efforts of many analysts to keep in touch with the relevant work going on throughout government and the research community, I was surprised to see how easy it is for an analyst to become isolated and not be aware even of previous work in his own agency. Research on the analyst's versions of "invisible colleges" is needed.

17. One can immediately point out that analyst Charles L. Schultze was the head of the Budget Bureau or that Alice M. Rivlin is Congress' chief analyst. But within the politics of an agency, most policy analysts are tied to the power of the client; and outside of the agency, compared with policymakers, they are relatively anonymous.

a particular identity. As Goffman points out, "an organization can therefore be viewed as a place for generating assumptions about identity."[18]

In chapter 1 we will start our exploration of these assumptions by examining bureaucratic analytical roles. We will see that some analysts become bureaucrats but others do not. Then in chapter 2 we will turn our attention to what analysts do. The bureaucratic context is such that the analyst does a variety of tasks, many of which are responsive to the policymaker's need for short-term, ad hoc advice and support. The scheduling of analytical work is accomplished through the bureaucratic hierarchy and is discussed in chapter 3. How the analyst works on a policy problem is our next concern, and in chapter 4 we point out the importance of working styles learned in the bureaucracy. In chapter 5 we concentrate on the bureaucratic context itself as a means to facilitate or inhibit the solving of problems. As it turns out, some analysts like some bureaucrats engage in advocacy and pathology. Then in chapter 6 we examine clients, and here the bureaucratic context encourages several different clients and a separation of beneficiary from client. The link between client and analyst is communication, and in chapter 7 the bureaucratic tendency to use formal communications is pointed out by discussing the various modes of interaction between analyst and client.

As political actors, policy analysts are part of the political process. They have the potential to stimulate the public bureaucracy with uncomfortable questions and fresh ideas. But there are obstructions in this path of innovation. Some of these originate from the analyst and his own conception of his role and the place of analysis. Other impediments are, to some extent, outside his control; they have to do with the inadequacy of policy knowledge and with deficiencies in organizational and political arrangements. As we shall see in the concluding chapters of this book, whether policy analysts can be different from their past and present colleagues in the bureaucracy is an open question.

18. Erving Goffman, *Asylums: Essays on the Social Situation of Mental Patients and Other Inmates* (Garden City, N.Y.: Anchor Books, Doubleday and Co., 1961), p. 186.

1

Analysts

Policy analysts are a highly variegated species. Neither their professional education nor their exposure to bureaucratic folkways has encouraged the development of a single standardized type. True, they are all staff men and women without a program of their own to manage, and all of them are in one way or another in the business of giving information or advice. But at that point similarities end and differences appear—not only, as would be expected, because of educational background, but also because of the policy area, the agency, and the client. A Harvard economist working on defense is not quite the same animal as a Chicago economist working on education. Even if we could hold these various situational and background factors constant, policy analysts would still differ. They come to their jobs with different incentives. They have different internalized standards of accomplishment and success, and even those with a common education rely on different skills or strengths in the performance of their tasks. Moreover, they have different views about policy analysis and its impact on policymaking.

During 1970 and 1971 my research assistant and I interviewed 116 federal policy analysts.[1] As an educated group of bureaucrats

---

1. A detailed discussion of the methodology of the study, along with a list of questions used in the interviews, will be found in the appendix. The interviews were nondirective and the questions open-ended. The analysts were not selected

they were certainly not representative of the nation's population: 99 percent had completed college and 90 percent had obtained graduate degrees. Thirty-nine had Ph.D.'s; six had legal degrees; and there was one M.D. and one C.P.A.; fifty-five had various masters' degrees. Forty-six were economists.[2] Fourteen had backgrounds in other fields of social science, such as sociology and political science; twenty-one came from science and engineering; and twenty-seven had studied in such professional fields as planning, social work, and business and public administration.

Because the analysts were selected mostly on the basis of personal recommendation (my own and other analysts'), the sample cannot be considered representative, in a statistical sense, of the entire population of federal policy analysts at the time of the interviews. I suspect that the sample was fairly representative of senior (more likely to be a CS-15 to 18 than a GS-11), central-departmental (none from the field and only a few from lower echelon bureaus or agencies), and highly educated analysts who then worked in Washington.

To provide a framework for discussion in this chapter, the interviews were analyzed and the 116 analysts were classified by their political and analytical strengths or skills. Twenty-seven analysts with high political and high analytical skills were classified as *entrepreneurs;* 41 analysts with high political and low analytical skills as *politicians;* and 48 analysts with low political and high analytical skills as *technicians.* Although we encountered no analyst without skill in either area, there must be a few in the federal government. These could be called *pretenders,* and they will not concern us in this book. The classification, therefore, yielded four types of analysts, as shown in Chart 1.

---

randomly but rather on the advice of analysts, other informants, and from a listing of 563 senior executive civil servants associated with program analysis. This listing was very kindly provided to me by the United States Civil Service Commission.

2. This bias toward economists was due to a number of factors. First, most of the analysts whom I had known and whom I selected initially for interviewing were economists. Their recommendations for possible interviewees usually led to other economists. Second, the program budgeting, PPB system, shops originally relied heavily on economists and many of these economists continued to work as policy analysts. Third, we picked up a number of economists simply by interviewing in departments where the profession was directly related to the policy area, such as public finance economists in Treasury. In my view, policy analysis continues to be dominated by economists or by those with an economic orientation.

Chart 1

Political Skill

		High	Low
Analytical	High	Entrepreneur	Technician
Skill	Low	Politician	Pretender

Before the reader starts creating his own typology, let me explain the underlying rationale behind this one. Since this book is about the bureaucratic context of policy analysis, I wanted to examine the extent of the effect of the bureaucracy on the definition of analytical roles. My notion was that a practitioner of a new and emerging profession would be more shaped by the forces around him (such as the client, and the politics of the agency and policy area) than a practitioner of a mature profession with its standards, relatively defined field, and organization to promote both. In short, I expected that policy analysts, as practitioners of a new profession, would have developed sufficient appreciation of bureaucratic folkways and methods to be said to have political skill. To my surprise, I found that, while many policy analysts had learned to be or were skillful bureaucrats, some had made only the slightest accommodation to their environment.[3]

Analyzing bureaucratic behavior by identifying types is of course a standard and useful technique. Dwaine Marvick, for example, in an old but solid study, examined laymen and experts in an agency. He identified three types: the institutionalists, who were laymen and "place-bound"; the specialists, who were experts (scientists, engineers, lawyers) and "skill-bound"; and the hybrids, who were "free agents" and "operators." My technician would be fairly close to his specialist with the exception that many technicians do not perceive themselves as being influential. The politician would be a hybrid because of the hybrid's interest in furthering himself. The entrepreneur, as both a free agent and skill-bound, seems to cut

3. Another explanation of the typology is that political scientists, by definition, usually look for the political aspects of their subject. Putnam, for example, found it useful to distinguish between "classical bureaucrats" and "political bureaucrats"; see Robert D. Putnam, "The Political Attitudes of Senior Civil Servants in Western Europe: A Preliminary Report," *British Journal of Political Science* 3 (July 1973): 257–90.

across both the specialist and the hybrid types. Probably none of our analysts would be institutionalists, because we are not dealing with laymen.[4]

The lack of fit between Marvick's bureaucratic types and my analytical types is one reason for not using a previously developed typology. But this reason is insufficient for explaining the use of a classification of analysts in the first place. Any typology, at best, is bound to be misleading because of its rigidity. No single technician or politician or entrepreneur has *all* of the faults or virtues I will describe in this chapter. Indeed no policy analyst who was interviewed corresponds precisely with my composite portraits. At the risk of reification but for the sake of clarity and as a shorthand device, I will talk about the types as if they existed. Policy analysts certainly do not go around referring to one another as technicians, politicians, and entrepreneurs.

After a systematic look at my interviews, I discarded the premise that there were just analysts. I saw that analysts had a variety of orientations to their jobs, and that they also placed different weights on what they do and how they do it. But to describe all of the variations would have taken volumes; thus, the typology became a convenient way of discussing some central characteristics. At the same time, the typology made it clear to me that policy analysts have some measure of choice in the definition of the roles they assume. That in addition to the effects of the bureaucratic context and the analyst's professional background and education, there is a personal dimension—made up of motivations and beliefs—in the definition of analytical roles. Because of this personal dimension, some analysts, for example, adjust to the bureaucratic context by becoming bureaucrats, while others adhere to the norms of their former profession, and some try to do both by stressing different aspects of their work.

---

4. Dwaine Marvick, *Career Perspectives in a Bureaucratic Setting*, Michigan Governmental Studies, no. 27 (Ann Arbor: Bureau of Government, Institute of Public Administration, University of Michigan Press, 1954). Anthony Downs has also developed a typology of bureaucrats based on differences in goals or motivation. My entrepreneur is probably in between his "advocate" and "statesman" types. The politician fits well with his "climber." I do not think that Downs has a corresponding type for the technician, but some readers might feel that technicians are "conservers." See Anthony Downs, *Inside Bureaucracy* (Boston: Little, Brown and Co., 1967), pp. 88–89.

THE TECHNICIAN

The technician is an academic researcher—an intellectual—in bureaucratic residence. No admirer of bureaucratic folkways, he weaves around himself a protective cocoon of computers, models, and statistical regressions. He knows about politics, but not much. Politics is somebody else's business. His main business is research which is linked to policymaking, and if left alone he will faithfully adhere to an internal standard of quality. "I'd rather be right than on time" is the common refrain of many technicians.

Some may think that most technicians are baby analysts who haven't yet been housebroken by the realities of politics and the bureaucracy. While it is true that some technicians are apprentices who, if they stay, will change their nonpolitical ways, others—the "inner-directed" technicians—will not. How long does it take to get housebroken? For the true technician, forever; and if his agency provides an inhospitable climate for research (which is not unlikely in the bureaucracy), he will shift his niche by hopping to another.

INCENTIVE TO WORK: POLICY RESEARCH

As one would anticipate, there are many reasons for technicians to work in the bureaucracy; but there is also convergence on one central motivation or incentive—the opportunity to do policy research in a policymaking environment. A technician at the Office of Economic Opportunity (OEO) provides us with some answers to the question of why the technician works in the bureaucracy. He chose to work at OEO for four reasons. First, he and his wife liked living in Washington more than in other cities where teaching positions were available. Second, he enjoyed the working environment of government. OEO had given him the opportunity to do research, but he did not want to work on research all the time. His job had an element of excitement and immediacy in that it allowed him to get involved in high-level decision making. He found it fun to work on revenue sharing, for example, because it gave him a chance to see how government operates. Third, his government salary paid him more than what he could get at a university. Finally, he felt that his work at OEO had a better chance of being used than did the academic studies which he could conduct elsewhere.[5]

Two decisions concerning work are the decision to join an organization and the decision to stay there. The reasons for the first decision may differ from those for the other. When one technician finished his graduate work, he began looking for a teaching position. Not successful in finding one, he considered employment in the private sector or in government. He chose the latter—the Treasury Department—because his advisor at Columbia University suggested that a year in Treasury would enhance his ability to get a teaching job. A Treasury Department supervisor, however, thinks that the main incentive for both new and continuing employees is the high salary; true, they may also join to prepare for a university career or as a way of tiding themselves over while completing their dissertations, but they remain long after they intended because their salaries are high compared with those of entry-level faculty positions. The supervisor may be partially correct. The technician who went to work at Treasury for a year in hope of getting a teaching job had been there for about ten years.

Supervisors keep their technicians happy by allowing them time to pursue their own research interests. Sometimes the research is related to the mission of the particular office. At other times it is simply a morale booster. In either case, the supervisor is quite aware that the technician is primarily interested in doing research.

Enter a technician's office and you will see a computer terminal. It is not for show; he uses it. His desk and shelves will be cluttered with papers—worksheets, charts, congressional and governmental reports. His books will be the same as those of academic social scientists. Behind him you will see a coffee pot and a brown-bag lunch. All of this tells you that here is a person who spends his time in his office, "making with the numbers." One such analyst said that he enjoyed his present position because "the Treasury Department has the best resources to underwrite serious research.

---

5. Stanley, using a sample of scientists and engineers, found that their main reasons for staying in the federal service were challenge of work (59 percent) and security factors such as retirement (41 percent); only 16 percent cited adequate pay as a reason. See David T. Stanley, *The Higher Civil Service: An Evaluation of Federal Personnel Practices* (Washington, D.C.: The Brookings Institution, 1964), pp. 64–65.

Here I have the opportunity to do independent research and participate in important decisions."

Oddly enough, at the policy level of the bureaucracy a research environment is maintained. There are bright and knowledgeable colleagues to talk to. There are data. In between budgeting and other legislative demands, an assistant secretary encourages a technician to do research to increase his own and the analytic office's capability to respond to the client's needs. Sometimes the technician negotiates his research agenda with his superior, but a great deal of the time he generates it himself: "Most of the staff is self-motivated; we don't discuss with anyone what would be useful research." Able to set aside months, with no interruptions, for personal research, one technician estimated that about half of his time could be devoted to projects of his own choosing.

The research has to be "interesting and relevant," but what is relevant is in the eye of the beholder. Thus, one HEW technician, a monetary economist, found working on social policy problems (such as the financing of education) more interesting than studying the demand for money. Another analyst gets a feeling of relevance and satisfaction when "he gets on top of a policy problem." Relevance for most technicians means a personal sense of high-level, long-range involvement. They like the opportunity to "operate on a high policy level within the department." In the case of President Nixon's price control program, it did not mean policing price controls; it meant doing the "thought work."

Occasionally a technician will become so involved in day-to-day assignments that it is almost impossible to get to talk with him. One Treasury Department technician said he could not schedule an interview even a few hours ahead: "I can't tell what's going to break. Call me just before you're ready to come over. I'll tell you if I can take the time." Nor did he have the same relaxed attitude as his colleagues: "I came here in 1966 after completing my graduate course work, figuring that I could complete my dissertation on the job. Other people have found time on the job to complete their Ph.D.'s and write journal articles. I can't find the time." Unlike him, most technicians do indeed find the time; for them, research is more satisfying than fire fighting.

Technicians, of course, are not completely wrapped up in their own models. Some feel a strong sense of personal involvement with their agency's programs. An analyst at the National Aeronautics and Space Administration (NASA), for example, postponed his interview because he wanted to see a lift-off. On his walls were photographs of Apollo missions, and during his lunch hour he would watch films of the missions. He enjoyed watching the space shots and took great pride in being part of NASA. Another analyst at OEO was deeply concerned about the welfare of America's black poor. As he said, "I have to test my soul on how much I will meet their need." His greatest concern was for the welfare of the urban black poor, but he was working on a rural project (affecting whites as well as blacks) which he thought was quite important: "If the report is read, rural people will have good housing. This is a real incentive because most of these people are blacks. I am tackling a real problem whose solution is badly needed." Another analyst liked his work at the Department of Housing and Urban Development (HUD) because he "always enjoyed building construction, even as a kid." At the National Science Foundation (NSF) it was the same story; the technician, a chemist, was attracted to NSF because of its support of basic research.

THE POLITICS-ANALYSIS DICHOTOMY

Notwithstanding the policy concerns described above, technicians, by my definition and in reality, still are the most apolitical analysts by far. They may gossip about shop and Washington politics; they may feel personally involved in their agencies' programs; they may even be active as private citizens—say, in leading an assault against a suburban city council. But in their work they generally do not see themselves as political actors. They tend to separate politics from analysis, perhaps because they lack political skill; they see other actors as the political experts.

"We're here for technical advice," one OEO analyst asserted, and "we're not experts in selling the program. The White House seems to want to keep the political aspects of its program under its own control anyway." Another analyst saw policymaking as a big pot that everybody stirs—"my study was a teaspoon in the Pacific," and "if you have a goal of really developing policy or influencing it, you may just be developing frustration and unhappiness for yourself." What it takes are "skills to engineer policy through."

Thus, the technician sees politics as "selling," and he does not want to be a "hustler." Instead, he adopts what one analyst called an "inside mentality" and lets others with an "outside mentality" do the hustling. Yet while content to do his research, he is not above criticizing the analysts who do hustle. He sees them as "intent on justifying their own existence," as "wheeling and dealing with research funds." Moreover, it is "easy to hustle when you have a naive client." And technicians feel that such salesmen are not really analysts. The hustlers may appreciate analysis, but they are really involved in personal "empire building rather than analysis. They have lost touch with their own academic field; they are victims of human depreciation. They leave the university and then make no further investment in their skills."

Because the technician thinks of politics as nonrational, he often omits or is blind to the political considerations in his analysis. He thinks political criteria should be avoided—let the White House worry about politics. As one analyst put it, "We try to stay away from politics. There must be *someone* in government whose purpose is to point to the best program rather than to the most popular one." Other analysts claim ignorance: "Even if we wanted to include political considerations at our level, we do not have the essential bird's-eye view of what the president needs."

Not having the presidential vantage point and living in a self-imposed political vacuum, many technicians work on what is "best" by taking goals or ends as given. Here the technician's prior education and belief in efficiency help him. He is able to demonstrate that the cost of training civil servants is greater in special institutes than in college and night schools. Indifferent to the political and major policy implications of his work, he sees no need to question the goal of training itself. Similarly, two technicians at HUD were dumbfounded that their research and the research they supervised might have political implications: "We are engineers and are systems oriented. We take problems and consider all the technical aspects of them. We are rarely confronted with political controversies." One of these technicians was asked about the origin of the urban goals of the federal government (for example, the provision of housing and the prevention of urban blight). He replied, "I am not really sure. They were given to me when I came."

Of course the more politically sophisticated technician understands that ends are just as likely to be modified as means and that analysis often involves playing with the relationship of ends and means. He sees that the ends, the objectives of the analysis, are "set by the political process." For this sort of technician, politics sets constraints on program development: "You know that what you recommend must pass a political test." You have to develop policy recommendations within "the constraints determined by what the administration is willing to do." But having decided that politics sets constraints, the technician still has a problem: what to do with policy alternatives that fall outside the constraints. Now the long-term time perspective of the technician comes into play. While he may limit his recommendations, he does not limit his analysis to current notions of political feasibility. Instead he broadens it, so that when the political climate changes he will be prepared. The infeasible alternative should be analyzed and discussed so that the policy debate will be clarified. In a study of the financing of higher education, for example, one technician satisfied himself by placing at the back of his report the discussion of an alternative that had no immediate congressional support and whose possible acceptance was far in the future.

Most technicians, however, are insensitive to the rationale behind politics. While they may understand what is going on, they do not appreciate it. Often they feel frustrated when decisions are made for noneconomic reasons and conflict with their own professional preferences. One analyst in the Treasury Department, for instance, felt that the Nixon administration's decision to accelerate depreciation rates of business equipment was politically motivated by campaign promises to specific industries. The analyst felt that it gave an unnecessary tax advantage to business and that there were other more effective ways of stimulating the economy.

The technician is convinced that he is objective, a scientist of sorts. If he has political views he keeps them to himself and separates them from his work for his agency, or so he says. Unlike the messenger of ancient times, the technician does not fear for his head when he has to bring bad news. No, he would not soften his findings; he would do "the best analytical job that can be done in conformity with the principles of economics." He refers to his work as "honest analysis," and he complains about analysts having to provide justification for a decision that has already been made. Or he may allude to when he was at OEO and some negative findings were suppressed and "that's what drove me out of OEO; the leadership simply didn't understand the proper role of evaluation."

But keep in mind that the technician is not oblivious to politics. He is quite interested in political gossip about an area he is investigating. He may have coffee with friends from his agency's legislative affairs office. Or he may be like one NASA technician who read the speeches made by NASA personnel, attended congressional hearings, and scanned the daily bulletins published by the NASA Office of Legislative Affairs. In general, however, the technician's interest in politics is passive.

THE INFLUENCE OF DETAILS

Although the technician (as well as other analytical types) will recall, say, how his study was smuggled into the White House decision-making process, he does not see his work as influential. His image of a large policymaking beach with analysis as a grain of sand may be quite realistic, but what we are interested in here is what it tells us about the technician's self-image—his perceived lack of influence and, in some cases, his impoverished sense of personal efficacy. Consider the situation of one HUD analyst. By 1971 the agency had been undergoing a process of reorganization and turmoil for several years. Besides being upset about the general working environment there, the technician was dissatisfied with his role of "pushing paper up to another level." Actually, there were at least three levels of review within the agency; it was difficult to see results because implementation was too remote from the analyst's technical contribution. He cited one of the programs he had worked on: "It bounced from person to person without allowing anyone an input of which they could be proud." Similarly, another analyst felt that there were so many people working on revenue sharing that he was unable to see where he was influential.

Then there is the hardworking technician in the Treasury Department who felt frustrated when his analysis was ignored, "even though it happens all the time." Another analyst from the Labor Department resolved this frustration by seeing himself as a "purist" who enjoyed technique regardless of the effect on decisions. When asked if he could recall an instance of one of his studies being misused, he sat silent for some time. Then, when the interviewer tried to restate the question, he laughed and replied, "Oh no, I understand your question. It's just that to answer it, I first have to think of an instance in which a study of mine was *used.*"

To get out of this uncomfortable psychological conflict between expected and actual influence, the technician turns to his research orientation. He figures that there is a trade-off between analysis and influence: the more opportunity to do research and develop analytical capability, the less time to be influential. If he wanted to have an immediate impact on policy, he says, he would be working in the White House, or for the Council of Economic Advisors, or in the Bureau of the Budget or its successor the Office of Management and Budget. Instead, he expects to be influential in the future by making a research investment in the present.

Sometimes the investment pays off. Consider the Treasury Department technician, a specialist in econometrics and forecasting, who had been with the department for six years. In discussing his work on a simulation model of the federal income tax, he said, "Because I was here and recruited others in whom I had confidence, we have increased the role of computers in the department. Now we have a computer terminal in our office and are called upon often. When I first came there was resistance to the computer, but the initial contact of the policymakers with the results of our simulation model were good—mainly because we found a good person to build a dependable simulation model that worked and filled the need." Evidently there have been two payoffs: increased computer capability and the ability to estimate the impact of changes in the income tax law.

Sometimes the payoff is not apparent, and here the technician is similar to those of us in the university who do research and justify our activity with feelings about the ultimate utility of knowledge. A case in point is the analyst who was thinking of leaving Treasury and returning to teaching. He had been working on the use of taxation to decrease pollution but did not see much immediate acceptance of the idea by Congress. Believing that in a number of years current law would be proved ineffective, he said, "It will soon be obvious that the Clean Air Act has failed and people will demand new solutions. I want people to look back and ask what we turned down. I want my proposal to be a good and intelligent proposal which can be revived and used as public policy. This position [in the Treasury Department] offers me the opportunity to take part in a fundamental change in pollution policy."[6]

6. The 1970 clean air law (Public Law 91–604) gave the Environmental Protection Agency a broad range of powers in a variety of areas affecting air pollution. The principal provision of the law is Title II, known as the "National Emissions Standards Act." See *Congressional Digest* 53, no. 3 (March 1974): 72.

This reliance on future consumption is initiated by viewing research as "making ready." Research then becomes the development of a capacity to respond, and its effectiveness depends heavily on someone's prescience. That someone can be the analyst himself, his boss, or a client; but in any case someone must anticipate what information will be needed. Thus, one OEO technician was only partially correct when he stated that the influence of the analyst resides in his ability to "expand the issue at the opportune moment," and that the analyst "must remain prepared by doing pure research." We are still left with the question of *what* research.

The technician believes that whatever influence he can muster will depend on his command of details. In his view, White House and congressional politicians who have a problem and are "in trouble" are open to a wide variety of suggestions so long as the solution meets the general problem. When desperate, politicians will let someone else worry about the details; thus, it is in the details, in the designing of a policy, that the analyst expects to exercise his influence.[7]

Being in charge of the details, however, may not be enough to win influence. A Treasury technician recalled that on one occasion, when the Senate was considering 1969 tax legislation, he worked with the staff of the Ways and Means Committee to formulate an amendment that would have altered an increase in the personal exemption to make it more progressive. He helped formulate the amendment and generate the revenue estimate. The Ways and Means staff "then set some senator up to propose the amendment on the floor. It did not fly through the Senate; the members just did not understand it." When accelerated depreciation rates were proposed, Treasury technicians were known to be opposed and the department's economists were publicly criticized by Ralph Nader's staff for not speaking out against the proposed change. One of the technicians reported that it was an advantage to be working for Treasury because of the opportunity to influence decisions before

7. This emphasis on details reminds me of Fritz Marx's portrait of the career bureaucrat and his comments on narrowness and breadth. While the career man's "window is usually quite small, . . . when he advises policy-makers on program questions . . ., he must be willing to unravel the raw data patiently, to spot as many relevant aspects of the problem as possible, and to assess the likely effects of promising solutions." See Fritz Morstein Marx, "The Mind of the Career Man," *Public Administration Review* 20 (summer 1960): 135, 137.

they were made. The price he had to pay, however, was that he could not speak against the decision after it was made. Now these technicians certainly knew the details, but despite this and their loyalty they were excluded from subsequent meetings on the subject. The final position papers were written by lawyers.[8]

MODEST EXPECTATIONS

To understand the influence of the technician, we must understand what he expects of himself. What is a successful analysis for the technician? Criteria of success can exist at many levels, ranging from appreciation for one's own work to having an impact on a segment of America through a particular policy. Most technicians crowd toward the modest and circumscribed end of the success scale. They see success in personal terms, in their ability to do work of quality and to develop models that work. As one technician said, "Success is the ability to construct a model which specifies the relevant policy variables and is capable of accurate prediction." Another said, "Success is based on the accuracy of the estimate as tested by real world outcomes." But what if there is no empirical test? How then does the technician measure his success? The answer is simple: "If other analysts think it's a good piece of intellectual work, then it is good." Success is acceptance among peers.

All analysts want to make their impact on the formulation of policy and legislation, but the technician usually puts the quality of his work first. He expects his models "to predict well"; after that it is natural to feel even more successful if the work has some effect. Confidence in his work is a primary consideration, and influence is an important afterthought. The two criteria come together in the choice of "small" satisfying problems where there are reliable data and the analyst can "distinguish his influence over the outcome."

8. There is a certain amount of antagonism between analysts and lawyers that should be investigated further. One reason for this antagonism may be due to the gap between analysis and the drafting of legislation. Because the analyst usually does not know how to draft legislation, a lawyer or someone with his skills is given the job. Storey, for example, reports that in the case of the Family Assistance Plan, the "separation of the analysis from the legislation-writing led to situations where an implicit policy upon which analysis had been based was implemented in a very different manner in the drafting of a bill." See James R. Storey, "Systems Analysis and Welfare Reform: A Case Study of the Family Assistance Plan," *Policy Sciences* 4 (1973): 6.

In large problems involving major legislative proposals, it is difficult for the technician to discern whether he has been influential.

Technicians who work as evaluators of existing programs are fortunate in being able to point to a particular change in a program as a touchstone of success. As one analyst said, "A successful evaluation demonstrates something about the way a program is working and results in a change in the program to make it better." Or as another put it, "Have people learned anything they didn't know before, and does that bring about a change in their action?" From these statements, one might think that the technicians' criteria of success are set at the level of discerning an impact on people. But no, they also have lowered expectations. According to an HUD technician, urban renewal programs are so complex that it is difficult to demonstrate their impact on the people they are intended to serve. Therefore, he attempts to concentrate on administrative procedures and mechanical factors, believing that it is more fruitful to improve a program's operation than to attempt to improve its impact. Since evaluation can be done for a variety of purposes, I am not criticizing the technician's emphasis on programmatic details, but this emphasis can also be interpreted as another example of circumscribed expectations.

Occasionally a technician will count an analysis as successful if it is persuasive. In 1969 one of the technicians at Treasury felt that contemplated reforms of tax law were unnecessarily favorable to real estate interests. He was able to convince HUD officials that eliminating certain tax preferences would not hurt the stock of housing as real estate interests claimed. Since the final legislation omitted these preferences, he believed that his analysis was successful.

"Correct and useful" analysis was one technician's convenient summary of short-term success. Long-term success for him was analysis that resulted in a journal article that was interesting, creative, and pathbreaking and that would stimulate other research. But why this interest in publication? Other analytical types are content to feed information silently into the policy process; but the technician, like the academician, feels compelled to publish.

At best his publishing has tenuous ties to policymaking. One OEO analyst, for instance, used his studies and research for journal publication in the belief that it would help him if he ever decided to return to university teaching. Another analyst, who was working on a paper for Congress' Joint Economic Committee, said that in his personal writings he intentionally avoided discussions about current policy issues because of the danger of appearing to use his position to influence policy. A Treasury technician (who said he doesn't like to write but is encouraged by his superiors to do so) had published several articles and was contemplating several more. Here is his reason for writing a piece on a particular simulation model: "I thought it would be useful for the universities to know about its complexity so that they would not duplicate it and could channel their work into another area."

Often the criteria of correct and useful will conflict, since the time pressures of policymaking do not allow for extensive research. In order to be useful one has to be less correct. This situation is sometimes necessary but often counterproductive, according to the technician. What does he do when asked for a "quick-and-dirty" study? Usually, after thinking the problem through, he tries to convince his superiors that the schedule is unrealistic. Failing that, "you fish out what you have in your head and just put it down, even though it may be wrong." At the Department of Health, Education, and Welfare (HEW) a technician recalled that he had to make some first cracks at budgetary recommendations for education. He was very unhappy because he knew little about the field of education and had no basis for allocating funds. He was unsure of his recommendations and would not have given them out if he had had the choice. Although somebody would take his advice, he would prefer not to have it taken if it meant he could not do quality work. When forced to do quick-and-dirty work, he said, "What I would do is leave my name off it."

But there are also quick and not-so-dirty studies. These come about when the technician is armed with sufficient research to be able to make a response that is both correct and timely. In Treasury a number of available models made it possible to respond overnight, for example, to demands for revenue estimates:

Unless we are timely we will not be able to have an impact. We are geared up for the congressional hearing and the opposition generally is not. Therefore, if we are able to respond overnight or perhaps the same day, the administration will have greater ability to influence the outcome of tax legislation. If we fail to respond quickly though, the initiative will be with the opposition to the administration's bill.

Nevertheless, despite this talk about timeliness or about "action-oriented positions where there is some chance of influencing policy," the technician is basically research oriented and only partially action oriented. A case in point is the technician who left the staff of a prominent senator because he was dissatisfied with his own work and was interested in pursuing something closely related to his background in economics. He went to OEO to do evaluation studies, and there—left alone to pursue his long-run research interests—he was happy. For major action on policy, the research orientation is a source of weakness because it shapes very modest expectations. On the other hand, this ability to do research is also a source of strength. The technician's concern for standards, honesty, and objective analysis provides much of the analytical backbone of the emerging profession of policy analysis. Without such a core of expertise, there might not be anything to act on or be political about.

THE POLITICIAN

The politician is more a bureaucrat than an analyst. Of course, he does not see himself as a bureaucrat. After all, he is a risk taker who has moved frequently to advance his career, and he is not "wedded to the federal bureaucracy." With some disdain, he contrasts himself with bureaucrats by saying that "most of the people in this office would say they enjoy today because it's payday." The implication is that he is not the average career bureaucrat—he has more important things to worry about than his salary.

Despite this self-image, the politician talks and acts like a bureaucrat. In controlled and measured speech he calls forth Office of Management and Budget circular numbers as easily as if they were the names of his children, and his language is filled with specialized jargon and acronyms such as FIFO (for "first in/first out"). Concerned about where he sits and whom he works for, he worries about his civil service rating being lower than those of some of the people he has to deal with. He thinks that differences in rank place him at a disadvantage for getting important assignments and in participating as an equal in discussions. An office to him is not just a place in which to work; it is a demonstration of past and present accomplishments and influence. His office, with its plush chairs and stained hardwood desk and heavy brass lamps, may be handsomer than his superior's. In one office, filled with beautiful native American art, the analyst gestured to a blank spot on the wall, noting that one of his outstanding paintings had been requisitioned from him for the office of the vice-president. In other offices a large bronze wall plaque commends the analyst's work, or there is a picture of him shaking hands with the president, or at least there are a number of charts and maps to illustrate his expertise. Soft-spoken and well-dressed, the politician is a bureaucratic operator.

Although most of them see themselves as generalists, they are still a disparate lot. Some have degrees in public administration, while others have graduate degrees in history or political science, or occasionally in a technical field such as civil engineering. Some are lawyers. Some started their public service careers as budget analysts in the Bureau of the Budget (now OMB) or in the Defense Department; some were management interns. Others, particularly political appointees, had extensive careers before joining the federal public service. In the Department of Housing and Urban Development we came across one senior civil servant who felt he was in "semi-exile" because of his association with a former Democratic administration; he described himself as "the last remaining political appointee of the Kennedy Administration." Another politician, a businessman with previous governmental experience and in his fifties, had done fund raising in New York City for the secretary of the department. He described his boss, the deputy undersecretary, as a close political associate of the secretary. To underscore his image of being part of the political staff, he said that he was serving at the pleasure of the deputy undersecretary and that it was the secretary who was actually his client.

THE VANTAGE POINT

Politicians, similar to technicians who do "private research," are just as likely to serve themselves as they are to serve the secretary: "I grabbed this project because I wanted to build a reputation and expertise in the area of housing; I guess it was partly opportunistic and partly because of personal interest in the field." They are in the federal bureaucracy for a variety of reasons. Some enjoy the feeling of political efficaciousness, of being close to real decisions and the source of power: "I came to Washington with vague ideas of impacting on big, important things." Others are satisfied by drafting their agency's responses to current legislative issues and watching the interaction between Congress and the agency. Some closely identify with their agency's programs ("I am committed to solving the problem of the cities"); others couldn't care less, seeing their agency merely as one rung on the ladder of advancement. One senior policy analyst (a GS-15) said that he wanted to work directly for the secretary of an agency and went to work for the first secretary to offer him a job. Besides his desire to move up (he had worked for an assistant secretary before), he liked the vantage point: "You can see immediate results because the interest of the secretary's office in the problem in itself brings action to the lower bureaucracy."

Policy analysis seems to offer the politician an opportunity to broaden himself. Those who come from technical fields, such as engineering, see the experience as expanding their careers to the social field and helping them learn about such activities as community development. Those who start out with broad social science backgrounds have similar feelings of personal growth. For example, one saw his office as a think tank which allowed him to keep abreast of some new ideas on labor-related subjects and at the same time explore his interest in sociology. He believed that he was able to transform social science research into public policy.

Regardless of where they sit, politicians want to work on the major problems facing the agency. They want to be where the action is. When it was suggested to one analyst that his evaluation office might get involved in reviewing a General Accounting Office report, he grimaced and said, "I sure hope I don't get involved in that; it is so dry. We don't want to be saddled with the type of evaluation which verifies that sums were spent appropriately. We want assignments that have the policy issue content." In short, the politician, like the other analytical types, wants to pursue his own agenda; but as we will see, he is more constrained than other analysts because of his close ties to his client.

MORE POLITICS THAN ANALYSIS

What the technician shuns, the politician embraces. To advance himself, he is political. As a staff man to the secretary of the agency, he knows he is "something to someone," but he hopes to become "someone." The route to becoming someone, as Tullock has pointed out, is to please one's superior.[9] Thus, an HUD analyst pointed out the importance of gaining the attention of the client and of maintaining a good working relationship with him: "If you come up with analysis that continually reflects your interests and not your client's, you will fail. You must also have a pretty good relationship going with your client before it's possible to press him to accept your conclusions after he has initially rejected them. It is far too easy to be frozen out. Sadly, this can happen simply because you don't say what the king wants to hear."

The politician knows that his future lies in protecting his client's future. The secretary "has only a few brownie points to spend, and he should know how strong or weak the opposition is." A senior politician in HUD, expecting his colleagues to be objective, would tell them, "You get the thing in here and we will put the political sheen on it." He explained, "Our role is to keep the secretary programmed so that when he feels the timing is right, he will be able to move." The same sentiment was echoed by an analyst at Agriculture: "It is my job to help the president and secretary get a handle on the operation of this department. Because it is so complex, we find ourselves far too often reacting to problems. I can help best by anticipating problems and calling them to the attention of my superiors."

As protector of his client, of course, the politican does more than merely raise a red flag. He evaluates agency proposals and gives the secretary some means for judging them, not only by providing cost and effectiveness data but by giving advice on the proposals' timeliness. Because of his reading of legislative hearings and his contacts with appropriations committees, the politician feels that he has a good sense of timing. Timing certainly played a dominant role in one analyst's study of public health service hospitals that provide health care for merchant marine personnel. His recommendation that the hospitals be upgraded emphasized that their current deteriorated condition was inconsistent with the president's recently announced policy of improving and subsidizing the merchant marine.

---

9. Gordon Tullock, *The Politics of Bureaucracy* (Washington, D.C.: Public Affairs Press, 1965), pp. 52, 64–68. Tullock's bureaucratic politician is quite similar to my policy analyst politician.

Once captivated by the nuances of the policy process, the politician exhibits an antianalytical bias. Policymaking at the Commerce Department, according to one analyst, was done "by the seat of the pants" and "by way of personal influence." The problems are too variable to be subjected to a logical form of decision making. "What about Vietnam and the C-5A?" an analyst questioned, and then went on to criticize McNamara and the Planning-Programming-Budgeting System (PPBS) at Defense: "Those whiz kids came in saying 'Here I am with my eight degrees and computers; I can't be wrong.' It was a kind of intellectual arrogance."

Another politician, this one at HUD, rejected the holistic or systems aspect of analysis. According to him, "dedicated people see too many sides to a problem," and so he "tries to carve out small parts of the problem and tackle them individually." And as any incrementalist knows, "by working a problem's component parts, we eventually solve the problem as a whole." And given the complexities of housing problems, the analyst may have the right approach.

Some politicians are so intent on pushing for a recommendation and making an impact on the client that they criticize analysis that does not focus on one alternative: "Decision makers will be confused by more than one alternative." If it makes an impact it is successful, "even if it is bad analysis technically." Although most analysts are supposed to be skeptical, one politician is dissatisfied with his job because he is expected to examine programs with suspicion. Finally, politicians, unlike technicians, tend to welcome the quick-and-dirty study. In discussing his work on revenue sharing one politician said, "We—the staff—had to get the program into effect in a very short time. The pressure and feeling that we were really needed made the job enjoyable."

ACCEPTANCE

How does the politician know whether he is successful? One responded candidly: "I know I'm successful because I'm still here." He went on to explain that he "happened to do right those things that people wanted." In a highly volatile environment, where the turnover is great, he was able to maintain his position over the long run because he was able to maintain the confidence of the secretary. As for the short run, he knew he had been successful when he received notes from his superiors congratulating him on his work, and he knew about his failures when people "stopped speaking" to him (more important and not quite so rare). This analyst stayed on after a change of administration and a change of boss, the assistant secretary. He realized that it was time to leave when there was a sharp decrease in the number of phone calls he was receiving. Another analyst also has a simple indicator: "Success is when something doesn't come back to me to be rewritten. That's the only criterion I have."

Most politicians, however, are more guarded. They talk about success in objective terms as involving various levels of acceptance. In this respect they are not different from other analysts. Typically their levels of acceptance—their criteria for success—involve changing budget allocations or "raising the level of debate." The final test of acceptance is when recommendations generated from the politician's work are transformed into legislative proposals.

When that ultimate acceptance is not forthcoming, the politician retreats behind a mask of professionalism. One analyst at HUD attributes his success to his familiarity with public housing projects: "In my work I live facts; I operate from what I know." According to a Department of Labor politician, success is determined by technical quality, objectivity, and—again—facts: "Policy officials want the best support the available facts can give them: as a civil servant, I must be responsive to that need." Providing facts can raise a new issue for the client or force him to reply to an issue he has been avoiding.

DERIVED INFLUENCE

It is not surprising that politicians, like other analysts, provide facts. But the politician's influence derives primarily not from facts but from political skill. He writes and talks well; he makes the complex simple. Indeed, one analyst described himself as a journalist. In technical areas he commands sufficient vocabulary to be able to write, for example, administrative plans for oceanographic and atmospheric programs. Not only is he good at communication, but he is able to anticipate issues and win the trust of his superior: "Very often the secretary says, 'Jack, take a look at this one and see that my backside is protected' "; or, "Those PPBS people who were influential have gotten there because the secretary trusts their judgment." And from one of the influential ones: "You really have

to understand the level you are dealing with; we are secretary-
trusted confidants. Our influence is usually very informal."

Trust and confidence, then, are the ingredients of the
politician's influence. In order to develop them the politician or his
superior must have access to the secretary. Three to four times a
week, one politician reported, his boss met with the secretary, and
when his boss was out of town, he would meet with the secretary.
Of course, the politician feels more influential when he has access
to somebody who has access. In one department the head of the
policy development staff was close to the secretary, and the
secretary in turn was close to the president. This set of relationships was maintained despite a change in administration and in the
occupants of the three offices.

Usually the politician knows when he has influenced the secretary because he will get some feedback either verbally or by memo.
Feedback from farther up the chain of influence is much less
direct, but the politician will ferret it out. He will pull out a
presidential report on housing and point to a particular page where
his ideas were included, inferring that this inclusion means presidential endorsement. Or take the case of an OEO analyst: Her
shop, concerned about a rumor that President Nixon was going to
veto a certain bill, quickly pulled together a memo showing the
effects of a veto and then sent it up the bureaucratic ladder. Aware
of other pressures on the president, this politician still felt influential when the president did not veto the bill.

In short, the politician works for and on the secretary. Once
trust is established, he sees his influence extending down into the
bureaucracy through the secretary's directives and up into the
White House through the secretary's contacts. With some skill he
gathers and conveys information in the pursuit of self-
advancement.

THE ENTREPRENEUR

The entrepreneur is both technician and politician.[10] He knows
how to work with numbers and people. Pragmatist, educator,
manipulator, coalition builder, he engages with relish his political

---

10. The existence of analytical entrepreneurs in the policy process has been
discussed in the literature. See Eugene Bardach, *The Skill Factor in Politics:
Repealing the Mental Commitment Laws in California* (Berkeley and Los Angeles:

and organizational environment. More politically aggressive than the technician, he may be a politician in the making; but for the moment he is technically competent and has internal standards of quality control. As a purveyor of knowledge, he does not let his immediate client constrain him. If one client will not listen, others will. Actually, he sees the public interest as his client. He has strong normative views of the scope of government activity. He is concerned about distribution as well as efficiency. Whether his views are that government should do more or less, he is much more aware than other analysts that his preferences guide the selection and solution of analytical problems.

With this combination of technical and political skills, I suspect that the entrepreneur is scarcer than the other analytical types.[11] Yet they are an important type. Much of the effectiveness of future policy analysis will depend on them, a subject to which I return in chapter 8 when I urge the need for greater political sensitivity on the part of policy analysts.

ANALYSIS IS POWER

Entrepreneurs know that the policymaking stage is crowded with a great many actors. But they are not intimidated by this, just as they are not intimidated by the lack of immediate applause. Unlike technicians, they see themselves as, and want to be, part of the cast. Why is an interesting question of motivation. Just what are the incentives to be a federal analyst? Intellectually competent, many entrepreneurs could have stayed in academia. Instead, they chose the bureaucratic life.

Some entrepreneurs will say that they do analysis because they are good at it—their skills give them a comparative advantage over others. Some may like the money. Some are intellectually interested in the problems and their dissection. They like roaming through an organization and seeing how the parts operate. How a government should spend its money is an interesting problem.

University of California Press, 1972); and David E. Price, "Professionals and 'Entrepreneurs': Staff Orientations and Policy Making on Three Senate Committees," *Journal of Politics* 33 (May 1971): 316–36.

11. Some readers may object to such an inference because of the nonrandom nature of the sample of analysts. If anything, the nonrandom sampling procedure should have resulted in a large number of entrepreneurs, because I deliberately sought out for interviewing analysts with good reputations who were politically sensitive, experienced, senior, and well educated.

Moreover, they often have freedom to chose their own problem, or so they believe. But freedom, interesting problems, money, and skill are secondary incentives to the primary incentive of power.

There is nothing so sad as to talk to an analyst who is in political exile in some think tank. Once he had power. He was making decisions by influencing decisions. Now, he has time to read, to write, to do the study right. But he is unhappy because he is out of the action. He fondly recalls the weekend when everyone worked through the night so that the secretary would have something to say at the president's cabinet meeting. "I don't really miss Washington; I miss power."

What these analysts want is to be in. And to get in, one has to go into the bureaucracy. The closer the analyst is to the bureaucracy, the more efficacious he feels. Perhaps the feeling is illusory with respect to actual outcomes. Nevertheless, being in the bureaucracy reinforces the entrepreneur's illusion: he works on critical budgetary issues; he writes memoranda the secretary may read; he is appointed to the staff of presidential commissions, and he may even attend cabinet meetings. Like the politician, he has the feeling of commanding the resources of the bureaucracy.

Although the entrepreneur is in the bureaucracy, ironically he (like the other analytical types) does not see himself as a bureaucrat. He is there to question the bureaucrat's stodgy premises, to shake the system, to take risks. It is particularly the short-timer, the entrepreneur who has been in government for about three to five years, who does not worry about maintaining the agency or conserving its jurisdiction. He can always retreat to a think tank. His problem is to be productive within his short stay without alienating possible future clients and employers. The analyst who moves in when there is a political changing of the guard has the same problem as the political appointee: he wants to make an impact. The opportunity to try is what gets him into the bureaucracy and keeps him there.

When he cannot make his impact on short-term decisions, the entrepreneur, like the technician, will take the long-range view. So what if the client does not accept a study's recommendations. Somehow and sometime in the future, someone will. Just as academicians may introduce an idea for future consumption and legislators may want to build a base for eventual acceptance, so entrepreneurs see ideas as having a long life span. They say that the value of an alternative depreciates slowly.

Entrepreneurs can be tenacious when they think they know something, and they are not wholly rationalizing a failure by taking the long-range view. They know that there are many points of access. If an idea will not fly in one part of an agency, it may in another. Or sometimes the analyst can get a new client; for example, he can transfer to the Office of Management and Budget or to some other vantage point in the bureaucracy where his ideas will be accepted. Or he may have a friend in the White House to whom he can slip his good idea.

As a final tactic the entrepreneur will leave the bureaucracy. Consider the analyst who left Treasury to work on the staff of a congressional committee. In his new position he enjoyed being "where the action is when tax policy is developed." He liked the variety of the work and the exposure to many topics of interest, above all, "the committee listens to my work, agrees with me, and places the suggestions in legislation." Moreover, he had a vantage point from which to criticize administration proposals: "My criticism will gain public attention whether or not the committee . . . wants it to become public. Someone is always interested in such criticism and will pick it up." By working for a congressional committee, he was not "buried in the bureaucracy."

Entrepreneurs firmly believe that knowledge is power. This belief is exhibited in several ways. First, analysts act on the premise that information from analysis makes a difference in decisions. Often they urge that one compare the way in which decisions were made before and after the introduction of analysis. The earlier decisions were ad hoc, seat-of-the-pants judgments. Since the information is better now, then obviously we have better decisions. Avoiding the obvious naiveté of that premise, many entrepreneurs also recognize that the effectiveness of analysis depends on a convergence of many external forces that push in the same direction as the analysis. Nevertheless, they still fervently believe that a little analysis is better than no analysis and that you do not have to know everything before you act.

Second, entrepreneurs believe that knowledge is an important input to their own power. One does not acquire knowledge solely to influence current decisions. Acquisition of knowledge is an investment for the future. Look at the leverage the entrepreneur can achieve from millions of dollars of research when he has a say in choosing contractors and the questions they will explore. Some of these entrepreneurs, a subspecies, do little analysis. They try to keep themselves free of the desk calculator so that they can be brokers of other people's work. They acquire knowledge because they are skillful in manipulating agency personnel, task forces, and consultants. Many entrepreneurs of this bent are or are likely to become project supervisors or heads of analytical shops.

BALANCED PERSPECTIVE

What are the entrepreneur's criteria of analytical success? Like the technician, the entrepreneur will be concerned about the quality and competence of his work. Like the politician, he may see success as getting a grade raise or expanding his influence over "what leaves the office." And like all analysts he responds with the typical rhetoric about improving decision making or moving toward superior policies. Of course he knows that improved decision making may only mean improved discussion or client satisfaction. "I put thoughts in other people's minds and make sure they look at the whole picture." Did the client read the analysis, spend time on it, do anything about it? Was it worth the money he paid for it? The distinguishing feature of the entrepreneur, however, is his balanced concern for short-term demands and the long-term implications of policy analysis. Politicians expect to be fire fighters; technicians anticipate the future payoff of research. Entrepreneurs accommodate both perspectives.

Success is not just "winning" on one issue; it is a relationship that is established with a client over time. It is measured by the number of times a discussion is illuminated and extended by analysis. Doing a quick-and-dirty study may be his price of admission, but the entrepreneur's objective is to establish a relationship of confidence and trust with his client. Over time this confidence leads to an expansion of the use of analysis, and this expansion is his indicator of success. One entrepreneur says that the more successful the office, "the more it is asked to do." Another recognizes success when conversations about decisions, over time, included more variables from his analysis.

Because there is always a delay between what is suggested and what happens, most entrepreneurs are concerned with implementation: "You are an intellectual eunuch if you don't care if it's not acted on. Analysis is not an end in itself." Conceptually, they believe, success should depend on whether the policy was implemented, and whether the implementation improved the program, and whether the target or beneficiary of the program actually benefited. But for many entrepreneurs—sitting as they do at the top of the agency—their concern to do something about implementation has been mostly expressed by developing new techniques and in encouraging a greater awareness of the problems of implementation. For example, entrepreneurs know that they cannot test the effectiveness of the policy alternative that was discarded; therefore, at the very least they have pressed for better measures of improved program effectiveness and evaluation studies of the chosen alternative.[12] In addition, a few have suggested that the investigation of an agency's capacity to deliver should have priority on the analytical research agenda; thus, Walter Williams, a former OEO analyst, urges that

the analyst's concern is with the agency's *capability to implement* recommended decisions derived from policy analysis. At any point in time, the analyst's interest focuses on the likelihood that a major decision concerning a substantive change in the agency's programs or policies can be implemented to yield a positive outcome for beneficiaries of the program; over time, this interest concerns the steps the agency may take to improve its capability to implement major program changes.[13]

Not many entrepreneurs have had the opportunity to put their implementation ideas into practice, to test their notions in the world. One exception, who was a kind of operations research troubleshooter, found that in implementing a centralized information system, the departments were afraid to pass information up the line because it might be held or used against them.[14] He

12. For example, see Worth Bateman, "Assessing Program Effectiveness," *Welfare in Review* 6 (January-February 1968); Thomas K. Glennan, Jr., *Evaluating Federal Manpower Programs: Notes and Observations*, RM-5743-OEO (Santa Monica: Rand Corporation, September 1969); and Joseph S. Wholey et al., *Federal Evaluation Policy: Analyzing the Effects of Public Programs* (Washington, D.C.: Urban Institute, 1970).

13. Walter Williams, *Social Policy Research and Analysis: The Experience in the Federal Social Agencies* (New York: American Elsevier Publishing Co., 1971), p. 131. See also pp. 144–48.

14. Operations research "analyzes the quantitative aspects of human activity, the operation; [develops] mathematical models which represent some of the interrelations between [operations]; and [uses] the model to predict the reaction

convinced the department heads that there were advantages to having a direct line to the boss by showing them that the boss was not trying to meddle in their affairs and by making the information system as invisible as possible. The experience taught him to be concerned about implementation, a subject he feels most analysts ignore.

Despite the uncertainty of seeing success in the long run, entrepreneurs have a concrete measure of their short-run success—their impact on the budget. They know that budgeting is incremental and is not always flexible enough for major trade-offs.[15] But a common refrain among them is the importance of the budget as a lever for reallocating resources. At budget time, an HEW analyst who transferred to OMB was able "to knock down some nursing programs even over the objections of the budget examiners." Success for another is when you cut the budget by one hundred million dollars and not let anything take its place. In practice he has not been able to do this and has had to be content with several $15+ million cuts in the NASA budget. Of course, not all entrepreneurs simply cut; some try to add on or to shift resources, which is harder to do when the president is interested in decreasing the budget. Consider the analyst who found from his work that governmental student loan programs should be preferred over guaranteed private loan programs. Officials were quite interested in his analysis but kept it quiet, because putting more money into governmental loans would increase federal outlays while guaranteed private loans were not considered in the federal budget.

---

of the operation to various possible changes in external or internal influences. These predictions are then available to [the decision maker] to assist him in choosing between alternative policies and plans"; see Philip M. Morse, ed., *Operations Research for Public Systems* (Cambridge, Mass. and London: M.I.T. Press, 1967), p. 1. Sherman Blumenthal defines an information system as "an evolving organization of people, computers . . ., communication and support systems, and their integrated operation to regulate and control selected environmental events to achieve systems objectives"; see Sherman C. Blumenthal, *Management Information Systems: A Framework for Planning and Development* (Englewood Cliffs, N.J.: Prentice-Hall, 1969), pp. 17–18.

15. Aaron Wildavsky, *The Politics of the Budgetary Process* (Boston, Mass.: Little, Brown and Co., 1964), pp. 13–16.

BE YOUR OWN EXPERT

As one entrepreneur told us, "PPBS people don't get to the top. Only analysts who use political considerations will do relevant and influential analysis. Administrators must make the decisions, and they don't always understand issues fully; therefore, their staff must include all the variables which would help the decision maker arrive at a solution." In short, entrepreneurs are their own political experts.

Like other analysts, the entrepreneur knows that politics introduces constraints into analysis; but he is more likely than others to convert constraints into opportunities. Suspicious of conventional notions of political feasibility, he will say, as one HEW entrepreneur did, that "everyone in Washington is his own political expert." This HEW entrepreneur attempts to get on top of the politics of his technical assignment. Besides reading or attending congressional hearings, he checks things with the department's legislative liaison staff or talks with the secretary's assistants who have been working in his area. He wishes that his agency could be like the State Department, which he believes keeps detailed histories and voting records of congressmen interested in foreign affairs. He would like to have such records to predict congressional behavior. He tries to understand political considerations and then to make them an integrated and explicit part of his analysis. If a third best alternative is recommended for a political reason, then that reason should be communicated to the secretary, either verbally or in writing. Another entrepreneur, this one in the Department of Labor, conducts political feasibility studies. When interviewed, he and his staff were reviewing the positions of members of the Senate Finance Committee in order to design compromise proposals that might obtain committee approval. The work was done quietly because the secretary and the White House did not want to indicate publicly that they were willing to compromise.

One way of turning constraints into advantages is to look for targets of opportunity. A Department of Agriculture analytical supervisor said, "I expect my staff to seek out public programs to attack and to look for opportunities for solution; we are constantly trying to identify new issues." One entrepreneur in an OMB evaluation shop had a simple recipe: avoid grubby, ad hoc work;

attack multimillion or billion dollar programs that no one else is worrying about. To circumvent the "sweetheart" arrangement which OMB examiners have with agencies, he used a contact in the White House to attack his target of opportunity.[16]

As his own political expert, the entrepreneur is sensitive to the politics of his immediate environment. He adjusts his analytical expectations accordingly. "If not initially accepted, the analysis can be placed on ice until the decision-making environment becomes more favorable." Analysis without a political environment is completely bounded or closed and exists only in textbooks. Unlike technicians who see politics solely as a constraint, entrepreneurs expect that the more political the environment, the more open the boundaries of analysis, and the more political considerations will influence their work. Consider this experienced entrepreneur who has worked in a variety of environments. When he worked in business and industry, company and office politics were an irritant, something to avoid but not much affecting his analytical work. In the Department of Defense with its supportive think tanks, politics became more obvious in the conduct of studies—sometimes determining the what and the how of a study. Finally, in working for the chief administrator of a major urban center, the administrator said that, while his decisions were usually 100 percent political, he would be pleased if the analytical input could be increased from zero to 20 percent. This analyst recalled a study in which the administrator wanted a coordinator to supervise 30 agencies involved in the city's youth programs. The administrator finally had to settle for three coordinators, one of whom was a friend of the mayor.

There are several limitations on the political tendencies of the entrepreneur. One limitation is the client's expectations. Imagine the entrepreneur who worked for a secretary and two assistant secretaries and other key departmental members, all of whom held Ph.D.'s in economics. What they wanted from him was "straightforward analysis"; besides, all of them were "capable

16. Often in budgeting, whether at the federal or at some other level of government, the examiner is captured by the agency he is supposed to be reviewing. In exchange for not raising fundamental questions, the agency gives the examiner information and access and makes his job comfortable. Soon the examiner becomes an advocate or a "sweetheart" of the agency.

politicians." Another limitation is the analyst's concern for maintaining his authority by not undermining its base, his professional expertise. To an outsider, he is likely to describe his work as the technician does: "It's good and objective analysis done in such a way as to be useful to the top decision makers." Although some bias may creep into his work, it is important to be objective and to "let the chips fall where they may." For entrepreneurs there is a time for advocacy and a time for holding to disciplinary values.

Despite (or because of) their political sensitivity, some entrepreneurs subscribe to a conflict model of bureaucracy. One such analyst would always take along a slide rule to meetings in order "to explode the enemy" by discrediting their numbers and them. He explained, "You have to have a dirty mind. You have to say, where did that number come from? Any number can be leaned on."

Another entrepreneur enhanced his pragmatism with a judicious image. He had previously been a professor, openly critical of policies and leaders. Now, as an analyst in OMB, he was more inhibited. He felt he had to speak in positive terms—otherwise he would lose friends and gain enemies. When looking into the subtleties of a problem, he felt he could not appear to be indecisive: when convinced of a solution to a problem, he could not appear to be too "cut and dried." To protect his superior, a politically appointed analyst, he couched the superior's comments in positive terms.

In the entrepreneur, pragmatism is married to expertise. One entrepreneur found that most of his colleagues on the staff of the Council of Economic Advisers shared a common liberal ideology and technical approach. If the problem was at the staff level, they could argue the merits among themselves, "regardless of political feasibility." But once a decision had been made, discussion stopped and they went along. The council operated by "democratic centralism." Moreover, if the president said, "we're going to have a social security increase in the 1967 bill," then their problem was no longer to question the increase but to package the bill. Walter W. Heller echoes a similar realism when he says,

The economist on the policy firing line clearly has fewer options than the academic economist because he has to operate within the limits not only of his scientific knowledge but of political reality, public understanding, and institutional rigidities. . . . Unlike his academic colleague who can abstract from reality, deal with ultimates, and envision quantum jumps in our progress toward the ideal economic state, the economic practitioner has to operate deep in the heart of realism, has to deal with movement *toward* rather than *to* the ideal, and has to be at all times multi-dimensional in his objectives.[17]

Coleman, attempting to disentangle the roles of advocate and researcher, suggests that a separation can be based on the "fact that certain stages of policy research lie in the world of action, while other stages lie in the world of the discipline." He states the following principle:

Those stages of policy research that lie in the world of action, formulation of the research problem, posing conditions for communication of the research results back into the world of action, and making policy recommendations based on the research results, should be governed by the investigator's personal values and appropriately include advocacy. Those stages that lie within the disciplinary world, execution of the research and statement of the research results, should be governed by disciplinary values and do not appropriately include advocacy.[18]

Undoubtedly most entrepreneurs would subscribe to this in principle but not in practice. They know that political considerations are everywhere in the analytical process. For one thing, their clients do not respect artificial boundaries of the stages of policy research.

Consider Sargent Shriver's experience as director of OEO. When he received a proposal from his analytical staff for a negative income tax experiment, he was for it, but the "possibility of severe political criticism bothered him." His legislative staff had told him that the experiment would be "political suicide." According to Walter Williams, an OEO analyst at the time, Shriver hit on the idea that the experiment could be administered and funded through the University of Wisconsin's Institute for Research on Poverty rather than directly through the contractor, Mathematica, the firm that had originally developed the proposal. Thus, Shriver could proceed with the experiment while heading off congressional criticism by emphasizing "symbolically the research aspects of the project." For their part, the "policy analysts at OEO were clearly

17. Walter W. Heller, *New Dimensions of Political Economy* (New York: W. W. Norton and Co. 1967), pp. 25–26.
18. James S. Coleman, *Policy Research in the Social Sciences* (New York: General Learning Press, 1972), p. 14.

advocates for the negative income tax" and had been "frustrated by their inability to get their ideas accepted by the key policymakers in the Executive Office." Although they "had doubts about whether or not Shriver was right in his belief that the Institute's involvement would reduce political pressure, [they] saw the great advantages of including the Institute, which had several staff members experienced in the income maintenance area, and pushed to work out the arrangements."[19] Here, analysts and clients alike were advocates in determining who would execute the research.

The entrepreneur has a refined sense of politics. He knows that the more that he questions the political implications of particular programs, the more he is exposing the legitimacy of existing programs. How indeed does one explain why a particular state has more military installations than any other state? The entrepreneur also asks a different question: How can we most efficiently get rid of an old bad program? He recognizes that while policy analysis and evaluation may give evidence that the government is engaged in a bad program, something still has to be done about getting rid of the program or providing a substitute for it. To admit that the program is poor, as the analysis indicates, is to expose the program manager in a particular agency to severe political costs. Thus, some analysts seek ways not only to compensate those who would be affected by a major program change but also to save face for the program manager. Other analysts, aware that analysis cannot stand by itself and must gain acceptance within and outside the bureaucracy, try to develop a consensus model of analysis. Such a model co-opts important actors during the process of analysis and, indeed, the analytical product itself is modified to gain acceptance as the study proceeds. An analyst certainly appreciates what it means for an agency head to call a presidential cabinet member in order to get acceptance for a particular recommendation in a study. Thus, the entrepreneur understands and uses his knowledge of politics.

19. The whole story is told by Walter Williams in *The Struggle for a Negative Income Tax: A Case Study 1965–70*, Public Policy Monograph, no. 1 (Seattle: University of Washington, Institute of Governmental Research, 1972), pp. 9, 12. See also Walter Williams, *Social Policy Research and Analysis: The Experience in the Federal Social Agencies* (New York: American Elsevier Publishing Co., 1971), pp. 76–82, 155–58.

Chart 2
Policy Analysts Are Not All Alike

Type of Analyst	Central Incentive/ Motivation	Standard of Success	Main Resources	Timing of Impact	Attitude Toward Policy Analysis
Technician	Opportunity to do policy-oriented research	Quality work that satisfies him and his peers	Comand of details and knowledge	Long term	Objective and apolitical; analysis an end in itself
Politician	Opportunity for self-advancement and personal influence	Satisfies his immediate client	Communication and coordination skills	Short term	Antianalytical; analysis a means for personal influence
Entrepreneur	Opportunity to pursue policy preferences	Acceptance of implementable policies which could aid beneficiaries	Knowledge plus communication and coordination skills	Balanced perspective: long and short term	Political and analytical; analysis a means for policy influence

SUMMARY

If this chapter has done nothing else, it should have made clear that there are a number of different sorts of policy analysts. Although the characteristics of our three general types do overlap, I have sorted out their main tendencies in chart 2. While to some extent most policy analysts work to please themselves, the technician does it most. Either he is his own client or he works to please his peers. The politician pleases himself by pleasing his immediate superior. The entrepreneur, in defense of his version of the public interest, either cannot admit to having a client or changes his client from time to time in pursuit of his policy preferences. The sources of the technician's political resources or power are his objectivity, expertise, and substantive knowledge. Not having quite the technician's command of knowledge, the politician relies on his skills of communication and coordination; trust, confidence, and persuasion are his tools for influencing the client. The entrepreneur, a hybrid type by definition, is both persuasive and knowledgeable; he is capable of providing timely, correct information and of building confidence with his client.

Depending on the type of analyst, there is either never much time or there is always time left. The technician does his work for the long term and for acceptance by his peers. The politician, at the other extreme, works for the short term and for acceptance by his client. The entrepreneur does both; he works on short-term assignments, but he also encourages long-term relationships with clients and works on studies that he will be able to use when the time is right. More so than the other types, the entrepreneur worries about implementation and the impact of policies on beneficiaries. In short, he is political but also analytical. The politician and technician complement each other's deficiencies in that one is almost antianalytical and the other is almost apolitical.

Enough of analytical types; it is time to move on to what they do.

2

Analysis as Advice

If our policymakers always knew where they wanted to go and how to get there, they would have no need for advisors or advice. Of course, in some policy areas their interest and expertise lead some of them to keep their own counsel. Yet when old policy problems are too complex or when new, unexpected problems arise, policymakers may feel directionless, full of conflict, and uncertain about the knowledge they possess. Wanting to avoid mistakes and do what is appropriate, they then turn to advisors. They may talk about the problem with a spouse at breakfast or with a trusted confidant at the office, or they may consult with a prestigious academician or the Joint Chiefs of Staff; but it is also likely that they will go to a policy analyst. Whether the policy analyst is writing a memorandum, or doing an analytical study, or administering a research contract, he is either getting ready to give advice or he is giving it. The policy analyst is an advisor, and policy analysis is advice.

Giving advice is as old as Adam and Eve. Moses took the advice of a relative when he organized the people of Israel. The pharoah had a department of planning to mark stones for shipping down the Nile and placing in the pyramids. Frederick W. Taylor, the apostle of efficiency, gave advice on shoveling; by studying how people worked, he improved their productivity. Then there were the scientists who were advisors during World War II and initiated the field of operations research. Others of us who were trained in public administration may recall the use of O & M (organization and methods) for solving management problems.[1] If you were an engineer involved in the selection of water resource projects, the "green book," with its impact on cost-benefit analysis, would be a benchmark.[2] And not too long ago, it was program budgeting, with its emphasis on systems and program analysis, that was in vogue. Every generation has had its "whiz kids," its bevy of experts who have advised and made themselves needed. According to Kelly, experts "have been indispensable in history." As he puts it,

New knowledge or new ways of putting the old, whether forbidden or public, sacred or secular, are the province of the expert, who "sees combinations we do not see," and by his vocation, as we presently define it, helps to translate them into action. He pronounces anathemas and justifications that serve us but are beyond our skill. Experts are revered or reviled; but they have been indispensable in history.

The expert as policy counsellor has been available to societies from earliest times, wearing among other transitory costumes those of magician, tax collector, confessor, constitution-writer, strategist, and

1. Organization and methods (O & M) "embodies . . . the idea of scientific approach to public management. Administrative bodies . . . have special branches whose job is to think objectively about their organization and methods of operation, and by thought and experiment to devise improved structure and procedures. [It is] the application of research methods to the conduct of . . . business"; see E. N. Gladden, *The Essentials of Public Administration* (New York and London: Staples Press, 1953), p. 204.

2. The complete title of the "green book" is *Report to the Inter-Agency Committee on Water Resources, Proposed Practices for Economic Analysis of River Basin Projects* (Washington, D.C.: U.S. Government Printing Office, May 1958). It contains the recommended principles and procedures to be followed in the analysis of river basin development projects. The green book is one of the earliest appearances of cost-benefit practices in the federal government. Cost-benefit analysis represents the application of welfare economics, public finance, and resource economics to questions of public choice; see A. R. Prest and R. Turvey, "Cost-Benefit Analysis: A Survey," *Economic Journal* 75 (December 1965): 683. The objective of cost-benefit analysis, according to Caiden, "is to enable decision makers to know the cost-benefit results of alternative programs and to allow them to allocate resources between competing programs, so that the estimated marginal returns would be equal on all programs. Cost-benefit analysis identifies relevant alternatives and clarifies their respective implications." See Gerald E. Caiden, *The Dynamics of Public Administration: Guidelines to Current Transformations in Theory and Practice* (New York: Holt, Rinehart and Winston, 1971), p. 196.

economic planner. The form has changed with convenience, values on the scale of knowledge, morale, and culture; but the function has stayed rather constant.[3]

Now comes the policy analyst, the latest in the family of advisors and experts who want to improve the management of public enterprises.

For years students of public administration have classified bureaucratic roles and functions as line and staff. Leonard D. White, for example, suggested that the function of staff is "to study administrative problems, to plan, to advise, to observe, but not to act. . . . It is always advice, however, and never command."[4] And the Dimocks concisely made the same point: "line connotes action; staff, advice."[5] Since policy analysts seldom run programs or implement major policy initiatives, by definition then they are in the staff business. Like other staff personnel, analysts answer congressional correspondence, write and deliver speeches for their bosses, and, like many of their predecessors, they share the same concerns.

Almost all advisors maintain a concern for objectivity. Often in competitive advisory situations, each advisor asserts his objectivity while attempting to impeach the other advisors. They seem to recognize that objectivity, or at least the illusion of objectivity, is a source of their strength. What is interesting about policy analysts is that many of them believe they are objective, and perhaps, within the limitations of analysis itself, they are. For example, in the late sixties a nursing manpower program was due to expire and an HEW analyst was assigned to a departmental team whose task was to recommend what to do. The team was dominated by nursing interests that wanted to build new schools of nursing. From his work, the analyst concluded that there was a surplus of slots in existing schools and that money should not be put into new facilities but instead ought to be used for scholarships and faculty in order to increase utilization. The analyst believed his analysis was

3. George A. Kelly, "The Expert as Historical Actor," *Daedalus* 92, no. 3 (summer 1963): 529.

4. Leonard D. White, *Introduction to the Study of Public Administration*, rev. ed. (New York: Macmillan Co., 1939), p. 42.

5. Marshall Edward Dimock and Gladys Ogden Dimock, *Public Administration*, 3d ed. (New York: Holt, Rinehart and Winston, 1964), p. 273.

straightforward and objective; and not wanting to participate in a "whitewash," he left the team and wrote his own 80-page report. As it turned out the analyst's recommendations were included in the legislation that renewed the nursing manpower program.

Most advisors, whether as outside consultants or as inside staff members, are also concerned about the consequences of being wrong or not sufficiently anticipating the needs of the client. The doctor or lawyer, if he is wrong, will probably not lose his entire practice but stands to lose only a single patient or client. If the analyst is wrong too often, he may lose his access to policymaking. Thus, a problem for the analyst is to ascertain when it pays to play it safe and when it pays to suggest an innovative idea that might backfire. In this respect, I found no evidence that policy analysts are any more or any less courageous than other staff personnel in their propensity to climb out on the proverbial limb.

Are bureaucratic policy analysts, then, different from other advisors? Not much, I think. After all, analysts are subjected to the same problems and pressures of incremental policymaking, and as a consequence both policy analysts and other staff have to respond to the demand for short-term, reliable answers. Perhaps technicians and entrepreneurs do have slightly more confidence than politicians and other staff in the value of policy research and so are likely to make investments of their own time and their agency's money in long-term efforts. Perhaps policy analysts are a little more skillful in quantitative techniques than other staff advisors. But these are not significant differences. It seems that the policy analyst has joined the ranks of the bureaucracy's anonymous advisors.

Some analysts, however, feel that they are not advisors. In their view, all they do is provide *information* to policymakers. The word "advice" sounds too much as though they were making, or at least suggesting, decisions. The word advisor, to them, means that they should have a close relationship to the policymakers, and they know that they seldom see the policymaker because they are buried in the bureaucracy. As we will see in this chapter, despite these feelings of some analysts, analytical information is used to make, explain, and support decisions. Often policymakers need the information and advice quickly and so the analyst becomes a "fire fighter." Sometimes there is more time and in-house studies can be done or contracts can be issued to undertake policy research. As the requirements of the policymaking process change, so does the advisory role of the policy analyst.

FLAPS AND FIRE DRILLS

In one agency an analyst was asked about his work schedule. He replied that he spent 30 percent of his time on "garbage" (mostly correspondence relating to internal staff operations), 50 percent on longer reports, and 30 percent on quick-and-dirty analyses for an assistant secretary. When it was pointed out that his percentages added up to over 100, he laughed and replied, "Well, I guess that's the way it is."

Sometimes bureaucracies are depicted as citadels of routine and stability where work can be easily planned and programmed. Tranquility does exist at some bureaucratic levels but not where the analyst lives. The analyst who is used and not ignored is by definition a busy analyst. Every day brings another crisis; and when there are no deadlines, the boss will create them. Instant information, quick-and-dirty memos, briefings, and harried analysts are the ingredients of this fire-fighting, flapping atmosphere. No wonder the analyst feels that he spends more than 100 percent of his time on the job.[6]

One typical analyst describes his work as "putting out fires for the secretary. We go where the heat is, but we try to anticipate the secretary's needs for information and problems before they arise. Hopefully the secretary won't need to call us out on a fire drill; we should spot the problem on our own." A desirable expectation, no doubt, but hard to live up to. No analyst can completely anticipate the demands of decision makers and the vagaries of the policymaking process. Certainly much of the short-term, short-fuse work involves responses to unanticipated inquiries. The analyst never knows when he will have to write a one- or two-page memo, answer specific questions on the phone, or give advice at meetings.

One day a Treasury Department analyst, for example, was asked by an assistant secretary to generate estimates of the effect on federal revenues should the Lockheed Corporation fail. On

---

6. One analyst told me that this crisis atmosphere is mitigated by the feeling that he has security and cannot be fired.

another occasion he was asked to comment on a draft report of a congressional committee that was studying the Lockheed loan issue. Not particularly eager to see Lockheed get governmental financial support and busy with other things, he did these short-term, off-the-cuff tasks but considered them an "interruption."

What is an interruption for some is bread and butter for others. Short-term work can be the payoff for having been ready at other times and for having shown a capability for analysis and research. The quick call from OMB, Congress, the White House, or another agency signifies acceptance of the utility of the policy analyst by his clients. Secretary Richardson of HEW, for instance, showed this kind of acceptance; and when he was going to the hill to defend the Family Assistance Plan (FAP),[7] analysts at OEO were able to respond by working overnight to bring together from the New Jersey experiments what information they had on the effect of FAP on work incentives.

Whether the quick response is made overnight, in a few days, in a couple of weeks, or at most over six months, short-term work is definitely a prevalent activity for the policy analyst. In such a situation the analyst often does not create knowledge. Instead he uses the knowledge that is available or the people he knows. Without a telephone he would be in trouble. He is like a manufacturer assembling a product out of somebody else's resources. In his assembling he adds an element of quality control by screening information. As a screen or filter he relies on his professional training but also uses his experience. And he learns to do everything faster; he cuts corners and, by working with rough assumptions, tries to do a one-year job in a couple of days. The aim is to be 90 percent rather than 30 percent right in two days; if one waits a year to be 100 percent right, the policy decision will have already been made.

7. The Family Assistance Plan (FAP) was proposed by the Nixon administration in August 1969. It was designed to restructure the existing welfare system. Under the FAP proposal, each family of four would receive a guaranteed $1,600 per year. In addition, the plan would have enlarged the federal role in other public assistance programs. For a discussion of the origins of the plan and the unsuccessful attempts to obtain congressional approval, see Theodore R. Marmor and Martin Rein, "Reforming 'The Welfare Mess': The Fate of the Family Assistance Plan, 1969–72," in *Policy and Politics in America*, ed. Allan P. Sindler (Boston: Little, Brown and Co., 1973), pp. 2–28. See also Daniel P. Moynihan, *The Politics of a Guaranteed Income: The Nixon Administration and the Family Assistance Plan* (New York: Random House, 1973).

The agenda for short-term policy advice can be set by an important political actor inside or outside the analyst's department. In one situation, for example, a White House aide called the administrator of the Federal Insurance Administration, a component of HUD, for policy positions on whether labor's fringe benefits should be frozen as part of one of the phases of President Nixon's efforts to control inflation. He also requested another policy paper on the treatment of insurance rates during the same phase. After clearing the project with HUD's Office of the Secretary, the administrator turned the project over to an analyst. Or OMB, another outside actor, may turn over a farm bill to the Department of Agriculture for its review. In the analyst's words, "We discuss it with them and try to speak for the rural interests. We may advise them that this is not the proper time to propose the issue, and that they should wait until an upcoming election." Reviewing legislative proposals is an opportunity for analysts who are in the policy and program "development" business. A proposal, whether from the agency's general counsel or congressional opposition, implies some pressure for change; therefore, the analyst can suggest new policies or modifications to old programs.

Short-term work does not always take the form of a policy memo or paper. The client may use the analyst as an extension of himself, and in such cases the analyst is not that different from other staff assistants. One policy analyst in the Department of Transportation said that he did a "great deal of troubleshooting for the secretary's office on problems dealing with FAA." Evidently the Federal Aviation Administration was not cooperating with other agencies in forming general departmental policy. The analyst described his work as not really being analysis but mainly "running over and wiping their noses." Another analyst, this one at OEO and an expert in the intricacies of revenue sharing, traveled as an assistant to Vice-President Agnew on two trips to various states. The vice-president would deliver off-the-cuff talks to legislators, governors' staff, and interest-group representatives on the merits of revenue sharing. After a talk he would answer questions; and when a highly technical question came up, he would turn to the analyst sitting behind him to answer it. By the second trip the vice-president was better informed and could answer the questions himself, so the analyst found that trip "boring."

Most analysts experience a tension between getting involved in short-term problems and wanting to think ahead about the long-range fundamental issues their agencies face. For some, short-term demands simply drive out important long-term basic research activities. For others, short-term work is attractive in its own right. Not everybody wants to stay out of the firehouse. According to the head of a large analytical office, analysts should be able to "pick up the bucket when the bell rings and conceive of their role as one of trying to have an impact on policy as it is being developed. That is, one would proceed on the basis of convictions that there is a great deal of latitude in how particular policy outcomes emerge, and that the application of analytical insight, well-thought-through data, and well-presented alternatives can make a difference in the short run." He goes on to note that "if you put together a group of people who are truly motivated to develop good policy ideas . . ., who are action oriented, who are creative and imaginative, they are inevitably going to want to be where the action is. They're inevitably going to want to be involved at least in those decisions in which there are bigger stakes, . . . and so . . . they will become very heavily involved and drawn into the short-run policy concerns."

THE ANALYST AS CONTRACT COORDINATOR

Reflecting on his experience in the federal government, William Gorham, president of the Urban Institute, suggests that when "the staff is small, the analytical operation is of necessity a bridging one." For those who are setting up analytical staffs, he cautions, "Make effective use of outside resources."[8] That effectiveness will depend on the analyst and on how serious he considers the job of contract coordinator.

When the analyst does not know what he thinks the agency should know, he gets into the business of supervising research contracts. Paying someone else to do research on long-term problems while fending off the short-term ones is a common, if not always effective, mode of operation. "If I only had the time," the typical analyst says, "I could come up with the answers." Not having the time, he turns the work over to a trusted colleague in a

8. William Gorham, "Getting into the Action," *Policy Sciences* 1 (summer 1970): 175.

university or research think tank, such as Rand or the Urban Institute. His natural predilection for research is also encouraged by the legislative earmarking of a small percentage of program funds for evaluation, by the desire for trial or test projects, and of course by those officials who feel good when they support research.

Of course, there are analytical and strategic situations when it does not pay to use contractors. Maintaining bureaucratic secrecy is one such situation. Another is when you know more than they do. As one analyst put it, "The other day some people from one of the major, profit-mad consulting firms came in with some 'great new' ideas. These guys were about eight months behind us. And the problem I faced here was, do I have to sit down with these guys and bring them up to speed or not. . . . Now, my answer to that was no. I would have had to spend an hour, and that was too much."

The trick to using contract research (or any analysis for that matter) is to anticipate future informational needs. In the early 1960s a senior policy analyst at Treasury (at the deputy assistant secretary level) saw that the department would face a critical issue over depreciation allowances by 1965. The problem hinged on departmental guidelines allowing for a shorter life for plant and equipment. By 1965 firms were either to replace their plant according to the guidelines or set up a reserve for replacement. The analyst suspected that many firms would be hard hit because they were probably claiming shorter lives without setting up adequate reserves. In any event, a nine-month study was launched using a Pittsburgh contractor to perform a simulation with survey data of the probable effects on various firms. The study confirmed the analyst's suspicions, and the department rescinded its 1965 deadline in favor of spreading enforcement over four years.

Even when informational needs cannot be anticipated and indeed turn out to be the opposite of what was intended, contractors sooner or later get involved. The National Aeronautics and Space Administration (NASA) provides an interesting example. In the early 1960s, in response to criticism that growth of space programs would draw scientists and engineers out of priority defense work, NASA cooperated with the Department of Defense in creating a data bank on the employees of contractors. The data bank included information on the work force, the area, contractor dollar volume of work, and specific projects; it was collected semiannually from about 600 contractors across the nation. By 1966 NASA reached peak employment; afterward, as equipment for the Apollo program was completed, employment by NASA's contractors decreased. For a while the manufacture of equipment for the Vietnam war absorbed the laid-off workers, but by 1970 this was no longer the case. At about this time NASA's administrator requested information on the effects of the cutbacks. NASA thought that Congress was assuming that a shift of one dollar from NASA to, say, HEW had no effect on national purchasing power. Under some time pressure, NASA's analysts produced a report showing that the assumption was inaccurate and that such a shift caused a decrease in total purchasing power. But the analysts were not happy with their report; they felt it provided only an interim answer to a set of complex problems.

With the administrator's support, the analysts expanded the question to use the data bank for an extensive study of the economic impact of aerospace layoffs. As one of the analysts told us, "It's not unusual that when we finally get around to answering a question the lag is so great that the question itself has changed." NASA then contracted with the Battelle Memorial Institute to do the study, and Battelle's work showed the effect of cutbacks on aerospace and national unemployment and on the migration of scientific personnel to nonscientific fields. The NASA analyst who headed the team that worked with Battelle was made responsible for developing further uses of the data bank.

Like Mary and her lamb, where there are policy analysts there are sure to be contractors. Resorting to contractors is a natural extension of the work of the analyst. For another example, consider the HUD office responsible for enforcing and developing standards for equal opportunity in the sale and rental of housing. At the time of my research, the staff of this office were in the process of compiling data on minority hiring and on the purchase and rental of homes by minorities. They expected that their analysis of these data would enable them to identify any discriminatory patterns that might exist. As part of this activity, the office contracted for a comparison of 1970 with 1960 census data which would analyze the distribution of minorities and determine whether communities were resisting equal opportunity in housing.

Some analysts become contract coordinators because they have expressed an intellectual interest in the problem at hand. One

OEO analyst, for example, thought it would be desirable to develop a simulation model that would examine the economic effects of concentrations of urban poverty. He had conducted a seminar on the subject at OEO. Then he took a leave. When he returned he found that the Urban Institute had submitted a proposal for a similar project, and he was assigned to supervise the contract.

What does the analyst do when he becomes a contract administrator? His activities may range from merely going through the motions and letting the available money and time determine the research agenda, to becoming so intensely involved that the distinction between contractor and administrator disappears. In the case of field experiments, for example, such as experiments with performance contracting in education[9] or with the negative income tax, analysts may try to issue a tight research design and become involved in the choice of contractors and locations and in most phases of the production of the research. Yet a limit to such intense involvement is created as funds for the contract research increase. When the funds for evaluation in one shop of the Office of Education increased from $1 to $16 million, the resident analyst, a capable technician, found himself consulting on more contracts, going to more meetings, and becoming more and more frustrated in his role, which he described as that of "midwife."

Coordinating contractors can have its payoffs. The design of the proposed research can be improved, and in areas involving considerable expenditures for equipment and "hardware," contractors' proposals can be screened for cost-effectiveness.[10] While the evaluation of proposals can precipitate an agenda for extensive studies, often just meeting with contractors can bring results. A NASA analyst, for example, was visited by representatives of RCA, who proposed adding a kit to the lunar rover to make it operable over a longer period of time. This would call for an additional

9. Performance contracting is a form of accountability in education. It usually means hiring a private firm to teach students and paying the firm on the basis of how much the students learn.

10. Cost-effectiveness analysis is concerned with determining "which of several alternative courses of action will provide maximum effectiveness for a given cost, or minimum cost for a given [level] of effectiveness." See Alfred Blumstein and Richard C. Larson, "A Systems Approach to the Study of Crime and Criminal Justice," in Philip M. Morse, ed., *Operations Research for Public Systems* (Cambridge, Mass. and London: M.I.T. Press, 1967), p. 160.

expenditure of several millions of dollars. The NASA analyst arranged a meeting of RCA and the manned space flight staff to discuss the addition. At the meeting it was determined that the project would cost more than RCA had suggested and that a number of technical difficulties would arise because of the addition of the kit at that particular stage of the space program. Therefore, NASA's personnel agreed that the RCA proposal should be rejected, and the analyst sent a memo explaining the reasons for the rejection to his boss, Dr. Wernher von Braun, a deputy associate administrator of NASA.

The administration of other people's research or experimentation can become such a large job that an entire office can be devoted to it, with little time or inclination to do in-house policy analysis. A case in point was HUD's research and technology unit. Headed by an assistant secretary, it had about 100 people and enjoyed a research budget running into the tens of millions. The assistant secretary, along with others, formulated the research agenda for the department while his staff contracted for and monitored approved projects. One of the unit's clients, a politically minded analyst, explained that he preferred to transfer the study of major policy issues to the Office of the Assistant Secretary for Research and Technology in order to keep his staff free to aid his own assistant secretary daily.

A major activity of the research and technology unit was monitoring Operation Breakthrough, a comprehensive program for increasing housing through technological innovation, volume production, and an aggregation of the housing market.[11] One analyst, for example, was responsible for preparing biweekly briefings on the status of Operation Breakthrough. The office also had an elaborate "control room" for viewing the progress of contracts under its jurisdiction. The room, reminiscent of rooms in Grade B movies (and of rooms I have worked in at the Pentagon and Rand),

11. Operation Breakthrough, sponsored by the Department of Housing and Urban Development (HUD), was an attempt to develop and test innovations in housing design, construction, financing, and marketing. It was designed to "develop a mechanism which would provide volume production of marketable housing at stable or reduced costs for all income groups, particularly those in the lower income range." The program began in fiscal year 1971 and was terminated in fiscal year 1974. The total cost of Operation Breakthrough was an estimated $65 million; see U.S. Department of Housing and Urban Development, "Operation Breakthrough," *HUD Challenge* 3, no. 6 (June 1974): 10.

was about 30 feet by 20 feet in area and had walls covered with color-coded charts and graphs. On one wall was the overall schedule for Breakthrough by time and money. On another wall were two exhibits displaying the current progress of various HUD contractors. The first exhibit categorized Breakthrough's pilot projects by identifying the six or seven contractors and the eight sites; each site had two or three contractors constructing housing units. The second exhibit monitored the progress of individual contracts: on the left side was a panel of cards, each containing information concerning a contract—its cost and completion date—and a string stretching from the bottom of each card to the right illustrated progress toward completion of the contract. The same wall was also equipped with a gigantic calendar on which a large red circle identified the day's date. A third wall contained a detailed listing of the goals to be accomplished by the department's research and technology program. These goals included, for example, "preventing the spread of urban blight," "providing housing to meet national needs," and "improving the environment." To the right of the goals was a display showing the budget allocation for contracts for various years. Contracts were designated by color to indicate the goal under which each contract was classified. The fourth wall contained a sliding panel for each pilot project of Operation Breakthrough. For instance, the project in Kalamazoo, Michigan, had a panel showing the various designs used by its three contractors, a picture of the building site, sketches of the housing models, and lists of the cost, schedules, and program plans.

My own experience with such rooms is that they are shown to everybody but used by practically no policymakers to make decisions.[12] They take up the time of creative people, deflecting

12. A similar feeling is shared by Sapolsky in his evaluation of the Management Center, an elaborate room designed to show the progress of the Polaris program. As he says, "Management graphics and the Management Center can also be eliminated as candidates for commendation. The brightly colored classified charts that lined the Management Center normally attracted the eyes of visitors only. The Management Center itself, though the site of many conferences and the weekly meeting, was not the place to which the Admiral or his staff would go for a 'quick look' at the program's progress or to handle a crisis. In the Special Projects Office up-to-date information on the status of the program was obtained by picking up a telephone and calling the relevant technical group or by ordering tickets and flying to the relevant location." Harvey M. Sapolsky, *The Polaris System Development: Bureaucratic and Programmatic Success in Government* (Cambridge, Mass.: Harvard University Press, 1972), pp. 107–108.

them from innovation to public relations. Generally, the displays are geared to past decisions and soon get out of phase with the policymaker's current demands for information. When the rooms do contain relevant information, there is too much of it. Some data reduction, some focus, some analysis is needed before the policymaker will see that action is required. Displaying everything provides advice on nothing. The policymaker who wants tight control over a program can be given the requisite information without elaborate displays. Such rooms, however, are important for organizational maintenance—they show outsiders that the agency is "on top of the problem."

THE WRITER

Writing is an essential link between the desires of the client and the standards of the analyst. Depending on its purpose, a written communication can clarify or obfuscate, inform or persuade (see chapter 7). Despite the prevalent image of the analyst tinkering with his computer, he spends a great deal of his time writing. His ability to write is an essential ingredient of his bureaucratic success. He writes speeches, answers to congressional and other inquiries, policy issue memos, study reports, presidential reports, critiques of periodical articles, procedures, and research designs. Bureaucracies thrive on written communication, and analysts do not escape the bureaucratic tendency to get everything down on paper, often if just for the file.

At the National Science Foundation (NSF), one analyst said that most of her work involved the preparation of written analysis. She had just completed a "discussion paper" on the question: "What should the foundation's role be in the support of education?" The paper discussed NSF's promotion of science through grants to assist in the education of high school teachers and seminars involving the university with the community.

One branch chief of an analytical shop at OEO was responsible for preparing summaries of research proposals for a selection committee. She would send the summaries to the committee even when "some of the suggested projects were clearly half-baked." The person in charge of the writing, in this case a summary, can have considerable influence. As the OEO branch chief said, "When something is a bad proposal, all I have to say is this is the problem and state the proposed solution in a way that clearly demonstrates that it will not have the desired consequences of attacking the problem. After stating that, it will be unnecessary for me to take the next step and recommend that the proposal be rejected." Another analyst at OMB spent his time writing "elegant questions" for White House officials to use for cutting out "bad programs."

Because of the constant reorganization of the federal bureaucracy, regional and local officials are often confused about who is doing what and how they should proceed. Writing operating procedures is supposedly one way out of this man-made mess. In HUD, with its transfer of personnel and program authority to a number of regional and area offices, procedure writing became part of the job of the Washington analysts. Consider HUD's annual arrangements program in which a city was encouraged to plan its use of federal funds for a year in exchange for a commitment by the federal government to deliver the necessary funds.[13] In 1971 HUD's operating officials held a conference intended to simplify the process, and after that a letter was sent out to the regional offices suggesting that each office develop comprehensive funding procedures. Back came a set of haphazard and diverse techniques from the regions. So some analysts were called in to develop an issue paper that would outline for the local offices the major components of an annual arrangement. As another HUD analyst put it, "When I was in evaluation I used to think of procedure writing as nit-picking. I now see that in a decentralized organization such as HUD, unless the procedure is very carefully and strategically written, the policy may have the reverse effect than that intended by the decision maker."

13. The annual arrangements process is an attempt to circumvent "the categorical structure of the Department of Housing and Urban Development's (HUD) grant-in-aid programs. Although [HUD] cannot shift money among the categories without violating the law, its annual arrangements attempt to give the mayor the ability to pick and choose among projects as if he had total discretion over a no-strings-attached grant of community development money." In March 1973, HUD had annual arrangements completed with 79 cities and was negotiating with an additional 150 cities; see *National Journal* 5, no. 9 (3 March 1973): 301.

STUDIES: ON TOP AND IN TEAMS

When the analyst is not flapping, administering contracts, or writing speeches, he does "studies." This analytical activity has a longer time fuse than his other advisory assignments and usually involves some continuing organizational responsibility. Either because of personal interest or an organizational division of labor of the policy turf, analysts shed their generalist clothes and become "experts" in selected areas. Typically, the analyst comes into a large analytical office after writing a dissertation—say, on medical manpower. At first he joins other health experts and his interest in manpower problems continues, but as time passes his work expands to include the problems of rising hospital costs and Medicare and even nutrition. So far so good, but then the office's expert on higher education leaves and the office needs a replacement. Our analyst is transferred and told to get on top of the new area. The head of the analytical office thinks that it is a small step from knowing hospital costs to understanding the financing of higher education.

The policy turf is divided so that studies cover the important areas. Usually there is a resident expert in each area doing studies in order to keep current and stay on top of new developments and issues. Thus, most heads of analytical shops encourage research projects; they feel that they must build in their staff a fund of knowledge in a variety of substantive areas, so that whatever problems arise can be attacked quickly. Such assignments also keep the analysts happy. An analyst in the Treasury Department, for example, keeps on top of the tax laws of other nations in order to anticipate problems in the interrelationships between the United States and other countries. Studying foreign tax laws may also suggest policy ideas for changes in our tax laws.

Being an "expert" can be embarrassing when the analyst has not had time to get on top. When I first joined Rand's Cost Analysis Department and was assigned to cover the area of aircraft engines, I didn't know one engine from another, so I ran to the library to get some books and started scanning various reports on production costs. After two weeks I began to know at least the names of the different kinds of existing engines. Then the trouble began; I started getting phone calls for information. A nationally known propulsion engineer wanted some cost data for some new designs, and a UCLA economics professor, who was doing a cost-effectiveness study, wanted to know the maintenance costs of a ram-jet engine that had not even been built yet. When I started backpedaling on the phone, the usual response was, "What's the problem, aren't you Rand's expert in costing engines?" In arcane subjects, where no one else is working, two weeks makes you an "expert."

A compelling argument among critics of analysis is that it lacks a coherent body of disciplinary knowledge and standards of its own. "The variegated experts who have chosen to invade the market for systems studies and designs," Ida Hoos tells us, "have been slower to acknowledge the inadequacy of their tools for the job to be done. . . . In the move into the systems field they have come from a heterogeny of intellectual backgrounds, in all of which certain bodies of theory and reservoirs of accumulated knowledge kept them within bounds. The farther from home base the experts have roved, the more attenuated has become the discipline."[14] Part of the explanation for this attenuation and lack of coherence, at least for bureaucratic policy analysts, is the very diversity of assignments the analyst is given.

At the time of my research, diversity was the norm. As part of NASA's planning efforts its analysts were working on a cost-benefit study of the space shuttle system, for example.[15] They were also responsible for coordinating the planning of NASA's various divisions and for developing a 20-year plan for the agency. At the General Services Administration (GSA), analysts were at work on what might be described as a records management study. GSA was responsible for storing some of the Internal Revenue Service's records. After one of their studies the GSA analysts were able to convince IRS that some records did not have to be retained. Another of their studies suggested that the National Archives should decentralize its stock of microfilmed documents. An analyst

14. Ida R. Hoos, *Systems Analysis in Public Policy: A Critique* (Berkeley and Los Angeles: University of California Press, 1972), pp. 245–46.
15. The space shuttle is a proposed two-stage rocket-propelled system whose orbiting component would fly back to earth like an airplane. It is designed to be an economical means of sending men and satellites into earth orbit; see *Congressional Digest* 51, nos. 6–7 (June–July 1972): 174.

for the Office of Education was concerned about forecasting educational trends, such as an expected surplus of teachers.

Other analysts work on distributional rules for governmental grants; for example, on what basis should HUD distribute its sewer grants or the Economic Development Administration its largess? Should everybody get a little or should distribution be based on some indicator of need? The general problem is that requests for grants amount to ten times the available money, and the complaints to congressmen pile up. So analysts are assigned the job of developing reasonable bases for distribution other than the postmark of the request. Then the president decides that so many millions should be spent in an area—say, child health care —without specifying *what* they should be spent on, and the analyst finds himself a member of a task force studying the effects of alternative programs. No doubt diversity of assignments and frequent transfers result in thin expertise and an inability to follow through; but there are possible advantages—organizational freshness rather than rigidity, analytical excitement rather than boredom, and open thinking rather than the closed thinking of professional orthodoxy.

Besides developing expertise in certain policy areas and having to cope with diverse assignments, another important influence on the analyst's advisory role is the frequent use of teams. While universities may encourage their researchers to work alone, governmental bureaucracies do not. Teams, task forces, and advisory groups are commonplace in the production of policy analysis. Working through a team is a convenient way of getting analytical resources—for example, people, access, and information—and of ensuring some measure of political support from the numerous tentacles of the bureaucratic octopus.

In such teams, however, one is never sure of who is co-opting whom. In the early 1960s I was working as a consultant day and night in the Pentagon. One day I was told that I was to be chairman of an office of the secretary of defense team on naval decision making. I knew that it was ridiculous to be given just a few weeks to analyze the central decision-making process of the whole Department of Navy (including the marines), but an assignment was an assignment. Before long I was presented with a room full of senior military men who had been delegated to help and to ensure that the interests of their various offices were represented. Throughout the following weeks I turned down invitations to take rides on aircraft carriers and submarines and instead steered the team onto a round of interviews with key admirals. During the interviews I tried to get some glimpse of the formal and informal planning and decision-making processes but was often presented with a justification of why the navy needed more planes or nuclear aircraft carriers. At one meeting of the team by itself, for example, I was trying to explain the importance of considering alternatives in military decisions. A marine colonel who had spent most of the meeting doing deep-knee bends jumped up from his crouched position and banged on the table, "In the marines, we have no alternatives." One of the blessings of a short study is that it comes to a quick end.

A more appropriate example of a team effort is provided by a study from the National Institutes of Health (NIH), a component of HEW.[16] After a major reshuffling of the health area in April 1968, NIH still faced a number of complex and difficult organizational problems. NIH had expanded considerably as a result of the addition of the Bureau of Health Manpower (BHM) with its budget of roughly $300 million and staff of 800. One policy problem was what to do with the bureau. Given the fact that its responsibilities were similar to those of other offices in NIH—most particularly to those of the Division of Research Facilities and Resources (DRFR)—how should BHM be organized and integrated into the scheme of things? By April 22 a study team was set up; it was composed of a chairman, an analyst who worked in the Office of the Director of NIH, and one representative from BHM and one from DRFR. Acting under some considerable time pressure, the team conducted 50 interviews, reviewed the advisory groups and legislative authority for a multitude of programs (for example, the Allied Health Professions Personnel Training Act of 1966 and the Health Research Facilities Act of 1956), evaluated four alternative organizational plans, and submitted their 249-page report by July 10, 1968. The various plans ranged from major reorganizations to a

16. U.S. Department of Health, Education, and Welfare, Public Health Service, National Institutes of Health, *Reorganization of the NIH: Bureau of Health Manpower and Division of Research Facilities and Resources*, A Study for the Director, National Institutes of Health (Washington, D.C., 10 July 1968).

status quo alternative with better coordination. One of the plans, which the director of NIH favored, would have restricted NIH manpower concerns to physicians, dentists, and osteopaths. Responsibility for nursing and other health professionals and service technicians would be transferred outside of NIH to the Health Services and Mental Health Administration. This separation of BHM functions was to preserve the traditional identification of NIH with scientific research. The chairman of the team, however, felt that the manpower functions should stay together. Because the team found that "a review of the primary organizational issues reveals matters subject to some considerable political as well as programmatic judgment," the members of the team decided not to endorse any particular plan in their report.[17] A perusal of the 1971 HEW telephone directory (always a good guide for traversing the tortured path of federal reorganizations), however, indicates that the team, for the most part, got its way as the manpower functions were not separated from the NIH family.

THE ANALYST AS EVALUATOR

Sometimes another word for policy analysis is evaluation. Like other professionals, policy analysts attempt to designate their activities precisely. Fine distinctions, however, are as likely to lead to obscuration as they are to clarity. The same word can encompass many different advisory activities, and the same activity can be called by different names. Moreover, some words are more fashionable than others; and if the analyst is going to remain an advisor he must call his work by the name that is *de rigueur*. When I was doing my interviews, the OK word was "evaluation." Analysts were quite interested in making distinctions between analysis and evaluation. The staff of the president's Advisory Council on Executive Organization was seriously considering a quasi-public institute for evaluation. Not only would the institute gather basic facts and information on federal programs, but it would also be a source for methodological innovation. According to the council's staff, the skills used in evaluation were different from those of analysis. Evaluation was a kind of "market research" which one did before

17. *Ibid.*, p. 7.

doing analysis. Without evaluation, the analyst would make up data out of whole cloth.

The distinction between analysis and evaluation is usually made in terms of time. Analysis of past and present programs is evaluation. When the work covers hypothetical or future policy alternatives, then that is analysis. As Joseph S. Wholey and his team of evaluators put it: "Evaluation's preoccupation with existing programs differs from 'program analysis' and 'policy analysis' which usually compare existing *and* hypothetical alternative program solutions to the same problem."[18] But when an existing program is evaluated and found to be deficient, then what? Suppose the program cannot be abandoned but has to be fixed: is the suggestion of alternative solutions evaluation or analysis?

The book from which the above quotation is taken is a study of the federal government's evaluation practices and deficiencies. It is based on a sample of 15 programs which "represents a range of evaluation efforts."[19] On the list is HEW's program for maternal and child health, an area in which Wholey has some expertise as he was the key analyst who produced HEW's *program analysis* on the subject.[20] Indeed, the lessons he learned in doing that program analysis were used in his book on evaluation and in an article for a congressional committee.[21] The deficiencies in evaluation that Wholey quite correctly points out, however, are deficiencies in analysis as well. Getting data about the effects of federal programs, for example, could have been discussed and sold in terms of

18. Joseph S. Wholey et al., *Federal Evaluation Policy: Analyzing the Effects of Public Programs* (Washington, D.C.: Urban Institute, 1970), pp. 23–24.

19. *Ibid.*, pp. 17–18.

20. U.S. Department of Health, Education, and Welfare, Office of the Assistant Secretary for Program Coordination, *Program Analysis: Maternal and Child Health Care Programs* (Washington, D.C., October 1966). The Department of Health, Education, and Welfare's (HEW) Maternal and Child Health Care Program was designed to increase the availability of health and dental care services to expectant mothers and children in "health-depressed" areas, that is, in areas with high infant mortality rates, poverty, and substandard housing. In fiscal year 1971, $118,600,000 was allocated for the program; see *Budget of the United States, Appendix, Fiscal Year 1971* (Washington, D.C.: U.S. Government Printing Office, 1971), p. 381.

21. Joseph S. Wholey, "The Absence of Program Evaluation as an Obstacle to Effective Public Expenditure Policy. A Case Study of Child Health Care Programs," in U.S. Congress, Joint Economic Committee, *The Analysis and Evaluation of Public Expenditures: The PPB System*, vol. 1, 91st Cong., 1st sess., 1969, pp. 451–71.

improving program analysis rather than instituting evaluation. Why wasn't it? Probably because program analysis was identified with a moribund and a not so popular program budgeting system (PPB) while evaluation was untainted.

Now that we know that some people think it important to distinguish analysis from evaluation, just where are we? Not very far from where we were in the first place, because analysts have different notions of evaluation, depending on what is being evaluated and how it is to be done.

An HEW policy analyst, working at the secretary level, felt that there were two kinds of evaluation. The first, target evaluation, reviews a specific program to see if it is meeting its objectives. The second, comparative evaluation, examines a function of the department by comparing the allocation of resources between health, education, and welfare programs. Another analyst, this one at HUD, saw evaluation as occupying a continuum: At one end of the continuum is the "sponge" evaluator. His type of evaluation emphasizes "sponging up all the information possible." He visits the project and observes in a nondirected manner anything he believes to be related to the project. (Another analyst has a similar conception when he describes evaluation as an informal process: "To most, evaluation sounds like a formal study; we prefer to consider it an assessment. Our evaluation is based on discussion with field personnel more than it is on a formal analysis of data.") At the other end of the continuum is the "academic" or "full-blown" evaluation; this involves hypothesis testing, research designs, control groups, and the like. The sponge type will lack consistency because different evaluators will look at the same project from different perspectives, but something close to it is necessary, so analysts say, when working within a restricted time schedule. The academic evaluation takes considerable time, probably employs contractors, and uses social science research to make judgments about policy.[22]

The prize for the use of distinctions should go to OEO. Who should do what, according to Walter Williams, was a problem at OEO. Analysts at the top had to work out a *modus vivendi* with program people, and this took the form of OEO Instruction No.

22. For an interesting discussion of evaluation research, see Carol H. Weiss, *Evaluation Research: Methods of Assessing Program Effectiveness* (Englewood Cliffs, N.J.: Prentice-Hall, 1972).

72-8. In the instruction, three types of evaluation were defined. The big area of assessing program impact and comparing programs (Type I) the analysts kept for themselves; the monitoring and within-project decisions (Types II and III) they left for the program people.[23] Wholey and his associates were impressed with the OEO distinctions and used them as a basis for their own list of four types: program impact evaluation, program strategy evaluation, project evaluation, and project rating.[24] They also thought that OEO could be used as a model for other agencies: "This study recommends that federal agencies adopt many of the evaluation procedures developed over the past few years at OEO. OEO is singled out as an example because evaluation has been used more effectively in that agency than in the other agencies examined in this study."[25]

No doubt OEO should be praised, but not for making such distinctions. Type I evaluation can overlap with Type II, and there is only a fine line between analyzing programs and evaluating impacts. What is one man's program is another's project. I suspect that there was confusion in using such distinctions but that they were necessary for settling internal jurisdictional conflicts or advancing territorial claims. In any event much analytical activity goes on under the rubric of evaluation. Whether sponge or scientist, the evaluator examining a particular program is a policy analyst in disguise. He looks backward for a diagnosis of experience, he looks to present experimentation for data, and he looks forward for great expectations.

MULTIPLE USES:

DECISIONAL AND SUPPORTIVE ANALYSIS

Policy analysis is like a hot dog because its ingredients can be varied according to the tastes of both producers and consumers. Up to this point we have been paying most of our attention to the producers, the analysts, and we have been ignoring the consumers and their needs for analysis. Assuming a uniform product, clients will still have many uses for analysis; and whether analysis becomes

23. Walter Williams, *Social Policy Research and Analysis: The Experience in the Federal Social Agencies* (New York: American Elsevier Publishing Co., 1971), pp. 108–11.
24. For definitions, see Wholey et al., *Federal Evaluation Policy*, pp. 24–26.
25. *Ibid.*, p. 61.

advice depends on its use. Benveniste, for example, in his discussion of the functions of planning, sees the primary use of expertise in reducing the policymaker's uncertainty about the choices he confronts. Then there are secondary functions: the analyst's expertise can be used to legitimate decisions or to provide the ballast for a trial balloon.[26] But how can we tell what is a primary or secondary function without understanding the specific context of policymaking?

In the bureaucracy, analysts are in the business of advising by providing information to policymakers. Knowing that they are informative, however, does not get us very far in understanding consumption or use. How do analysts, these "facts-and-figures men," satisfy the intelligence function?[27] Just what is done with analysis? Rather than discussing the use of analysis in terms of functions, which leaves open the question of intention, let us think for the moment of two categories of use or consumption: decisional and supportive. These categories are derived from the analyst's perceptions of the impact of his work. The analyst's world is fairly simple. Either the client wants to use the analysis to help make a decision or he has some other purpose in mind. For the analyst there is something immediate and direct about the first situation. He hopes decisional analysis will somehow influence the client to take some action; and the action will lead to an improved policy and to the effective behavior of both citizens and officials. The other situation, that of supportive analysis, is something most analysts do not like to talk about. They feel (often mistakenly) that it belittles them. Supportive analysis, they say, is an empty ritual. Who likes to work on a problem to justify a decision that has already been made? Yet justifying a policy is as important as determining it. Since much analytical activity is a matter of extending, explaining, and justifying the decisions of others, and since the line between information for a decision and information after a decision is blurred anyway, there is little point in tagging one secondary and the other primary.

Like Benveniste, however, most analysts make such a ranking. They do so because of their exaggerated trust in the efficacy of

26. Guy Benveniste, *The Politics of Expertise* (Berkeley, Calif.: Glendessary Press, 1972), pp. 23–60.

27. See Harold L. Wilensky, *Organizational Intelligence: Knowledge and Policy in Government and Industry* (New York: Basic Books, 1967), pp. 14–16.

ideas and knowledge. It is only after some seasoning in the bureaucracy that they begin to appreciate that ideas can be efficacious both before and after a decision, although in different ways. Katzenbach, in discussing the trend of government to contract for advice, reports that

One policy position, initiated within a government department, was finally sent out for editing and the appropriate imprimatur to a private analysis group simply to ensure its being read further up in the hierarchy. The cost was a thousand dollars a page, but the man who let the contract was content: the maneuver had actually saved the government many times that sum, he claimed, simply because it got the study read.[28]

This tactic is unique neither to government nor to policy analysis. In the late 1950s, when I was a novice beginning my analytic career in the private sector, I found myself working with a group of engineers who had studied a problem of whether there should be a central warehouse and where it should be located. After considerable effort we produced a study report that recommended a central warehouse and specified its location, but our superiors were reluctant to proceed because of the capital requirements involved in our recommendations. Instead they farmed the problem out to a well-known management consulting firm. The consultants took our study, put it between their covers, and the recommendation was implemented.

That consultant's "study" is a perfect example of supportive consumption. The clients, our superiors, already had agreed with the warehouse policy that emerged from our study, but there was some risk in proceeding without something to fall back upon "just in case." Sometimes an in-house study will provide the necessary support; sometimes only an unblemished outsider will do. In either case, supportive consumption is a ubiquitous phenomenon, as Wilensky points out: "When experts describe their functions as 'window dressing' and say they are 'there for front, for the show'; when they observe that 'really it boils down to public relations,' or 'supplying slogans,' they point to activities common to all experts everywhere—the defense of established policy."[29]

Whether for support of established policy or protection against the failure of a new venture, the policy analyst is the first line of

28. Edward L. Katzenbach, Jr., "Ideas: A New Defense Industry," *The Reporter*, 2 March 1961, p. 20.
29. Wilensky, *Organizational Intelligence*, p. 16.

defense. Whether to support an agency, a program, a client, or for that matter the analyst, a study helps. Consider NASA struggling against budget cuts in a climate of unmet social needs where space flight is viewed as a frivolous activity. I found that its analysts were (somewhat vainly) seeking social applications of space flight or trying to determine what effect the diverting of NASA funds would have on social needs. They tried to defend their budget in numerous other ways, from showing that inflation would affect them more than other federal agencies because of their labor-intensive nature, to indicating what impact the cancellation of this or that program would have on unemployment in a particular location. When a NASA official suggested the simultaneous development of a shuttle booster and orbiter, the analysts did a quick study which showed that the proposal would tie up resources for three to four years, thereby limiting efforts to produce private-sector applications of NASA's technology and thus damaging congressional support of the agency. Discussing NASA's lack of a constituency, one of its analysts said, "We are very wrapped up in justifying our program. People seem to be interested in what we are doing for them today."

Supportive analysis is particularly important when a policy of the administration is before Congress. When the supersonic transport (SST) was an issue, analysts at the Department of Transportation were busy answering questions on the economic effects of its cancellation. Their work was used in testimony and speeches, and they described their role as "strictly to justify the SST." Some analysts become so good at understanding their agency's viewpoint that it becomes their regular duty to answer congressional correspondence and prepare positions on pending legislation. They do not see such an activity as analysis: "Most of what we do is write justifications for the assistant secretary. He tells my boss what he wants and my boss tells me what to write; there's not much room for policy analysis."

To support or not to support, that is the question. On the one hand, the bureaucratic analyst must be loyal to his client. Thus, on the basis of his studies an analyst at Interior recommended against the Alaska pipeline; but he knew that, if his client, the secretary, approved the construction of the pipeline, he would write an analysis to support that decision. Clients who expect such loyalty are encouraging dishonesty in analysis. Honesty demands that the analyst also be loyal to himself and his feelings of objectivity.

Neither the analyst nor his work should be misused. An analyst at the National Science Foundation told me that frequently, when a problem is referred to her, she suspects that the decision has already been made but that someone is questioning it and the decision makers want support. As a case in point she cited her evaluation of an institutional development program. The main thrust of her report was on the quality of education delivered by the institutions, but her superiors used the report to emphasize the increased number of scientists enrolled in NSF-supported programs. Another analyst was assigned to a presidential task force on business taxation. The task force's main concern was to liberalize taxes on business without large losses of revenue. The analyst's job was to develop a computer program to estimate changes in revenue. As a conserver of the government's revenue he was not happy with the task force; he said it "was stacked in favor of a preconceived set of conclusions."

Bureaucratic analysts have to live with the psychological conflict of wanting to be both objective and supportive. Some technicians resolve the conflict by believing that presenting objective analysis is supportive, at least in the long run. Resolving this conflict is difficult for other analysts because supportive analysis involves not only the legitimation of the client and his policies but also the maintenance of the analyst and his shop. It is fortunate when an objective analysis is also supportive—as was the case, for the most part, with an evaluation of HUD's building code enforcement program. OMB had precipitated the need for a study when it decided that the program should be canceled and the money distributed to other HUD programs. HUD's undersecretary informed the assistant secretary in charge of code enforcement that, if the program was to have a chance of being reinstated, they would have to present a strong case to OMB. The evaluation would have to make the program look good. It was not surprising that the assistant secretary asked his new evaluation office for a report supporting and verifying the effectiveness of code enforcement.

The head of the evaluation office had different ideas. He wanted to conduct an objective evaluation which could result in either positive or negative findings, or both. One of his analysts found the study difficult because "we were a new office and wanted to demonstrate our credibility as objective evaluators. Also we felt the need to make our data useful to the assistant secretary." The head of the office went to the assistant secretary and told him not to "jeopardize your credibility over a 55-million-dollar program." He argued that if they came up with negative findings it would enhance the assistant secretary's reputation, which would work to his credit in future battles with OMB; and if they came up with mixed findings they would have the facts with which to defend the program and improve it. The assistant secretary decided to go along with the head of the evaluation office, to the surprise of his colleagues. At a breakfast of the senior staff he was asked if he was going to defend the code enforcement program. He replied, "I don't know whether we will or not. I have asked for an impartial evaluation to see whether code enforcement is any good."

The analysts had a practical problem because it takes some time to see the effect of code enforcement on the condition of housing, but they had to proceed anyway. After going on a whirlwind tour of twelve cities, they were told by a member of the assistant secretary's staff that it would be desirable to have cause-and-effect data that would support the program and emphasize its success; but that if the data did not warrant such conclusions, they should write the report in such a way that would show the success where it existed but also mention deficiencies. In the report they wrote over the following weekend, the analysts concluded that the program should be retained with the correction of certain deficiencies.

On the basis of this report, the assistant secretary went before OMB and successfully defended the program from elimination. Feeling good about the outcome of the study, the head of the evaluation office said,

I was brought here for both my understanding of programs and my understanding of methodology. I was told to give relevancy to analysis. Code enforcement was relevant and significant because we beat OMB. They wanted to kill the program, and in reaction the assistant secretary presented a factual report. His facts were sufficiently strong to make them back down and establish his credibility over theirs. He beat them at their own game and established a beachhead with them. They won't try to attack one of our programs again unless they really have something. There is nothing more relevant than beating OMB on facts.

Since the study only took about a month to complete, with most of the work done in one to two weeks, I would be skeptical that it was only the facts that beat OMB. A persuasive secretary and report might have had more to do with it. According to one of the analysts,

If we had had more time we could have given a much more useful indication of the program's strengths and weaknesses. The nature of the available data was our greatest limitation. The data that local code enforcement project officers had been gathering were very poor and related only to production (number of sites improved, average costs of sites, increase in value after improvement, etc.). We had to depend on our field visits, which gave us a general feel for the effect of the code enforcement projects. In the end we could not give a strong defense of the program based on data, but we were confident of the effectiveness of the program because of our observations.

Another participant had similar feelings:

We got many windshield tours of renovated neighborhoods and received complimentary comments from city and local officials. All of this, though, was simply a show put on by local program personnel and beneficiaries of the program. We discovered soon that the data vital to our study simply had not been collected. The lack of such data was a result of operating personnel being concerned with producing their program but oblivious to the need for demonstrating its effectiveness by getting quantitative measures. The lack of data hampered us greatly in producing what we believed was a respectable and objective evaluation.

Given the pressure for support, we must leave open the question of how objective the final report really was. Certainly all the participants felt that they were trying to be objective, and they did approach the evaluation openly and not with a whitewash in mind. But it is never quite realistic to expect political actors, bureaucrats or otherwise, to sponsor completely objective and neutral studies. The analyst, even when he thinks he is objective, does have preferences which he pursues through his studies; and his client cannot afford *not* to use an analysis, whether decisional or supportive, as a political resource. What we learn from the code-enforcement example is that an "objective" analysis can be supportive not only of the policy and its manager but of the analysts as well. One wonders what would have happened to the fledgling analytical shop if the evaluation had turned out to be completely negative.

Another thing we learn is that the analyst's distinction between decisional and supportive analysis breaks down. Both types stem from and lead to decisions. The same sequence—problem stimulus, search for information, action on information—is there whether the decision is to justify an old policy or initiate a new one. What is at stake seems to be the degree of openness with which the client allows the analyst to approach his task. At one rare extreme is the client who knows exactly what he wants to do, tells his analyst to back up his conclusions, and will not tolerate any deviation or opening up of the problem. Then there is the more typical case where the client partially delimits the analytical problem. For example, the president adopts revenue sharing as a policy worth pursuing; then it is entirely appropriate and reasonable to use analysts to explore alternative formulas and determine the policy's consistency with other financial aid measures and its possible effects on intergovernmental relationships. It seems unduly cynical to view such analytical activities as only justification and support for the preconceived notions of a political actor. Would we rather have our public officials so devoid of policy ideas that all they can do is plead with their analysts to tell them what to do?

CONCLUSION

No doubt some clients are the victims of their analysts, and some analysts the victims of their clients. Analysts are occasionally put to work to show that an agency cares about a problem when in fact a decision has been made to do nothing about the problem for a while. And both the producers and sponsors of a study can be surprised at its use in the political arena. That some bad analysis can get so much mileage while some good analysis turns out to have been part of an empty ritual is nothing but testimony that analysis is advice—to be used and abused as it has been through the centuries. Although analysts can influence the use of their work, I am inclined to agree with the analyst who felt that he had had his "day in court" when he "provided a really good basis of action." He explained,

If you have made available, to whomever the important decision makers are, well-developed analyses, good definitions of problems, good insights into how they can be solved, and good notions about alternative ways of solving them, and if you're confident that they have been taken into consideration, read, and digested, then even if portions of them ultimately have to be ignored, rejected, or (inevitably in the democratic process) compromised, nevertheless you've done your job as an analyst.

You've provided the input that you were trained to provide and by your professional occupation want to provide; and it has been left to others, rightfully so, to decide how that information will be used.

No definition of policy analysis will sufficiently encompass the staff activity of the analyst. Whether providing advice or a service, comfort or support, the policy analyst is largely what his clients want him to be. He is an analytical jack-of-all-trades, called upon to be a fire fighter, contract administrator, procedure writer, team captain, and hand holder. He explains policies as well as analyzes them. He keeps on top of a substantive area; and out of the mass of information that enters the policymaking process, he filters the good from the poor. He generally works on the subject matter that is of concern to his agency and not necessarily of interest to his discipline. Nor do his assignments always stem from his particular discipline. One can find an engineer working on child-health problems and a medical doctor working on an organizational question. This tackling of diverse assignments has its strengths and weaknesses: the analyst may well endow his agency with a capacity for flexibility and adaptation, but at the same time he sometimes works with only a veneer of expertise. His total activity contributes to formulating and justifying public policy, to making decisions and supporting them—a distinction that is often blurred by the relationships between advisors and policymakers.

3

Problem Selection

A common complaint among policy analysts is that old programs have a constituency and new programs have no information. Does this mean that analysts have nothing to do and that there are no problems to be solved? Despite the cynicism that exists within the analytical community, there are indeed many problems to look at and a few to solve. Indeed, selecting a problem to work on is a primary economic and political decision. It is an economic decision because the analyst is a scarce resource whose talents should not be wasted on trivial assignments or on problems that defy even approximate solution. And it is also a political decision. Choosing the right problem has crucial implications for the political efficacy of the analyst, the policy, and its sponsors. It is one of the critical steps the analyst takes toward ensuring his own success. In addition, which policies are analyzed and which issues are raised influence who wins and who loses from governmental programs.

In our discussion, we will see bureaucratic forces at work on the behavior of the analyst. Particularly the structural feature of hierarchy—of many levels, ranks, and superior and subordinate positions—is a central force in the selection of problems.[1] Where

1. For a general discussion of hierarchy, see Robert Presthus, *The Organizational Society: An Analysis and a Theory* (New York: Vintage Books, 1965), pp. 31–36; and Anthony Downs, *Inside Bureaucracy* (Boston: Little, Brown and Co., 1967), pp. 50–58. For a more specific discussion of the distorting effects of hierarchy

an analyst sits can determine how he perceives and selects problems. Both analyst and client *accept* cues or signals from superior levels in the hierarchy. They also *take* cues from their environment and select problems to influence these superiors. While cues can come from Congress, the press, or practically anyone or any place in the arena of policymaking, it is mainly through the hierarchy of the bureaucracy that the cues are converted into actual selections for analysis.

We will start our discussion, somewhat artificially, with selection by the client; then we will focus on the analyst, concentrating on his criteria for selection. I say artificially because we are dealing with a situation of multiple causation. Not only do clients and analysts exchange cues and attempt to influence each other in problem selection, but they are often subjected to the same cues from external forces in their environment.

SELECTION BY THE CLIENT

THE BUREAUCRATIC CONTEXT

No policy analyst exists in a vacuum. Rather, he is part of a social organization in which he interacts with other analysts and particularly with a set of policymakers, whom I have called clients. The relationship between client and analyst sets in motion a complementary process of problem selection. The more passive the client, the more freedom the analyst has in making selections. Not all clients, however, are indifferent or passive; they do make demands if analysts have something they want.

As many sociologists have pointed out, the analyst, advisor, expert, or intellectual is very much dependent on his client. Supposedly it is the client who tells the advisor what to do. Consider Florian Znaniecki's insight about technological experts:

But it is the leader, the man in power (or the group in power), who imposes upon experts the theoretic problems to be solved. Even when experts take the initiative in investigating facts and communicating the results of their research to the men in power, they select such problems as will presumably interest the latter.[2]

---

on the processing of information, see Harold L. Wilensky, *Organizational Intelligence: Knowledge and Policy in Government and Industry* (New York: Basic Books, 1967), pp. 42–48.

2. Florian Znaniecki, *The Social Role of the Man of Knowledge* (New York: Octagon Books, 1965), p. 48.

Or Robert Merton's description of the fate that awaits the intellectual in the bureaucracy:

Once he finds himself in a bureaucracy, he discovers that the intellectual task itself is closely connected with social relations within the bureaucracy. His selection of problems for study must be guided by what he knows or thinks he knows of his clients or prospective clients; his formulation of the problem, his analyses and reports must be geared to the same relationship to a client. . . . he now becomes aware of *visible controls* over the nature and direction of his inquiries.[3]

Or Lewis Coser explaining the conversion of the free intellectual to the kept expert:

When intellectual autonomy is relinquished and the constraints on inquiry imposed by policy-makers are accepted, when no independent basis of power is available, the intellectual becomes an expert. When the intellectual is not allowed to select his own problems and is forced by the exigencies of the situation to work on the problems posed to him by the policy-maker, his role comes to resemble that of a public servant who possesses peculiar skills but who must execute whatever the policy-maker may dictate.[4]

No one denies that every policy analyst must have his patron. But these statements make it appear that advisors are castrated intellectuals without much discretion. Actually, even in the most hierarchical situation the relationship between superior and subordinate is much more symmetrical than we usually imagine. Clients need ideas and help, and policy analysts can provide it. But more important, client and analyst are a bureaucratic pair, linked to each other in responding to external demands. Both are presented with similar cues for an analytical response. It is not so much that the client tells the analyst which problem to select, or that the analyst usurps the client's prerogative, but rather that they both face similar constraints. If the policy analyst has little discretion in selecting problems, then it is likely that his client also has little discretion. Of course, the client may act as a filter and distort the response to a demand because of his own values and objectives, and it is equally true that the analyst's influence is derived from his sponsor. But to understand the criteria for selecting problems, it

3. Robert K. Merton, *Social Theory and Social Structure* (Glencoe, Ill.: Free Press, 1957), p. 222.

4. Lewis A. Coser, *Men of Ideas: A Sociologist's View* (New York: Free Press, 1965), pp. 139–40.

would be better to view the client and analyst as manning the same rowboat. They may argue about styles of rowing, and one may row better than the other, but they do agree on the destination—and if not, the analyst will leave the boat or be dumped overboard.

The manner in which the client sets the agenda and the mutual dependence between analyst and client may become clear if we look at a few examples. When asked how he selects problems, one analyst replied that he works on "whatever is a problem for the secretary." At the time he was reviewing a road-construction project between the United States and Mexico, because conservation groups were protesting that the project would destroy the beauty of the area and he was delegated the task of heading off broader public protest. Or for another example, there is the surgeon general who was going to testify to Congress and wanted something to say; so he called in his analyst and told him to write a position paper on what the National Institutes of Health should be doing in the behavioral sciences or in the area of heart transplants. Then there is the executive director of the Civil Service Commission who was asked several questions by his general counsel on hiring policy because a key position had become vacant; the director referred the questions to his analysts. Finally, we have the client who was concerned about a General Accounting Office report that criticized one of the agency's programs and threatened to lead to its termination; an analyst was assigned to evaluate the program. Clients can't do everything themselves, and the delegation of day-to-day demands on one's time is not unusual. What's a staff for if you can't use it?

Consider the analyst who was working on educational policy problems for an assistant secretary in charge of policy analysis at HEW. The assistant secretary's client, and therefore one of this analyst's clients, was the secretary of HEW. One day, President Nixon decided that it would be a good idea to smooth the troubled path of school desegregation by spending 1.5 billion dollars. Of course, he could not send the legislation up to the hill without stating why he had named that amount and on what the money would be spent; so a committee was formed. The vice-president was put in charge, and one of the members of the committee was the secretary of HEW. Quite suddenly the analyst found himself a leading member of the committee staff and working on understanding some disparate findings of compensatory education programs.

Certainly, through the bureaucratic command system, the secretary as client selected the problem for the analyst; but it is also clear that a presidential decision set the analytical priorities for both secretary and analyst. In such situations the analyst has many clients and many people to please. He is working for and is part of a policymaking process, and he considers his work a "decision-driven" analysis. Somebody else's decision, not his own, has set the analysis in motion. Another analyst has a similar perception. Analytical problems, for him, are of two kinds: first, there are the "sensitive" problems, which are generated externally by important political actors such as the president; and then, as we shall see, there are the "critical" problems, which are mostly generated internally by the analyst and his immediate bureaucratic context.

Such distinctions between external and internal usually break down. No bureaucratic boundary is that inviolate, and there is a continuing stream of cues from the environment that influence the selection of problems. While the client does direct that a study be undertaken, he is actually only an intermediate actor in the process of environmental communication. To the analyst it may appear that the client has generated a thoroughly internal request, but this is because the analyst is several levels lower in the hierarchy. As an example, there was the costing problem that universities were having with the Department of Defense. For their defense contracts, the universities were using average instead of marginal costs for calculating their computer costs. Concerned about the problem, the president of Stanford wrote a letter to Secretary of Defense McNamara asking if he could do something about it. McNamara then wrote a notation on the letter—"take care of this"—and sent it to his assistant secretary of defense for systems analysis. Finally, the assignment was delegated to an analyst.

CHANGING AGENDAS

Because of environmental influences, the agenda for analysis is often in flux despite attempts to set priorities and order analytical efforts. Most analysts, other bureaucrats, and clients want to lay out the work rationally but find it difficult to do so. Usually at some particular point in time, such as when a new secretary arrives or when preparing for the budget, the analytical shop will initiate a list of issues or policy problems. The list may represent an intended work program for, say, about a year, or it may just be a shopping list for the client to add to or choose from. How long it is depends on how extensively the analysts consult with other officials. OMB will already have sent over its own list of worthwhile issues, and assistant secretaries and other chiefs will get their projects on the list.

A senior HEW analyst recalls a "hysterical discussion" with members of the Bureau of Budget (now OMB). The bureau's analysts and examiners would get together and argue with each other over what ought to be done. Generally, the examiners raised questions of management and efficiency, while the analysts raised questions of whether a program ought to be funded to begin with or at which level. (This difference in perspective comes about because the examiners have been around for some time. They are tied to the program managers, accept the programs, and try to work with them. The analysts have not been around long enough to have something to protect, and they feel free to question the arrangements of their colleagues.) Usually the examiners and analysts would leave with the same disagreements with which they had come. Then the bureau would react to an HEW list by sending back its own list, which was somewhat similar to HEW's original suggestions.

The idea of compiling the list is to anticipate policy problems that may require a decision in the future. But in addition, for the analyst the list is a way of getting his client to pay attention to him; for the client it is a way of knowing what his key people are worrying about. Depending on whether the analytical shop restricts the list to its own resources, the list can contain anywhere from 10 to 200 policy issues. Then the secretary or a committee of assistant and deputy assistant secretaries will choose about 50 of the 200 issues, or about 5 of the 10, and supposedly by this process a work program for the analytical shop and for other of the agency's analysts has been set. In the Department of Labor, for example, the analytical office asked around, drew up a list of issues, then added a few issues of its own, and finally came up with a 50- to 60-item agenda—which was reduced to 17 issues, 6 of which were actually worked on.

No sooner has the work program been set than it is unset. The annual work program will never be completed in the year because the analytical shop will be called in to fight crises and write speeches. Moreover, the secretary will have new issues to displace those on the agenda. In the Department of Interior, for example, after the analysts had completed a work agenda of about 50 items, the secretary asked for a study of resources on public lands, an item not on the original list. With the exception of technicians, most analysts appreciate that the interruptions are more urgent than the items on their list. "The crises usually involve important policy decisions," according to one analyst, "and generally imply a readiness on the part of the assistant secretary to make a decision; these circumstances do not generally exist with the issues in the annual work program, because the annual program contains issues we anticipate a year in advance."

Analysts are no better than their clients in keeping out environmental influences and keeping to the analytical agenda. In one major shop, the key analysts were concerned about not getting any of their scheduled long term work accomplished. Short-term work was driving out long-term work, so they decided to contract with Brookings for some long-term efforts. Several of the key analysts were to make up lists of problems for Brookings to handle. As time passed, however, the analysts kept changing their lists and shifting priorities according to what was topical; so the shop, lacking internal agreement, was not in a position to use Brookings.

THE CLIENT'S POLICY PREFERENCES

Beyond the short-term disturbances that must be dealt with, the personal interests and preferences of clients come into play in the direction of analytical activity. An analyst at HEW, for instance, expects to be working on a study of health and welfare policies for alcoholics because of the secretary's interest. It seems that when the secretary was involved with criminal justice, he was interested in removing alcoholics from criminal procedures; and this interest led to a general concern for increasing their well-being. For another example, at the Department of Labor the secretary believed that large numbers of slum residents probably were not included in the official unemployment rates, and that the figures for these slum areas were artificially low.[5] Giving his analysts two

5. National unemployment rates are determined largely on the basis of the Current Population Survey conducted by the Bureau of the Census. The monthly survey covers 50,000 households in 449 sample areas. Various criteria are used to determine whether one is employed or unemployed, and not having a job does not mean that one is considered unemployed. For example, persons not looking for

months to come up with a response, he asked them to identify and measure these pockets of unemployment and to design a program to concentrate the department's resources in those areas. The result was the department's Concentrated Employment Program (CEP), established in 1967.[6]

A client's policy preferences also influence whom he assigns to a study. In the Department of Transportation, a task force submitted to the secretary a report recommending the use of STOL (short take-off and landing) aircraft in combination with ground transportation systems. The secretary sent the report to the analysts in his Office of Economic Policy for review. After this review, the responsibility for the task force was shifted to the secretary's immediate staff to promote "broader consideration of the problem." The "broader consideration" was that the final report should emphasize ground transportation, such as high-speed rail systems, and not a combination of air and ground systems. Evidently, the railroad segment of the agency had made its impact on the secretary, and he in turn had expressed his preferences to the analysts, one of whom said, "we changed the results of the study 180°."

The Client's Concern for Jurisdiction

In a bureaucracy, members have their own sets of motivations which loosely mix with some almost common, but confused, set of organizational purposes. If there is no single overriding organizational goal, at least there is concern for jurisdiction.[7] The keepers of jurisdiction are usually the clients for analysis, and their concern for "what business we are in" is equivalent to their criteria for problem selection. Their concerns soon spread to other members of the organization, and the criteria of the keepers soon become the criteria of the analysts. Thus, an OEO analyst states three criteria

---

work because of the belief that no work is available would not be considered unemployed. In addition, people who were working part time or had a temporary job but would prefer full-time employment would still be considered employed. See Herbert Runyon, "Counting the Jobless" (Federal Reserve Bank of San Francisco), *Monthly Review*, September 1972, pp. 10–11.

6. In fiscal year 1971, CEP provided benefits for about 60,000 people at a cost of $76 million. *The Budget of the United States Government, Appendix, Fiscal Year 1971* (Washington, D.C.: U.S. Government Printing Office, 1970), p. 655.

7. A concern for jurisdiction is an externally oriented goal; see the interesting discussion in Lawrence B. Mohr, "The Concept of Organizational Goal," *American Political Science Review* 67 (June 1973): 470–81.

for selecting problems. First, the problem has to be related to the poor, broadly defined. Second, it ought to be a problem that cannot or should not be handled by another agency; for example, the Office of Education should not test the effectiveness of educational vouchers because it has "too many vested interests with too much to lose in the institution of a voucher plan."[8] And third, the problem should speak to congressional and White House requests, because OEO lacks a strong constituency.

Responding to a request is too mechanical a way of putting it. Requests, of course, are answered, but they can also be anticipated or engineered. Clients, just as analysts, look to increase their influence in the policy process. Policy solutions not only pursue problems but attract policymakers as well.[9] Policymakers look around for policy ideas that can be suitable vehicles for self-advancement. When the Family Assistance Plan (FAP) was the big domestic policy push of the Nixon administration, many clients asked themselves what they could do to get into the act. The client wants to jump on the policy bandwagon.

OEO was already involved with FAP with its experimental and analytical work on income maintenance, but clients can never get enough of a good thing.[10] Consider the OEO analyst who had his agenda changed. He had been working on a study of citizen

8. Educational vouchers represent a market approach to education. In its most general form, parents of school-age children would be given vouchers worth roughly the per pupil cost of education in a given locale. The vouchers would then be used at the school—public or private—of the parents' choice. For a recent example of this type of policy proposal, see John E. Coons and Stephen D. Sugarman, "Family Choice in Education: A Model State System for Vouchers," *California Law Review* 59 (1971): 321-438.

9. See Michael D. Cohen, James G. March, and Johan P. Olsen, "A Garbage Can Model of Organizational Choice," *Administrative Science Quarterly* 17 (March 1972): 2, where an organization is defined as "a collection of choices looking for problems, issues and feelings looking for decision situations in which they might be aired, solutions looking for issues to which they might be the answer, and decision makers looking for work."

10. According to Walter Williams, "The various government money-transfer programs making payments to the poor, such as Social Security and Public Welfare, were a major concern at OEO, starting with the Office of Research, Plans, Programs and Evaluation's first analytical activities (summer of 1965)." See his *Social Research and Analysis: The Experience in the Federal Social Agencies* (New York: American Elsevier Publishing Co., 1971), p. 76. For a discussion of the various programs that are addressed to the problem of insufficient income, see *Poverty Amid Plenty: The Report of the President's Commission on Income Maintenance Programs* (Washington, D.C.: U.S. Government Printing Office, 1969), pp. 89 ff.

participation, but quite gradually and without a specific order his attention was turned to a study of rural housing. His boss, Thomas K. Glennan, Jr., deputy director for planning, research, and evaluation, kept asking for more information on rural housing. Over a period of three months, the requests became more frequent and the analyst realized that he was really working on rural housing and not citizen participation. The increased frequency of requests was evidence to the analyst of what was now acceptable. But why the shift in requests? Several federal housing programs (such as Section 235 of the Housing and Urban Development Act of 1968) provide for subsidies, and eligibility for a subsidy is based partially on family income.[11] Passage of FAP would increase the income of families, particularly in the rural South, and therefore change the number of families that would be eligible for housing subsidies. What the impact of FAP would be on the demand for housing and how to meet this demand were serious problems to address.

OEO's leaders, such as Deputy Director Wesley Hjornevik, wanted the agency to be involved in the housing question and in shaping the implementation of FAP. When Congressman Carl D. Perkins—chairman of the House Committee on Education and Labor, which is responsible for the poverty program—inserted funds in an OEO bill for a rural housing program, OEO's leaders had the green light and became concerned about responding to Congressman Perkins's initiative. According to the analyst, "As soon as Congressman Perkins inserted that appropriation, all of us housing cats suddenly became very important." Glennan, the analyst's boss, told him to work full time on rural housing after a meeting of the senior staff in which the deputy director asked *Glennan's* boss how the housing study was going. Office scuttlebutt has it that the boss replied, "Just fine," and then, immediately upon returning to the office, ordered the full-time effort.

In short, the client does influence the selection of problems. He can order a particular problem to be studied. Or he can express general concerns which the analyst can adopt as operational

11. Section 235 was an interest subsidy, mortgage insurance program designed to make home ownership more readily available to lower-income families. Since 1968, the program has accounted for almost 500,000 new housing starts at an insured value of approximately 8 billion dollars. Section 235 was among several subsidized housing programs suspended by the Nixon administration in January 1973. See Office of Management and Budget, *1974 Catalog of Federal Domestic Assistance* (Washington, D.C.: U.S. Government Printing Office, 1974), p. 367.

criteria. No one should doubt the importance of the client in shaping the use of his advisors, but it should be clear that the client is also an intermediary in a process. Every client is somebody else's analyst or advisor. Both client and analyst are links in a complex chain, and it is important for both to understand the forces behind the analytical agenda.

CUES FROM THE ENVIRONMENT

Many of the political actors, groups, and institutions involved in policymaking, although not necessarily clients and users of policy analysis, are still forces that generate cues for selecting problems. Typically, congressmen, interest groups, and constituents provide cues to clients for using their analysts. But there are other forces—such as natural disasters, new scientific knowledge, and the communications media—behind problem selection as well. As an example, let us consider the press and how its cues stimulate clients in their selection of problems.

Analysis is sometimes a response to criticism in the press. What could be more dramatic and newsworthy than a person who almost dies on the streets because it took too long for an ambulance to arrive? Such was the situation in New York City, and the newspapers picked it up. Then, after a series of attacks in the press, Mayor John V. Lindsay formed a task force to study the city's emergency ambulance service. At the federal level, the same thing goes on. For example, Jack Anderson wrote a column criticizing one of the bureaus of the Department of Commerce. The secretary of commerce called in an analyst to do a quick two-to-three-day investigation and evaluation of the administrative problems within the bureau.

Probably as important as its role of critic is the press's role as source of policy ideas. A Department of Labor analyst recalls that, when Daniel P. Moynihan was assistant secretary of labor for policy planning and research, he brought in a short *New York Times* article which stated that large numbers of draftees were being rejected for physical defects. This fact of rejection could be used to support programs to convey services to the poor, such as health services to teenagers among the poor. Using selective service records it would be possible to identify the location of the rejected persons. According to the analyst, Moynihan easily received permission to undertake the project from the secretary of labor. In the fall of 1963, the White House staff was debating whether to use a suburban-oriented program or a poverty-reducing-oriented program as the basis for the 1964 presidential campaign. In the analyst's words, "Moynihan entered in late November with our statistics and individually approached key White House staff members. This turned the issue around and decided it in favor of the war-on-poverty program." The analyst uses as evidence for Moynihan's victory a press announcement of the war on poverty that justifies the program largely on the basis of the number of draft rejectees coming from ghetto areas. Moynihan has a more complex explanation of the origins of the poverty program, but the story is still a good example of how the press can stimulate analysis and the creation of policies.[12]

Another example also involves the Department of Labor. President Nixon had read an article by Pete Hamill in the April 14, 1969, issue of *New York*. The article dealt with the growing resentment of the lower-income working class, and it stimulated the president to send a memorandum to some members of the cabinet. At Labor, Secretary George P. Shultz took the memorandum seriously and turned it over for action to Jerome M. Rosow, his assistant secretary of labor for policy, evaluation, and research. What constructive suggestions could the department come up with in response to the president's request for assistance? The analysts were given only two to three weeks to formulate their response, so they decided to "broad brush" the issue with the hope of expanding their analysis in the future. The result was a memorandum, "The Problem of the Blue Collar Worker."[13] In the summer of 1970, some members of a White House working group leaked the memorandum to the *Wall Street Journal*. The *Journal*'s article made it appear that President Nixon was simply after the working-class vote and that the Department of Labor's blue-collar program would benefit only whites. The analysts were dismayed at this misinterpretation of their work, but because of the leak they had no time to expand their analysis. Instead, they were given the responsibility of writing speeches and articles defending the content of their memorandum and the administration's interest in the

12. See Daniel P. Moynihan, *Maximum Feasible Misunderstanding: Community Action in the War on Poverty* (New York: Free Press, 1969).
13. U.S. Department of Labor, Assistant Secretary of Labor for Policy, Evaluation, and Research, "Memorandum for the Secretary: The Problem of the Blue Collar Worker" (April 1970).

blue-collar worker. Here the press acted to stimulate policy ideas and then to foreclose them by pushing the administration into a defensive position. Criticism from the press, it seems, can be an innovative or a stifling force, but in either case it makes work for the policy analyst.

Cues for selecting problems can come from a variety of forces —from academicians, for example, or from Brookings on the East Coast to Rand on the West—so we will return to this topic when we discuss the analyst's selection of problems.

SELECTION BY THE ANALYST

THE DESIRE FOR RELEVANCE

A cynic might argue that, when the analyst is allowed to choose his own problems, it's because no one wants analysis. Not knowing what analysis is, clients can easily shunt the analytical activity off to plannning for future organization while they take care of immediate administration. But this type of conclusion ignores the motivation of the analyst. Whether he is a technician, politician, or entrepreneur, the analyst in a bureaucracy—despite the cliches—wants to be in, to be relevant, to do something meaningful. He does not want to be involved in doing nonoperational planning studies, studies that will gather dust on the shelf. His desire to be loved, to be appreciated, to be taken into account pushes him to select problems that can be marketed. He does not wait to be asked to do something. Because he wants his work to be significant, he anticipates the decisions of his clients and estimates the future payoff of his product.

"Win some soon," William Gorham urges.[14] Policy analysis has to be shown to be useful. At HUD, the head of an evaluation office "is searching for the hot issues." At Treasury, an analyst is working on alternative ways of decreasing the income tax for low- and middle-income people because he expects that Congress will try to offset the credits given corporations in a presidential tax proposal. It was important for him to initiate the study himself, otherwise, "if you wait around for instructions, you will never get the bone."

14. William Gorham, "Getting into the Action," *Policy Sciences* 1 (summer 1970): 174.

SELECTING PROBLEMS WITH PAYOFF

Analysts themselves distinguish between the good and bad, the perceptive and imperceptive, analyst according to the ability to select problems that have significance. What is significant? A problem with payoff is the answer. What is payoff? The typical answer of many analysts is in disciplinary jargon: maximizing effectiveness with fixed expenditures or minimizing expenditures given fixed effectiveness. What is implied, but not always stated, is that the analyst enjoys having his advice accepted. Payoff is acceptance. How then does an analyst become good? How does he select problems?

Before an analyst can become good at selecting problems he has to satisfy a few conditions. Obviously he must *choose the right client,* one who will allow him the discretion to make selections (see chapter 6). Most clients are fairly free with their staff, but still the client should have a predisposition to the brand of advice the analyst is prepared to offer.

Second, the analyst must *have a good vantage point* from which to perceive problems. Such a vantage point can be gained either through experience or position. In the analytical shop, the more inexperienced the analyst, the more likely it is that the problem will not be chosen by him but handed to him. Fresh from the university with his diploma, the policy analyst really does not know what a strategically good problem is. He is more likely to be called into an office by the head of the shop and told, "Why don't you look into such and such." The experienced analyst is more likely to know something about a policy area. He can sit down and list ten perennial problems worth exploring which are bound to come up in five years, and he will already have established the confidence of his superiors so as to be allowed to work on these problems. He is strategic in his thinking and in his choice of how he allocates his time.

Experience is usually accompanied by an advantageous position in the bureaucracy: project leader, section or branch head, deputy director, or head of the analytical office. The higher the analyst goes in the hierarchy of the analytical shop, the more he is in a position to influence the selection of problems. At the top of the analytical hierarchy the head of the office, the chief analyst, has an opportunity to pick problems strategically—not only important social problems but problems that will gain support for his shop. Gifted with unusual verbal ability, many heads of shops and project directors are the entrepreneurs and salesmen of the analytical team. Since they may not do studies but rather peddle them, it is important that the proper problem be selected at the beginning.

Position also provides the analyst with the opportunity to see a broader range and perhaps a more significant set of problems. With position, he can avoid trivial or low-level problems. Since he is not locked in the closet with the calculator, as are many of his colleagues, he can perceive cues from his environment and increase his range of choices. Because of his exposure to the outside, he is also better fit to convince his client that what he is working on is truly significant.

Like any other actor in the policy process, the analyst needs success stories. But, depending on his situation, he balances his need for success with his willingness to undertake an interesting but risky problem. He tries to *screen out low-payoff and high-risk problems according to three categories of criteria:* technical, organizational, and political. Technical criteria focus on the study itself; organizational criteria deal with the analyst's immediate environment in his agency; political criteria help judge events outside the analyst's agency.[15]

Technical Criteria

Choose big-dollar programs. No analyst likes to waste his time, so he always looks for work on the big-dollar program. As one analyst in the Office of Management and Budget put it to me, there are plenty of budget examiners working on trivia; analysis has to go after the big program. In a big program, one is more likely to find some fat or something wrong. Bigness is also a good way to help compensate for error in analysis. The crudity of cost and benefit measures, for example, can be tolerated in multimillion or billion dollar programs. But for small-dollar programs, there may not be enough room for the requisite number of statistically significant digits and refined measures may be unavailable.

---

15. The categories are mine; the criteria are the analysts'. I have couched the criteria in the form of prescriptive rules for the sake of clarity, but I do not intend to recommend them. The specific conditions under which the criteria will be efficacious, operational, and not in conflict are yet to be determined.

In the early days of evaluation at OEO, the analysts could have started anywhere since little analytical work had been done, so they decided to look at the big-dollar programs like Head Start.[16] Aimed at preschool child development, Head Start was a popular component of OEO's program. In 1968, for example, the cost of Head Start was $331 million, 18 percent of OEO's total budget of about $1.8 billion.[17] It was not only big but was bound to get bigger. Moreover, its expansion was not related to any hard evidence of its effectiveness, despite talk about its worthwhileness. Big programs usually involve big issues. At HEW it was the same story. Medicare and Medicaid are big programs, and the escalating costs of delivering health services created increased demands for information.[18]

Choose problems with quite different alternatives. Often the available data and analytical methods will not support a refined choice, and that is why the analyst plays it safe by choosing problems with different policy alternatives. A big-dollar program can sometimes involve quite different alternatives that offer the prospect, although rare, of a clear-cut solution. Of course, there are big-dollar programs where the choice is between similar alternatives—for example, the selection of an automobile sedan for the government—but such problems are more suitable for competitive bidding than for analysis.

16. Head Start is designed "to provide educational, nutritional, and social services to preschool children of the poor and their families, and to involve parents in activities with their children so that the child enters school on equal terms with his less deprived classmates." Since 1965, Head Start has served approximately 5 million children. Office of Management and Budget, *1974 Catalog of Federal Domestic Assistance* (Washington, D.C.: U.S. Government Printing Office, 1974), p. 275.

17. United States Office of Management and Budget, *The Budget of the United States Government for Fiscal Year 1970, Appendix* (Washington, D.C.: U.S. Government Printing Office, 1969), p. 91.

18. Medicare and Medicaid are authorized by Public Law 89–97, the 1965 amendments to the Social Security Act. Title 18, Medicare, "provides health insurance under Social Security to persons 65 years and over." Title 19, Medicaid, "offers health benefits to persons on public assistance and to other persons unable to pay for medical care who fall into certain legal categories." See Herbert E. Klarman, "Major Public Initiatives in Health Care," *The Public Interest* 34 (winter 1974): 108. For a history of the origins of the Medicare legislation, see Theodore R. Marmor, *The Politics of Medicare* (Chicago: Aldine Publishing Company, 1973).

Build on what you know. The analyst tries to choose a problem in an area about which he knows something, where he can build on experience. His education and previous investment in learning his discipline bear fruit in his selection of the problem and in his orientation toward it. The time allowed for performing an analysis is often so short that the analyst must choose a problem about which he already knows a great deal. An analyst now at Brookings did his dissertation on social security, which then led to work on income maintenance. Having always been interested in problems of income distribution, he took a short step to explore the question of who benefits from public housing. The analyst's objective is not simply to do the same thing over again but rather to extend his base of knowledge, capture a policy area, and become a recognized expert.

Be able to do it. It is not enough for the analyst to choose a problem that is in his area of substantive expertise: he must also know how to handle the work. In order to reduce his risk, he chooses so that the methodology for "solution" lies within the state of his art. And in addition to having a handy methodology, he is likely to know the relationships between important variables that are related to the problem. This is why the analyst pays attention to the relationship of inputs to outputs, or to the importance of ascertaining a production function. There is little point in conducting an analysis whose results are likely to be ambiguous or likely to be shot down because of technical or theoretical difficulties.

Consider the example of OEO, asked by the Department of Agriculture to do a study of the spending patterns of people enrolled in the food stamp program.[19] After a review, OEO turned down the request because the results of the study would be statistically inconclusive. The analysts suspected that there would be wide differences in the spending patterns of food stamp beneficiaries and that they would be very limited in their ability to gather data from a sample. Since it was likely that the results could come out in a variety of ways, OEO felt that supporters and

19. The food stamp program began on a pilot basis in 1961. Those eligible for the program can buy for a small amount stamps worth a larger amount when presented in local food stores. In fiscal year 1971, approximately 7.5 million people participated in the program at a cost of 1.2 billion dollars. *The Budget of the United States Government, Appendix, Fiscal Year 1971* (Washington, D.C.: U.S. Government Printing Office, 1970), pp. 146–47. See Gilbert Y. Steiner, *The State of Welfare* (Washington, D.C.: Brookings Institution, 1971), pp. 191–236.

opposers of the program might seize the report to prove their own points of view, with possible damage not only to the program but to OEO.

Organizational Criteria

Make sure there's enough time. The analyst must choose problems that allow him sufficient time to gather reliable information for the policymaking process. Although much analytical activity, the back-of-the-envelope kind, is devoted to short-term needs and to getting a quick feeling of success, some analysis is conducted as an investment for a future decision. Therefore, the analyst has to be strategic about calculating the time it will take to do a study, so that events will not pass him by. It takes time to do the required research. Analysts for the central administration of my university decided in 1965 that the establishment of tuition was going to be a significant issue; so they started studying the effect that tuition would have on the demand for higher education, and by the summer of 1967 the results of their study were used in responding to pressures from the state capital.

Time constraints are partly a function of how long the analyst expects to be in his job. He has to stay around long enough to complete the analysis and communicate its results. He may not have any control over the timing of the decision, but he does have control over his own commitment to work for a particular agency. One analyst, for instance, felt that he was going to be working at HEW for only three years, so he picked only those problems which could safely be done within that period.

Make sure your agency has operational control. The analyst should choose problems that are controlled operationally more by his own than by some other agency. Here he may have to trade off a significant problem for a narrow and small one with greater likelihood of implementation. The solution may not work because of this narrow selection, but at least the agency can make the attempt with a minimum of interference. When a problem is under the control of a particular agency, there is less negotiation and less opportunity for solutions to be attenuated by competing or conflicting forces. This criterion is probably more ignored than followed, because analysts are also looking for important problems, which almost by definition involve the cooperation of other agencies, or state and local officials, or beneficiaries. Take the example of one analytical office, which works for the under secretary of the Department of Labor. This office, interested in the "job satisfaction of the working man," initiated a study of the four-day work week. Within the department, the study idea was met either with indifference or with responses such as "what can you do about it?" The analysts were interested but no one else was, because the policy problem was perceived to be outside the control of the department. To make matters worse, the analysts' sponsor, the boss of the shop, was an effective political leader; the analysts expected that he would be called to do White House work and then, they concluded, "we will be unable to do our own work." It appeared that the study was not going far.

If the problem is not under the control of his agency, then the federal analyst should at least settle for a problem that is under the control of the federal government. Since the notion of control is relative, the idea is to look for a "clean problem." Explaining why he chose to work in the area of social security (public assistance and income maintenance), a former HEW analyst said, "It was really just a guess, and what is really important is what you can effect." In further discussion it became clear that his selection was not really a guess but a matter of careful calculation. He wanted a problem that had the element of "directness." Social security was handled as a trust fund and was outside the usual budgetary process; so he could avoid the typical recurring question of "what can you do to cut?" At the same time, all that was needed for a change in the system was to have Congress pass some legislation. Since the program was mostly under the purview of the federal government, the analyst could safely ignore state and local operations. In retrospect, however, the trouble the Family Assistance Plan ran into is one indicator that the area of social security legislation was not as clean as the analyst expected.

Know your client. The analyst hopes that what he is working on will capture the interest of the agency's decision makers. The problems he chooses should be those that also interest the client or, at the very least, be of enough interest so that the client will sit still and listen while the analyst presents his recommendations. The analyst should be "sympathetic" and know "what bugs the decision makers." This criterion is often ignored. Analysts raise issues they think are important to the client, but the client couldn't care less. An analyst who worked for the director of the Bureau of the Budget reports that his boss would often tune out and approve policy memoranda out of indifference. The effectiveness of the analysis was lost because the consumer of it did not really care; it was not relevant to his concerns.

Be sure you can get cooperation and information. The analyst sitting for the most part at the top of the agency has his techniques and models, but he is very much divorced from the program managers, who have control of the requisite information and understanding. One Treasury analyst working on the behavior of high-income taxpayers is lucky; he says that it's an advantage to be working for the department because "no one has access to the data as I do here."

Without the cooperation of program managers, an analysis will have trouble getting off the ground. The analyst needs informants who will tell a straight story and if they do not know something, say so. But since many bureaucrats feel threatened by the policy analyst and will not be helpful, he has to be able to tap into a precultivated group of friends, such as an "old-boy" network—and this means choosing problem areas that the friends know something about.

Political Criteria

Choose problems for which there is a consensus on objectives. With well-chosen problems, questions revolve not around objectives but around which alternative is better. Although there is some talk about analysis coping with the basic problems of a society, the analyst who wants to make an impact often chooses current problems that may have an efficiency solution. He is just as likely to see some areas as being sacred cows, unable to be changed, as any other actor in the policymaking system. He will not want to investigate ways of cutting down NIH cancer research, for example. Or he will be concerned with how the federal government supports higher education, not with whether the government should support it. He will assume that there is a consensus on the objective of supporting higher education and proceed from there. Shunning areas of high societal conflict, the analyst seeks out areas of consensus.

Find new areas where no one else is working. Most policy areas are crowded with a variety of actors; but analysis is still a relatively scarce skill and it is possible to look for problems that no one else has broken into and achieved a reputation for an approximate solution. Consider the entrepreneur at the Department of Labor who is interested in initiating an organizational study of the various state employment services. Evidently the state employment agencies are in an enviable position: although they receive federal funds, when federal officials ask them what they are doing, they answer that they work for the state; and when state officials ask the same question, they say they work for the federal government. Ignoring some of the other criteria for selecting problems, he believes that he found an area worth investigating because nobody else seems to be doing it. New areas imply new programs, and a new program is easier to shape because neither administrator nor constituent rigidity has set in. In the area of teacher training, for example, an Office of Education analyst tried to shift resources to a new program, the training of preschool teachers. Rather than concentrating his efforts on primary and secondary teachers, where there was a likelihood of a surplus and where the training was locked in, he set off into a new area.

Choose problems whose solutions have political support. The source of political support might be OMB or the White House, but when the analyst thinks about politics he also thinks of Congress. Known congressional opposition, although subject to rapid change, can be reason enough to screen out a subject for analysis. An analyst formerly with the Office of Education reported that he did not fool with areas in which there would be no receptivity to his ideas. Responsible for analyzing the impact of the Elementary and Secondary Education Act of 1965 (Public Law 89–10), he avoided looking at one of the five titles or parts of the act mainly because Congresswoman Edith Green, an influential member of the House Education and Labor Committee and chairwoman of the Special Subcommittee on Education, wanted to keep that part small.[20] Not knowing what was happening with the money and feeling that it

20. The Elementary and Secondary Education Act of 1965 is a major federal program which provides local public schools with fiscal assistance particularly to assist the children of low-income families. For a description of its various titles and the problems of implementing them, see Stephen K. Bailey and Edith K. Mosher, *ESEA: The Office of Education Administers a Law* (Syracuse, N.Y.: Syracuse University Press, 1968), pp. 48–60, 98–159.

was in the hands of the states anyway, the analyst felt that "it didn't pay to fight Edith Green."

Generally, the analyst's political awareness acts to screen out problems. He does not want to work on something that will not sell. As an OEO analyst put it, "I'm not going to spend time on a study that has no chance of being accepted." But analysts often misperceive the chances for acceptance; many, being politically naive, fail to question prevailing political wisdom or act to change political forces. To choose one problem is to avoid another; and the analyst uses his political knowledge, inadequate as it is, for avoidance. The implications of such political pessimism will be explored in chapter 8.

After this long recitation of criteria, one should not believe that problems are always selected through planned calculation. Sometimes an inexperienced analyst cannot select because he does not know what to work on. Sometimes an analyst wants to expand his influence by working on the client's selection but does not know how to answer the question. Moreover, substantive interests often develop by accident. Some work may need to be done when the resident expert is sick or on vacation, and the policy analyst called in to do it may find himself developing a new field of expertise. When one analyst was at HEW, he had to do a quick piece of work on college student loan banks for some legislative requirement because the shop's expert was out of town. He found that he liked the policy area. One thing led to another, and he became an expert on the financing of higher education.

THE ILLUSION OF SELF-GENERATION

Just as their clients think they direct their subordinates to study something, so many analysts think they generate their own analytical problems: "What we do is dependent on what we feel like doing." But here they ignore both their origins and their environment. Like Athena, analysts come into the bureaucratic world fully garbed, intellectual clothes and all. After all, they wear the garments of a liberal society and a particular education. Thus, analysts throughout the federal government in the mid- and late 1960s shared a concern for the poor that stemmed from general egalitarian norms and a conception of an enlarged role of government that was more likely to have been learned at Harvard rather

than Chicago (at least for economists).[21] Alice M. Rivlin, assistant
secretary for planning and evaluation at HEW during the Johnson
administration, is a good example of an analyst who has this
orientation. In her book, which in part reflects her HEW experience, she states, "The first step in making public policy is to get a
picture of what the problem is. Social action programs should be
based on answers to questions like these: How many people are
poor? Who are they? Where are they? Why are they poor? Who is
in bad health? Who is not receiving treatment? How many people
need more education or better job skills?"[22]

This concern for the poor, shared by both analyst and client,
resulted in a plethora of studies on improving the welfare of the
poor. Looking for an area with payoff, one in which a policy
decision might be made, a senior policy analyst at HEW, for
example, initiated a study on the financing and delivery of health
services to the poor. He thought that there might be gaps in
health-service coverage, and perhaps different ways of delivering
health services should be explored. The secretary of HEW received the analyst's study proposal, struck out the financing part,
and the result was an important study on the health problems of
the poor.[23]

I am not arguing that analysts do not and should not initiate or
select problems. Indeed, and this is particularly the case with the
entrepreneurs, they do and should continue to do so. Selecting
problems is such a critical task, however, that analysts should be
sensitive to the stimuli behind their selections. The background
and education of the analyst are a source for such stimuli. An OMB
analyst, with an education in the physical sciences before he turned

21. An illusion of self-generation and the biasing effect of education is not
restricted to policy analysts or those who do policy research. Similar behavior can
be observed among physical scientists. For example, Kuhn has pointed out the
importance of a "shared paradigm" in the conduct of "normal science": "One of
the things a scientific community acquires with a paradigm is a criterion for
choosing problems. . . . To a great extent these are the only problems that the
community will admit as scientific or encourage its members to undertake." See
Thomas S. Kuhn, *The Structure of Scientific Revolutions*, 2d ed. (Chicago:
University of Chicago Press, 1970), p. 37.

22. Alice M. Rivlin, *Systematic Thinking for Social Action* (Washington, D.C.:
The Brookings Institution, 1971), p. 9.

23. U.S. Department of Health, Education, and Welfare, Office of the Assistant Secretary for Planning and Evaluation, *Delivery of Health Services for the
Poor* (December 1967).

social scientist, believes that it is pernicious for government to be involved extensively in science; science belongs in the academy. The big scientific programs of government are a subsidy to business and industry. If the power industry, for example, wants nuclear reactors for electricity, it should pay for developing them. Thus, he goes after the big science programs of AEC, NASA, and DOD. When the analyst selects problems solely to extend a private notion or to advance professional interests in a discipline or methodology, he runs the risk that the analytical products may not be of much use to policymakers. His answers may be wrong because of his biases. Or his answers may be right but still out of phase with the informational needs of policymakers.

The illusion of self-generation is maintained by anticipation. Pick a policy area that will be hot in so many months and then muster up all the information before the debate begins. Gorham says, "Be clairvoyant about forthcoming issues. Predict next year's major budgetary or program issue. Play strong hunches on possible major program redirection."[24] An analyst at HUD believed that if his office was to be effective it must be able to anticipate problems, arising from OMB or Congress, for the assistant secretary. "It's nice," he said, "to be able to predict or guess what the problems will be, because otherwise, by the time [the assistant secretary or his assistant] get involved in an issue, it is usually behind them." In the Department of Agriculture, an analytical office tries to bring in new issues by producing about five unsolicited analyses a year; at the time of this writing they were pushing credit assistance for mobile homes.

How does the analyst anticipate problems for analysis? He uses his criteria for problem selection and relies like his client on cues from his environment.

CUES FROM THE ENVIRONMENT

The analyst takes his cues from wherever he finds them. Besides reading newspapers, journals, reports, the president's speeches, and the *Statistical Abstract*, he tries to attend meetings to see what's going on. An offhand remark by the client or a presidential assistant can often determine the agenda for analysis. A former head of HEW's analytical shop, for example, was in the office of

24. Gorham, "Getting into the Action," p. 175.

Joseph A. Califano, Jr., special assistant to President Johnson for domestic affairs, when he overheard that the president was interested in a child health-care program; picking up this bit of information gave the analysts a year to prepare a package.

The analyst also takes advantage of the routines of government, such as the creation and cycle of legislation. He thinks he should look into the Hill-Burton hospital construction legislation because it is coming up for renewal.[25] Or the two-year legislative cycle of social security may be a cue. Then there are the various reports that Congress expects from the executive branch; for example, 1970 legislation required that the president issue an urban-growth policy report every two years, so HUD analysts were writing the report. In the Department of Agriculture, an analytical office was responsible for reviewing specific legislation for the secretary. A bill, for instance, that would increase the number of railroad cars was of interest to the department because of the extensive use farmers make of railroads for transporting their goods. When this issue was studied, the analysts attempted to expand the issue to consider subsidies to transportation in general. Their report included a discussion of the movement and scheduling of boxcars, their distribution within the country, and alternate methods of transportation, such as trucks. The purpose of the report was to attempt to make the secretary and under secretary aware of the broader implications of the legislation.

The routine of budgeting is also an important stimulus. The analyst may not have direct control over budgeting, but he is usually asked or encouraged to comment on an agency's program. Since the analyst deals with resource allocation, his work on the budget often marks his entry into the policymaking process. He has to write issue memoranda on various programs, so he looks for budgets that seem to accomplish nothing and may be inconsistent with his own preferences.

---

25. The Hill-Burton Act, passed in 1946, "subsidized 25–30 percent of the nation's post-war hospital construction" (Marmor, *Politics of Medicare*, p. 2). The current version of the act, Title VI of Public Law 91–296, provides direct grants, loans, and guaranteed mortgage loans to states for the construction, replacement, or modification of health facilities. Through January 1974, 180 loans have been committed under Title VI for a total loan face value of 654 million dollars. Office of Management and Budget, *1974 Catalog of Federal Domestic Assistance* (Washington, D.C.: U.S. Government Printing Office, 1974), p. 157.

Cues can come from anywhere in the analyst's organizational and political environment. A National Science Foundation analyst was developing the beginnings of answers in several problem areas; as he said, "You know that some questions are coming." How does he know which questions? After reading a report of the Carnegie Commission on the Future of Higher Education and looking at other "evidence," he felt that the roles of educational institutions in our society are changing and this change should require a change in the policies of the National Science Foundation (NSF). The Nixon administration was pushing revenue sharing which might affect NSF. Also, he has noticed that during the past few years the demand for "pure" scientists has leveled off; and since NSF supports scientific research, he felt that he should be ready to assess these changes in demand on NSF programs.

What is an issue to the public or its representatives will soon be an issue for analysis. An HEW analyst felt that the public provides reliable cues for selecting problems. "Sooner or later the public gets to you," he said. How does it get to you? "Well, you hear everybody complaining about pollution, so you think this will be a topical issue." The head of an HUD analytical shop judged the "hot issues" by "vibrations." He or his staff might get a call saying that they should watch a particular issue because "it is not a hot issue now, but will be shortly." In discussing his office's role in HUD's annual arrangements program, he said, "We had no business doing that. I thought that it probably would be important and no one had really moved ahead on it yet. I sent people to San Francisco, Kansas City, Chicago, and Gary, Indiana. From their reports, we found that an issue was brewing. We just jumped into the void."

Given such an abundance of cues (and faulty memories as well), the exact stimulus that puts a study into motion or stops it is almost impossible to determine. The analyst may think he is setting the analytical agenda, but as the following story from OEO will show, he is only one factor in a complex human equation.

An Example from OEO

An OEO analyst specializing in housing policy was interested in studying the effect of housing on jobs for minorities. Industries and manufacturing firms had been moving to the suburbs, but black citizens were unable to follow the jobs because of transportation difficulties and discrimination in housing. Professor John F. Kain of

Harvard had done some of the initial work on this suburbanization problem using data from the Chicago and Detroit areas; these data suggested that segregated housing in the suburbs may increase the unemployment rates of central-city blacks.[26]

Sensing that Kain's work was being used to pressure the administration to change suburban housing patterns and that President Nixon was interested in increasing his political support in the suburbs, the analyst felt that Kain's work "needed verifying by defining and quantifying before the administration formed its response to this pressure." He was skeptical because he thought that Kain had slighted both the increase in minority suburban jobs outside of manufacturing and the need to differentiate by "quality" of job, and that mass production techniques might require a different type of labor (white females instead of black males). Besides these political and substantive reasons, the analyst thought that working in the area would expand his analytical ability. He was especially interested in attempting to use a particular data bank, the Social Security 1% Continuous Work History File, which contained a 1 percent sample of the social security population by sex, age, race, and employment.

The analyst and a partner started discussing the study around the office, and their colleagues were quick to point out the inadequacies of the data and the difficulty they would face in testing a hypothesis that explored the relationship between suburban housing patterns and minority jobs. After about three weeks of informal discussion, they took the study proposal to their boss, Thomas K. Glennan, Jr., deputy director for planning, research, and evaluation. Glennan was concerned about whether the results of the study could be used for policy. According to the analysts, he asked them, "How are you going to use the results?" and "How do we disseminate the resulting recommendations into policy?" In the end, although he had some reservations about its relevance for policy, he approved the study. The analyst thought it was approved for three reasons—because it would not cost much, it would help the analysts improve their skills, and it might conceivably be useful to the administration.

26. See, for example, John F. Kain, "Housing Segregation, Negro Employment, and Metropolitan Decentralization," *Quarterly Journal of Economics* 82 (May 1968): 175–97.

The analyst's partner has a slightly different version of the origins of the study. He recalls that the Rand Corporation had submitted a proposal to conduct a study that would relate the hiring of minorities to discrimination in housing. Rand had developed its proposal from its work with New York City. Glennan's superior, John O. Wilson, assistant OEO director for planning, research, and evaluation (PR&E), met with representatives of Rand, knew of Kain's work, and decided that OEO should do an in-house study of seven metropolitan areas to see how patterns of minority residence were related to patterns of employment.

In any case, the study proceeded on a low-priority basis. It was difficult to get the time to work on it. As one of the analysts said, "We keep having new problems thrown at us. Although my understanding was that we were hired to do research, we have had so much else to do that I have not worked on this for four weeks. My field of expertise is housing, and I keep getting small problems assigned to me which interrupt my work on the suburbanization issue." His partner reported that they would have been finished months ago but were interrupted by the revenue-sharing issue and also held up by the unavailability of data. The data bank, for example, did not contain all the information they needed; they lacked data on population shifts between city and suburbs and on changes in location of labor groups by race. The issue was much more complex than they had anticipated, and the data requirements were not as confined as their academic preparation had suggested they would be. They did make a number of computer runs, for which they paid the Department of Commerce $8,500 for its computer time and assistance.

As the study proceeded, the analysts were informed that a competing office within OEO—the Office of Program Development (OPD)—was developing a program, based on Kain's work, to create housing and employment opportunities for minorities in the suburbs. It was pushing a study, Operation Mobility, that would generate ways of eliciting the voluntary cooperation of suburban communities. OPD's analyst believed that HUD's "coercive" practice of using water and sewer grants to encourage open housing would backfire, and that it would be better to survey the leaders of suburban governments to find out what federal help was necessary to achieve the same objective. As part of the study, data on suburban employment and housing opportunities would also be gathered. The survey was to be completed within nine months, and the first nine months of putting its results into operation were to cost about $300,000.

The OPD analyst took his proposal to OEO's Project Selection Committee, which contained several members from the Office of Planning, Research, and Evaluation who criticized Operation Mobility. As one of them said, "We sometimes take two years just to design a study properly. OPD wanted to design the project, complete it, and place it in operation in less than one year." However, OEO Deputy Director Wesley Hjornevik, who had created the Project Selection Committee to begin with, liked the proposal; and after about five weeks it was approved. Probably one reason for its approval was that Wilson, director of PR&E, had emphasized the need for the study to Hjornevik.

Just prior to the formal advertisement for the contract for bid, a "political operative" (the analyst describes him as a Goldwater supporter) in the contract division of OEO contacted a conservative congressman and reported that OEO was about to initiate a program to move minority groups to the suburbs. The congressman contacted John D. Ehrlichman, executive director of the White House Domestic Council, to protest the contract. Ehrlichman called OEO Director Frank Carlucci to the White House to defend the program. Operation Mobility was canceled.[27]

One might think that after the command of the White House, all work on suburban minority housing and employment would cease. But as any bureaucrat would expect, such was not the case. With the support of Hjornevik, the OPD analyst pursued the proposal but under a different approach. The problem was now one of "metropolitan dispersion," and a task force with a less action-oriented mission was formed to gather data on the movement of jobs and population within metropolitan areas and on the structure of metropolitan government. Meanwhile, the two PR&E analysts, when they found the time, continued with their analysis of the "impact of the suburbanization of industry on the employment prospects and patterns of central city minority groups, specifically blacks." Glennan, their boss, still wanted the study and asked for

27. The *National Journal* (12 June 1971, p. 1242) quotes a HUD official as saying that "Ehrlichman and the Domestic Council—not OMB—were now handling the politically sensitive issue of dispersing federally assisted low-income housing into the suburbs."

periodic reports. Clearly the analysis, however, had a low priority, if for no other reason than that the Nixon administration was not terribly interested in increasing jobs for minorities in the suburbs; but one of the analysts (who is carrying anticipation of payoff a little too far) lamely said, "I feel that this is something for the next Democratic administration."

Where did the cue, the stimulus, for problem selection come from? Obviously, the published work of a professor, John Kain, laid the groundwork, just as Milton Friedman's suggestion of a negative income tax gave rise to the Family Assistance Plan.[28] It stimulated the intellectual curiosity of the analysts, who, knowing that HUD's policies were not working, became convinced that something more should be done. The Rand Corporation proposal got the suburbanization study onto the agenda because it indicated that something more could be done. Wilson and Glennan, as heads of the analytical shop and gatekeepers of analytical time, kept the study on the agenda. When the White House tried to kill the study, top OEO officials simply adjusted their priorities but did not take the study completely off the agenda.

Besides pointing out the abundance of cues that set the analytical agenda, the OEO experience shows how easy it is for analysts and their bosses to miscalculate. With the benefit of hindsight, we can see that it is not a simple matter to use the criteria for problem selection or to estimate payoff. The suburban employment of minorities is a complex problem which the analysts did not know how to solve and for which they had inadequate data. Moreover, their work would not be unique; they would not be the only ones working on the problem. Undoubtedly, HUD and the Department of Labor were equally concerned; but more important, within OEO itself there was competition. Finally, their sense of political timing was off. When an issue is politically sensitive, there is likely to be more disagreement than agreement, more trouble than votes. Why else was the issue assigned to the Domestic Council? Even if the analysts could have come up with some clever policies, they would have had nowhere to go with them because of a lack of congressional and public support. No one should doubt the importance of anticipating payoff—except when the payoff seems to be awaiting a future political administration.

28. See Milton Friedman, *Capitalism and Freedom* (Chicago: University of Chicago Press, 1962), pp. 190–95.

CONCLUSION

Charles L. Schultze sees the analyst as caught between the "criteria of efficiency and political reality." He does not want the analyst to be restricted by conventional political wisdom and at the same time to ignore practical political constraints. Similar to other policy analysts, he says that "one of the major ingredients of success . . . will be a perceptive selection of issues to be examined and alternatives to be considered."[29] Recognizing that problem selection is an art, he suggests some rules to follow: know your political constraints; choose pure public goods because they are less political and more technical in nature; pick new and expanding programs; and, finally, work in areas that have good data. The last two rules are in conflict because it is the old programs that offer the better data, and so he concludes, "What we can do best analytically we find hardest to achieve politically." The perversity of the old programs with their intense clients and rigid politics he leaves to the nonbureaucratic analysts in the universities and research institutions who can help "widen the range of feasible alternatives facing the systems analyst in government."[30]

Schultze's advice and the other criteria suggested by policy analysts throughout this chapter seem a little bit too simple and pure. Do these criteria really work? Will not one rule conflict with another? One can start off on a technical problem and find that the very act of analysis creates debate and the issue becomes politicized. How is one to know that his work will have the requisite political support? Surely there are times when the analyst must follow his convictions and ignore the cues that filter down through the hierarchy and those who say it can't be done. Yet these are the rules of good analysts, as judged by their peers. Most of these analysts are initiators and believe in "hitting the deck or ground running." Their rules, however, may not be much help to the novice who waits to be told what to do, nor can we be certain when these rules will work for the experienced and ambitious analyst.

One difficulty in assessing the analyst's criteria for selecting problems is that problem selection is just one small piece of the general question of how policy issues are raised in a political system. Some issues stay submerged or seem to take forever to get

29. Charles L. Schultze, *The Politics and Economics of Public Spending* (Washington, D.C.: The Brookings Institution, 1968), p. 82.
30. *Ibid.*, p. 89.

onto the public agenda. Other issues require a crisis of events to
make them salient to policymakers. And it may be that it is the
timely arrival of an issue that makes a hero of the analyst rather
than his refined exercise of political skill and timing.[31] Since the
generation of policy issues is a murky and slippery area, we should
be a little cautious in applying the analyst's criteria for selecting
problems. Nevertheless, it is clear that the policy analyst when
selecting problems tries to anticipate policy issues and decisions.
Seeking personal influence, he relies on his conventional wisdom
for problem selection, coupling it with his own notions of success,
cues from the environment, and, with luck, the luxury of a passive
client. And in doing so, the subjects of analysis, for the most part,
become more operational, topical, probably more conservative,
and less differentiated from other bureaucratic research activities.

It would be elegant if we could set forth a flow chart of the
problem-selection process, showing each rule, criterion, and cue in
the appropriate sequence. Instead, what we have is a rudimentary
understanding that policy problems exist, that they are perceived
by both client and analyst, and that they provide a stimulus for an
analytical response. In gauging the outcome of this process of
stimulus and response, offer and acceptance, much depends on
situational factors: on the willingness of a chief analyst to allow his
analysts to pursue their policy interests, on a client bereft of ideas,
and on the aggressiveness or timidity of the analysts.

Of course, some central tendencies can be discerned. Technicians, when free to choose, are more likely to pick interesting
problems from which they can learn and expand their knowledge of
techniques and substance. In selecting problems to protect their
client and advance themselves, politicians listen to and anticipate
the client's wishes. Entrepreneurs willfully choose problems according to their policy preferences and assume that their clients
share similar preferences.

What happens if the client does not select the agenda for
analysis? First, mismatches between what the client needs and

31. Robert A. Levine, an ex-OEO analyst, having cited several examples of
the influence of analysis on policy, concludes that "rational analysis and planning
on specific ideas can become immensely valuable when the time has come
politically for a specific idea that might be provided by such analysis." See Robert
A. Levine, *Public Planning: Failure and Redirection* (New York: Basic Books,
1972), p. 147.

what he gets will be more frequent. If left alone, analysts, regard-less of type, will go their own way. What is interesting for the technician may not be interesting for the client. What the politician anticipates may not be consistent with the client's needs. What assumptions the entrepreneur makes about his client may be wrong and out of phase. No matter how intimate a client and his advisor may be, the advisor does not sit where the client does. Second, the client is less likely to listen to his analyst. When the client and analyst do not share in the selection of problems, the analyst must work harder to convince, to sell the client. And third, there is no guarantee that the analyst will be an innovative force in the life of the bureaucracy. As advisors become more technically sophisticated and specialized, they may also lose perspective and the willingness to be venturesome. The analyst may have more time to reflect than his client, but he may reflect on the wrong things. In short, both client and analyst are linked in the broader context of policymaking, and each of them has something to contribute to the selection and solution of policy problems.

4

Working on the Problem

Policy analysts know that there is no such thing as *the* answer, *the* solution, but they keep trying to reach for tentative answers. What accounts for the way policy analysts solve problems? How do policy analysts work on problems? What techniques, tools, and heuristics do they use? Conceptually, the policy area, the bureaucratic context, and the analyst's professional orientation and education would probably be the central determinants in explaining the analyst's solution of policy problems. In practice, there is such a diversity of method and activity that these determinants merge and blur. What emerges instead are combinations of cognitive and working styles. A cognitive style seems very much a function of the analyst's professional education. Sometimes it provides substantive knowledge, but more often it determines which questions are relevant and it helps the analyst think through the problem. A working style, on the other hand, seems to be a function of the analyst's past and present organizational experience in which he has learned certain rules of thumb and norms that help him do his job.

Analyzing problems involves two overlapping stages—problem definition and problem documentation. For most analysts the first stage is the creative aspect of the job. Identifying crucial variables, relationships, and insights or hypotheses that can be tested are what the analyst sees as "wringing out" the problem. Problem definition as such is a first-cut approximate solution; it provides a central theme around which the rest of the work will be organized. Besides pointing to a possible solution, to define a problem very often means to state policy objectives, to constrain the analysis, and to provide a framework for future discussion of policy. Moreover, this approximate solution by problem definition is an aid to calculation.[1] Aids are also used in the problem documentation stage, which is mostly an elaboration, a hedging against future questions, a gathering of more detail and computation to substantiate the analyst's initial insight into the problem.

Let us begin with the influence of professional background on an analyst's cognitive style and then consider the operation of both cognitive and working styles in problem definition and problem documentation.

PROFESSIONAL ORIENTATION AND EDUCATION

Once a noted economist was asked to define economics and he replied, "Economics is what economists do." Taking the hint, I have been defining policy analysis by what policy analysts do; and if my definition has been confusing, that is at least partially the fault of the idiosyncratic and newly developing nature of the analyst's variable activities. Even if we cast the discussion in the restricted terms of short- and long-range studies, different policies and situations probably require different analysts and techniques. If there is a common thread, it is in the use of some sort of scientific method. By this I do not mean some rigid approach to knowledge. What I have in mind is an open spirit of inquiry and a tendency to be systematic or methodical in the gathering and presentation of information. As problem solvers, analysts select problems, try to define them, bound them, and cut them down to size. Once they begin to understand what they are trying to do, they look or search for information. With such data they make calculations, looking for order and explanation. Then they sit down with their results and try to interpret them. If the results fit the problem, fine; if not, the analysts will repeat the process of inquiry. Of course the process is actually intertwined and is often not as ordered or neat because, for

1. For a discussion of aids to calculation, see Aaron Wildavsky, *The Politics of the Budgetary Process* (Boston: Little, Brown & Co., 1964), pp. 11–17.

example, data gathering can take place before the problem is understood.

To this general process of inquiry, the predecessors of the policy analyst, such as the systems analyst, have added their own vocabulary for the elements of analysis.[2] Today we still talk about *objectives*, or the ends of policymakers, and the *alternatives*, or means for achieving the objectives. Then there must be *criteria*, rules for choosing which alternative is desirable. In order to apply a criterion, there must first be some understanding of the consequences, the *costs* and *benefits*, of adopting each alternative. All of this information must be put together according to a theory about reality, and this theory is called a *model*. Finally, the results must be communicated, an element of analysis that is often overlooked. Although there has been an expansion of techniques and applications, this vocabulary is still very much a part of the argot of the policy analyst. We will find it useful for indicating the relationship of professional background to cognitive style.

COGNITIVE STYLES

If we could hold constant the effect of clients and the bureaucratic context, then the importance of the analyst's professional education and orientation on his cognitive style would be apparent. Policy analysts with a background in economics, for example, have reported to me that their experience with graphics, supply and demand curves, and the like help them to conceptualize and work through the problems. One analyst who is also a physician feels that medical training is quite useful and compatible with doing analysis. Making a diagnosis on the basis of incomplete information is similar to breaking down policy problems and gaining insight into what to do. Moreover, in the policy analysis team effort, each analyst brings his particular professional orientation to bear on the problem. For example, in the preparation of the blue-collar memorandum, discussed in the previous chapter, one analyst

---

2. An expanded description of analysis and its vocabulary can be found in E. S. Quade and W. I. Boucher, eds., *Systems Analysis and Policy Planning: Applications in Defense* (New York: American Elsevier Publishing Co., 1968), pp. 7–19; and Richard S. Rosenbloom and John R. Russell, *New Tools for Urban Management: Studies in Systems and Organizational Analysis* (Boston: Division of Research, Graduate School of Business Administration, Harvard University, 1971), pp. 279–98.

perceived the problem in terms of an economic squeeze between the worker's expenditure and income; another analyst emphasized psychological and sociological variables, such as the worker's goals, perception of life style, and feelings of frustration and alienation; and the leader of the team, sensitive to political implications, was concerned about the harm (such as increased racism) that might result from blue-collar resentment, the effect on the Nixon administration, and the necessity for having policy recommendations that could be used by the White House.

But the bureaucratic context does interfere. It attenuates and modifies the analyst's professional background. Policy analysts, as we have seen, do assume roles. Economists or political scientists may become technicians or entrepreneurs; engineers and lawyers may become politicians.[3] So in order to illustrate the importance of professional background throughout the process of inquiry, I will compare some of the premises or considerations of three hypothetical policy analysts: an economist, a social scientist who is an organizational analyst, and for convenience a political scientist who is a political analyst.[4] Examples of the considerations used in working on problems are arranged by the process of inquiry and the elements of analysis in table 1.[5] This arrangement is to help us understand analysis within a general framework of rational problem

3. One suspects that those in the "softer" skill professions (e.g., public administration, law) would gravitate to the politician role and that those with "harder" skills (e.g., mathematics, statistics, operations research) would choose to become technicians or entrepreneurs. One complication is that skills are acquired on the job, at night school, and in in-service programs. Thus, one can find an analyst with a graduate degree in history who also has quantitative skills. Unfortunately, our sampling and interviewing procedures were such that we cannot provide any clear answer on the relation of roles to professional education.

4. The organizational analyst could be a professional psychologist or perhaps a political scientist. He would be familiar with the change agent literature, organizational development, and books such as Warren G. Bennis's *Changing Organizations: Essays on the Development and Evolution of Human Organization* (New York: McGraw-Hill, 1966) and Chris Argyris's *Intervention Theory and Method: A Behavioral Science View* (Reading, Mass.: Addison-Wesley Publishing Co., 1970). The choice of analytical backgrounds is similar but not exactly the same as K. A. Archibald's in "Three Views of the Expert's Role in Policymaking: Systems Analysis, Incrementalism, and the Clinical Approach," *Policy Sciences* 1 (spring 1970): 73–86.

5. These considerations may appear too simple or not realistic. Since I am not trying to describe a discipline but only to suggest the centrality of disciplinary orientations in policy analysis work, these examples should suffice.

TABLE 1: Cognitive Styles of Hypothetical Policy Analysts

Process of Inquiry[a]	Elements of Analysis[a]	Illustrative Considerations		
		Economist	Organizational Analyst	Political Analyst
Select problem		Allocation of resources	Increase support for and effectiveness of agency	Increase support for and effectiveness of president/party
Define, formulate, and delimit problem	Objective	Explicit Agreement Stable	Not as explicit Agreement with payments Can tend to stability	Confusion Conflict and disagreement Instability
	Criteria	Maximize difference between benefits and costs	Acceptable level of organizational conflict	Maximize probability of political acceptance
Determine and search for relevant data	Alternatives	Exclude the infeasible Present solution/policy	Exclude the infeasible Present solution/policy	Exclude the infeasible Present solution/policy
	Costs and benefits	Program related Quantitative	Program related Mix of qualitative and quantitative	Program and nonprogram related (political costs and benefits) Mostly qualitative
Calculate and explain	Model	Closed General Parsimonious	Open Idiosyncratic Complex-contextual	Open Idiosyncratic Complex-contextual
Interpret results, test, or start over if unhappy	Communication	Technical A good study sells itself	Persuasion Sell the members of the organization	Advocacy Sell the president and other actors

[a]Based on E. S. Quade, *Military Systems Analysis*, RM-3452-PR (Santa Monica: Rand Corporation, 1963), pp. 7-26.

solving, but the sequence of the steps in the framework should not be taken too seriously given the convoluted nature of the ways analysts actually do their jobs. As we will see, the professional background of the analyst can influence his cognitive style, or the way he thinks about a problem and the questions he asks.

To start at the beginning of the process of inquiry, the economist will select problems that deal with the allocation and distribution of resources. The organizational and political analyst, perhaps, will focus on problems of increasing the political support and effectiveness of an agency or of an important political actor such as the president. A concern for organizational effectiveness is just another way of expressing an interest in the allocation of resources; after all, forms of organization are a resource. But differences occur among analysts in that economists may not fully appreciate the strengths and weaknesses of these social forms and therefore analyze resources in nonorganizational terms of aggregates, such as the supply of nurses. And the organizational analyst, for his part, will talk about improving effectiveness and productivity but also pay attention to questions of jurisdiction or territory and adaptation, often finding that adaptation may require the inefficient use of resources.

In defining his problem, the economist assumes that some explicit set of objectives exists, that there is some consensus on these objectives among policymakers, and that these objectives will remain fairly stable over time; otherwise such tools as discounting make little sense. The organizational analyst knows that he will not necessarily have an explicit agreement on objectives, but working within one agency with the availability of monetary and other payments allows him to assume also some stable set of management objectives. The political analyst knows he is working in a milieu of many policymakers in which there is great confusion, conflict, and instability of objectives.

The three use different criteria. For each alternative the economist will have a calculation of benefits and costs, and his rule will be to choose the alternative that maximizes the difference between benefits and costs. The organizational analyst may have several rules in mind, but above all he will choose alternatives that permit a tolerable level of conflict without the organization falling apart. Maximizing political support is behind the political analyst's rule of choosing the alternative having the greatest chance of acceptance.

All three analysts will search for alternatives around the present solution or policy. The pull of current practice plus the lack of knowledge about innovative alternatives encourages a measure of conservatism despite the rhetoric about creative alternatives. All three will be concerned about feasibility, but their own kind of feasibility. The economist will exclude the alternatives that exhaust the gross national product or some lesser budget constraint. The organizational analyst will exclude alternatives that the members of his organization will not accept. The political analyst will be concerned about whether the alternative can get through Congress.[6] Costs and benefits will be computed but they will not necessarily be just dollar or other economic measures of resources. The political analyst, for instance, will concern himself with non-programmatic costs and benefits, with indicators of gain and loss in political resources. An alternative may be fine from a technical perspective but be deficient in its ability to get its sponsor reelected.

The influence of cognitive styles is especially evident in the different models of the three analysts. The economist deals with a closed system of relatively few but strategic variables. Usually he can quantify these variables, knows the relationships between them, and pushes for generality. Both organizational and political analysts operate with many variables, some of them quantifiable, many of them not. The more these analysts learn, the more they want to learn; so little is excluded as they build a contextual richness about a particular organization or political system.

All the analysts communicate their results, but the use of persuasion and advocacy is probably more legitimate for the organizational and political types than for the technician-type economist, who believes that a good study sells itself.

Hypothetical examples can easily be misleading, but our understanding will not be impaired if we keep in mind the variation in analytical problem solving. Even within a profession there will be some diversity in cognitive styles. The economist may not use a cost-effectiveness framework but employ a rate-of-return approach.[7] The political analyst may have as a criterion the stability

6. See my "Political Feasibility and Policy Analysis," *Public Administration Review* 32 (November-December 1972): 859–67.
7. In "internal rate-of-return" analysis, the analyst determines "the rate of discount which makes the present value of the benefits [of a proposed project]

of the regime rather than a notion of acceptability. In addition there are a variety of disciplines and technical fields I have not even mentioned that introduce other considerations into analysis, and these considerations may modify the cognitive and working style of the analyst. Analytical work at the Atomic Energy Commission, for example, obviously must rely on some considerations of physics and engineering. A conclusion from one of its studies shows what I mean: "The breeder can produce not only large direct money benefits from the low cost of electrical energy, but also other tangible quantitative benefits, such as those associated with reduced uranium requirements, reduced uranium separative work requirements, and the large production of plutonium."[8]

POLICY CONGRUENCE

The importance of the analyst's professional education and orientation is also probably related to its congruence with a policy area. The Treasury policy analyst who has been trained in public finance has, besides the cognitive style of the economist, the theory and knowledge base of his field. He already knows about concepts of equity, incidence, tax shifting, progressivity of taxes, and fiscal neutrality and does not have to invent them. He is obviously much better prepared to work in his field than he would be if he were working in an area new to him, such as prison reform.

Many analysts, however, do work in new policy areas that are less congruent with their backgrounds. Their professional education helps them to think about the problem and to ask certain questions, but they often lack the requisite intellectual support and substance. In the extreme case of incongruence, there will be little basic knowledge and theory to build on and few professional peers to encourage standards and quality. What is known will have been

---

exactly equal to the present value of the costs." This discount rate is called the "internal rate of return" of the project. If the costs were higher or the benefits less, this internal rate would be lower; conversely, if the costs were lower or the benefits greater, the internal rate would be higher. The internal rate of return attempts to sum up and express the goodness of the project in interest-rate terms. The alternative that yields the greatest return will be the preferred option. See E. J. Mishan, *Cost-Benefit Analysis: an Introduction* (New York and Washington: Praeger Publishers, Inc., 1971), p. 198.

8. U.S. Atomic Energy Commission, Division of Reactor Development and Technology, *Cost-Benefit Analysis of the U.S. Breeder Reactor Program* (#Wash 1126), April 1969, p. 9.

gathered casually about some past and present policies. What insights and direction exist will come from the analyst's bureaucratic colleagues.

PROBLEM DEFINITION

Depending on their cognitive styles, policy analysts have several ways of defining problems. Some who have been trained in quantitative methods and model building try to take some of the significant variables of the problem and put them together in simple algebraic expressions and then work toward a solution. It is this ability to cut quickly into a problem in one's head or with just pencil and paper that distinguishes the quality of the analyst. Some analysts can work through a problem without much substantive exposure in only a few days. Others feel it necessary actually to make a first cut or to work through a "dummy study" of the problem, which might take up to six months. This dummy study lays the groundwork for a more expanded and refined analysis, and it can tell the analyst who should be assigned to a task force and where the information is buried.

INITIAL INSIGHTS

Problem definition is a preanalysis, a formulation of what the problem really is and of what might be done. Often this process of thinking, of gaining insights, is fortuitous. A number of years ago, for example, a few defense analysts who worked for a navy think tank were sitting around at night having coffee and talking about the Department of Navy's desire to get into the business of fast deployment of troops and supplies. At the time there was considerable interest in using large-sized aircraft for this military mission. After some discussion, the analysts thought that it would be possible to have a certain kind of ship do the mission and do it in a more economical way than other forms of transportation. They did some quick checking and some crude cost estimates and found that the idea seemed to have even more merit. At this point a large study was launched, essentially to document and validate the initial insight of using fast-deployment logistic ships. Similarly, when some HEW analysts were faced with the possibility of reforming the country's welfare system, they wanted to find a breakthrough tactic that could serve as a major lever for such reform. Having known about the negative income tax proposals, they gave these some thought and came to the conclusion that some type of income maintenance program could be the tactic they were looking for. After that initial insight, the rest of the work involved tracing out the impact of different tax rates and different levels of income support on different groups of people in the country.

CUTTING DOWN TO SIZE

Avoid being inundated by data; shun the computer most of the time; ignore simpleminded models such as linear programming—that's the analysts' advice. What they are saying is that there is no substitute for thinking through the problem. One analyst believes he gets 80 percent of the answers by the end of the problem definition phase. But before the analyst can get answers, he must "cut the problem down to size," and the various ways he cuts illustrate the operation of the working style of the analyst.

Omit Part of the Problem

One way to cut the problem down to size is to leave out part of it. In a study of disease control programs, analysts started out with a list of diseases and then, after some thought, analyzed only five programs. Alcoholism was left out because no one could define it, and heart disease was left out because of the difficulty of understanding the benefits of treatment. Other diseases were left out because of possible political hurdles to reshuffling the money.[9] Often the same concerns that lead to the selection of a problem help to define it. A typical question analysts ask is whether they will be able to get information and cooperation from the people who will be involved. For example, some analysts who wanted to do a study of air pollution decided to concentrate on sulphur oxides rather than on some other pollutants because of the availability of data. Using a contractor, a simulation technique, and the data, they developed a working model of the dispersion of air currents. Picking an exemplar is another common way of cutting down complexity by omitting part of the problem. For instance, an OEO analyst concerned about the connection between public works and

9. For a brief description of the study, see Robert N. Grosse, "Problems of Resource Allocation in Health," in *Public Expenditures and Policy Analysis*, eds. Robert H. Haveman and Julius Margolis (Chicago: Markham Publishing Co., 1970), pp. 532–36.

health looked only at a limited number of communities and their water and sewer programs. To analyze a thousand communities and their many public works activities would have made the problem impossible to handle. Of course an exemplar should be representative of the policy problem; otherwise the analysis is likely to be misleading and in error.

Critically Examine and Discuss Assumptions

One can also cut by assuming away aspects that in fact may be relevant and important. The analytical task is to determine which assumptions are central to the conclusions of the analysis. Often there is no behavioral evidence on the consequences or effects of various types of public policy; and in whatever model is created, these effects will be treated as assumptions with a value of zero. For example, prior to the income maintenance experiments, much of the analysis that was done assumed that there would be no change in work incentives, given some sort of income subsidy. Moreover, beyond the question of work incentives, other behavioral implications of income maintenance were not explored; for example, what impact will income maintenance have on voting in the South, or what aggregate effect will it have on price and demand in various regions of the country? Obviously, many (if not most) possible effects have to be assumed away; otherwise the possibilities are endless. But the analytical problem is to determine which effects can safely be ignored. Unfortunately, the critical examination of assumptions is frequently slighted; rather than gathering strategic information that could qualify the nature of the assumption, effort is diverted into asserting the assumption's original validity.

One appropriate procedure is to explore the policy consequences of different assumptions—to convert an unexamined constant into a visible element of the analysis. "The point of analysis," Enthoven and Smith tell us, "is not to give the answer, but rather to show how the answer depends on various assumptions and judgments." Quite correctly, they urge that assumptions "be put to the test of debate and common sense," and that "in any analysis, the assumptions drive the conclusions. There can be no doubt about that, nor about the fact that there is no single 'right' set of assumptions, but only a variety of sets of relevant assumptions,

each more or less equally defensible."[10] Thus, while it is quite
sensible to cut the problem down to size by assuming away trivia or
irrelevant aspects, it is not appropriate to assume away central
policy implications if you know enough to know what these might
be.

Talking over assumptions with the client, or with someone close
to him, can help determine centrality. Both client and analyst can
benefit from such a discussion, because accepted and tacit assumptions can be questioned. An analyst at the National Science Foundation recalled an instance in which her office was asked to analyze
the effectiveness of an "institutional development program." In the
discussion between the analyst and her boss there emerged a basic
assumption, that "the schools we support are growing, and that,
therefore, there is a causal relationship between our support and
the productivity of the school." The analyst, however, argued that
the schools were growing regardless of NSF support and that
NSF's role should be to increase the quality of education. On the
basis of the analyst's assumption the analysis proceeded, and the
final report attempted to draw a relationship between school
quality and NSF support.

Isolate Technical and Political Components

What is central will also depend on how the analyst breaks down
the problem. Policy analysis does not linger for long at the level of
broad questions, such as what to do about education. The analyst
takes these broad questions and converts them into smaller operational ones. For each small question, which is a policy problem in
its own right, the analyst identifies a number of variables or policy
components. Studying student financial loan programs, for example, an HEW analyst developed "analytical categories," such as the
extent of governmental subsidy, the length of the repayment
terms, and the effect of repayment on future income. For a
health-service problem, the analyst might be concerned about the
mix of professional skills, or their distribution, or the availability of
laboratory facilities. If the analyst is working on emergency health
care, he should not be concerned only with the response time of an

10. Alain C. Enthoven and K. Wayne Smith, *How Much Is Enough? Shaping
the Defense Program, 1961–1969* (New York: Harper & Row, 1971), p. 64.

ambulance from the emergency facility or hospital to the accident and then back to the hospital, but also with what happens to the patient while he is in the ambulance and after he gets to the hospital.

In breaking down a policy problem into its components, most analysts first think of the important variables that can be measured. I call these variables *technical components*. For a public housing problem, technical components might include: number of units, location, density, type of construction, and rent structure. At NASA, analysts were studying the space shuttle system by looking at the timing of development, the configuration of boosters, sites for testing, and general management approach.

Then there is another group of variables which are probably qualitative and sometimes ignored by analysts. I call these variables *political components*. In the Department of Transportation, for instance, analysts were interested in comparing alternative forms of transportation. When examining the comparative safety of air travel versus travel on federal highways, some analysts felt that they would have to take into account more than the cost per life saved for each policy alternative.[11] The political currency of a life saved was different. There was bound to be greater public concern over a single air crash involving relatively few deaths than over the many individual deaths in automobiles across the nation. An airplane crash can create political repercussions because of the specter of mass death, while the vast numbers of people killed in highway accidents on weekend holidays are likely to be ignored. Professor Robert N. Grosse, a former HEW analyst, also emphasizes the importance of political components:

Analysis of major policy areas like health is not just a mechanical exercise of mathematics; we have to consider qualitative factors as well which may affect the outcome of our studies. Indeed, sometimes this is all we have to work with. Knowing the number of beds in a hospital or the beds' utilization rate is only a rough index of capacity and not a measure of the quality of care. Similarly, there are tradeoffs between health services and education for improving the communication flow between patient and doctor; such tradeoffs may actually involve value conflicts.[12]

11. A common argument among analysts is whether and how to quantify the value of human life. For a discussion of FAA's attempts in this area, see Steven E. Rhoads, *Policy Analysis in the Federal Aviation Administration* (Lexington, Mass.: Lexington Books, 1974), pp. 70–84.

12. Grosse, "Problems of Resource Allocation," p. 521.

Getting Help

Usually the analyst knows something about the problem before starting the analysis; for example, a Department of Labor analyst knew that the Concentrated Employment Program was in trouble, because enrollments and placements were dropping and the program was not reaching the hard-core unemployed. The head of an analytical shop, in making assignments, looks for people who know about the policy area and have in mind a working hypothesis that can be tested. In another agency the first step is to formulate a hypothesis—although the analysts do not call it that, to avoid "scaring off the program people in the department." Being on top of a policy problem certainly helps to define it, but what does the analyst do when he is assigned to a new area? How can he get help?

The client can help. Some analysts would like their client to work along with them in a mutual enterprise, but not many clients are that active. Besides, much of the client's help in defining problems is indirect and comes about through intermediaries and anticipation. The client is particularly helpful when he sets the objectives for a study. For example, while serving on a White House committee that was deciding how to spend $1.5 billion for easing the process of school desegregation, an HEW analyst felt that "presidential guidelines" were useful in cutting the problem down to size. At meetings of the task force, Attorney General John Mitchell would read the text of President Nixon's speech and say, "This is what we have to do because the president has said it." The money was to be used to encourage integration for educational achievement and not for any other purpose, such as promoting integration of housing.

Through the mechanism of anticipation the client also helps the analyst define the problem. One analyst likes to follow his client around for a week and attend the meetings he does, and the like, to see what "is hurting the client." At HUD, a secretary's statement on future federal funding of projects, derived from Domestic Council guidance, altered an analyst's thinking about the department's programs. The secretary had said that the department was going to work directly with mayors, so the analyst concluded that the model cities program should be restructured and that redevelopment funds should no longer go to a separate redevelopment agency.[13] No

13. "The model cities program was designed to concentrate public and private resources in a comprehensive . . . attack on the social, economic, and physical problems of slum and blighted neighborhoods. It was authorized by Title I of the

doubt, as he put it, "the statement caused some change in our thinking." The analyst anticipates what the client wants. He figures out the client's reasons for requesting the study; otherwise, "if the analysis proceeds in isolation and a decision maker receives his results and sees a bunch of irrelevant options, he will ignore the entire work."

But there are situations in which the analyst does not trust the client's definition of the problem or in which that definition does not go far enough. What then? Because he is under time constraints, the analyst must look for shortcuts to knowledge and insight that are readily available. He reads everything he can lay his hands on, and then he talks to trusted informants. Talking to program people at various levels in the bureaucracy and, if time permits, perhaps to outside academic experts and some beneficiaries, the policy analyst gets an impression of the various perceptions of the problem. But how does he know whom to trust? One analyst's technique is to ask some simple questions, based on his reading, to which he already knows the answers. Seeing whether the responses are consistent with his reading helps him calibrate his informants. If all external help fails, he has no other choice but to rely on himself and his own judgment.

COMPLEXITY AND CLOSURE

Thinking through the problem is an important means of cutting down the complexity involved in problem solving. The solutions are supposed to be better too. Enthoven and Smith express this practitioner's view in discussing how to get the most out of study groups:

the instructions to study groups should make clear that their goal is to identify the important questions and to get the answers roughly right. Too many groups spend too little effort defining the problem they are working on and developing a logical way of relating data to it. The design phase of a study is by far the toughest and most critical. It may take up most of the total time. But there is little to be gained from charging off to gather data and make detailed calculations until one knows what is really needed and how the parts of the problem fit together.[14]

Demonstration Cities and Metropolitan Development Act of 1966"; see Department of Housing and Urban Development, *The Model Cities Program* (Washington, D.C.: U.S. Government Printing Office, 1971), p. 3. In fiscal year 1971, the Congress authorized 575 million dollars for more than 100 model cities; see *Congressional Quarterly Almanac* 26 (1970), p. 742.

14. Enthoven and Smith, *How Much Is Enough?* p. 322.

Defining the problem also results in closure. The analysis becomes more constrained by inserting what is relevant and by excluding what may be infeasible or irrelevant. There is a danger, however; for preliminary diagnosis, coupled with a short deadline, can result in premature closure. At the beginning of a study, for example, a common device to force problem definition from a group of analysts is to direct them to indicate what the final conclusions of the research report will be, or to ask them actually to outline and sketch briefing charts which might be used in communicating the results of the study to the client.

This is not to suggest that the analyst is always locked in with his preconceived notions but rather that the line between correct problem definition and premature closure is not always clear.

CHOOSING OBJECTIVES

Questioning the Client's Definition

Most analysts feel that the problem definition stage is the most crucial one; an indication of this is that they often reserve this part of the analytical activity for themselves and then contract out pieces of the work of the problem documentation stage to other agencies or to think tanks and other research corporations. Because analysts know that it is the definition of the problem that drives the analysis, they may be reluctant to accept the client's definition. It is very much part of the working style of analysts that one should attempt to redefine the problem.[16] Sometimes the very fuzziness of the way the problem is stated by a client allows the analyst to substitute his own preferences or "to raise the level of optimization" in the guise of restating the problem. "The good analyst forces the pace and pushes the decision maker." Of course, some technicians do hold to a textbook view that the goals or objectives should be stated by the client and that then, and only then, can the analysis proceed. But most entrepreneurs are ready and willing to define a set of objectives. Indeed, we are told that, "initially to set tentative objectives, the analyst searches his own experience, knowledge, and attitudes, and talks with decision-makers, experts, other

---

15. Robert K. Merton comes to a similar conclusion about applied social scientists when he says, "The researcher has the task of ascertaining the *central* pragmatic problem rather than passively accepting its initial specifications by the policy maker." Robert K. Merton, *The Sociology of Science: Theoretical and Empirical Investigations,* ed. Norman W. Storer (Chicago and London: University of Chicago Press, 1973), p. 82.

analysts or anyone connected with the problem."[16] They may be tentative objectives, but it seems that it is the analyst who sets them. They are tentative because the analyst or client can reformulate the objectives as the analysis proceeds.

The Analyst's Preferences

In defining problems and selecting policy objectives, analysts cannot escape their own preferences and values. Even when analysts try to be "objective," eschewing the role of entrepreneurs or politicians, their preferences creep into their work. Most analysts are aware of their own biases. As one analyst says, "When you know one alternative would favor what you want to push, you include it." Clients, however, should be made aware of the bias, if for no other reason than to calibrate the utility of the analyst's advice. At the National Science Foundation, one policy analyst's superiors have never asked her to work on a program with which she does not agree. She believes, for example, in the general value of education and is less concerned with the linkage between education and future career. In her view, this belief is consistent with the goals of NSF, so it does not interfere with her work. One wonders whether her clients share the same feeling.

Another analyst, interested in achieving equality of opportunity in higher education, includes that objective and examines its implications when analyzing student aid programs. He knows that the legislation on such programs does not preclude selecting equality of opportunity as an objective. One can always find an official statement to justify the selection of a particular objective. "If politicians say it, it is fair play to hold it up to them."

Predetermined Preferences

Preferences often exist before the analysis. Thus, an HEW analyst who was committed to improving the education of poor minorities felt that Title I of Public Law 81–874, a financial aid program for federally "impacted areas," must be thoroughly bad because it benefits the middle and upper classes. It may be that providing funds to schools in areas that have federal installations is an inappropriate policy; but in this case it is the analyst's policy preferences that are driving the analysis, rather than the analysis

16. Rosenbloom and Russell, *New Tools for Urban Management*, p. 283.

determining his preferences. In this respect, the policy analyst is not unlike other bureaucrats, such as the HEW budget official, a Catholic, who did everything he could to stop programs of population control. In the policy process, neither analyst nor bureaucrat is neutral.

Imagine the Department of Labor analyst who grew up in a poor working-class neighborhood. He identified with the working man. For him, pointing out that the blue-collar worker was disadvantaged was not a mere policy exercise; it was an opportunity to express a deeply held personal view. If he had a concern, it was not that his own beliefs had crept into his work but that he had not been able to do as well-written and exhaustive a job as he should have. He had had to write the initial report in less than three weeks, after reading only a limited number of periodicals and holding internal discussions with only the three staff members involved. The second draft had to be completed in less than one week. Irritated because the short time span restricted him from developing and verifying his ideas, he said, "I'm not sure what the hurry was. Obviously, from the time it languished in the White House, unread, our rush was not warranted. But whenever the White House is involved there always seems to be a hurry. Our office was told by the secretary to get the information together right away, implying that this project had high priority in the White House."

As was pointed out in chapter 2, the goals of government are often not explicit, and when they are they may conflict with one another. Nevertheless, in defining a problem, the analyst is likely to make an implicit choice of objectives. It's not easy. An HEW analyst, studying child care and the use of nursery schools, found himself caught in between two HEW factions. One faction saw nursery schools as a means of improving the quality of life for children; the other faction saw them as a device for getting mothers out of the house to go to work. To choose one objective over another is to choose a different problem—getting people off welfare is not quite the same thing as improving the welfare of children.[17] At the Department of Interior, analysts were concerned about our diminishing supply of natural gas and wanted to use coal as a source for gas, but across town the Environmental Protection Agency was

17. Sometimes the policy problems and the situation are such that a choice of objectives does not have to be made and instead alternative sets of objectives are examined.

planning to restrict the use of coal because of advice concerning the ecological effects of mining. Even when clients are mushy headed about what they are trying to do, analysts are supposed to be clear and explicit about objectives. Consider the hard-nosed analyst who criticized his colleagues for introducing "sentimentality" into their analysis: "When you have limited funds, you can't use such funds to increase social equity if your objective is to improve education."

In discussing program budgeting (PPB), Charles L. Schultze has made it quite clear that the analyst is involved in setting objectives:

There is no simple division of labor in which the "politicians" achieve consensus on an agreed-on set of objectives while the "analysts" design and evaluate—from efficiency and effectiveness criteria—alternative means of achieving those objectives.

As experience in the Defense Department has taught us, systematic analysis is itself intimately concerned with the specification of objectives.[18]

Some analysts, however, feel that it is easier to specify the objectives of defense and space policy than to specify objectives for other governmental programs. Work in social policy, they say, is not like putting a man on the moon by a specific date. Objectives are not clearly identified, and analysis is "like driving on a Los Angeles freeway, guiding yourself by what you see in the rearview mirror." But while it is true that there are different analytical techniques and bases of knowledge for each policy area, part of the perception that it is easier in defense and space is a matter of ignorance. Analysts who have worked in NASA and DOD have also had their share of working in an environment of confusion over objectives.[19] Both in defense and domestic policy, analysts have had to set their own policy objectives.

CREATING ALTERNATIVES

Analyst as Innovator

A policy analysis without alternatives is like a sheik without oil wells. Not only is the policy analyst supposed to examine alternatives, but the legacy from defense analysis tells us that he

18. Charles L. Schultze, *The Politics and Economics of Public Spending* (Washington, D.C.: Brookings Institution, 1968), p. 3.
19. Once a policy decision is made, clarity of objectives and consensus about goals are apparent to everyone. But before the decision, the potential for conflict and confusion over objectives is there, even for such a straightforward policy as getting to the moon; see, for example, Howard Margolis, *Technocratic and Political Models of the Decision to Go to the Moon*, Note N-823 (Arlington, Va.: Institute for Defense Analyses, September 1972).

is supposed to create them. Consider Hitch's and McKean's statement:

The alternatives are frequently referred to as *systems* because each combines all the elements . . . needed to accomplish the objective. . . . The great problem in choosing alternatives to compare is to be sure that all the good alternatives have been included. Frequently we lack the imagination to do this at the beginning of an analysis; we think of better alternatives (that is, invent new systems) as the analysis proceeds and we learn more about the problem. The invention of new and better systems in this fashion is indeed one of the principal payoffs from this kind of analysis.[20]

This emphasis on invention is repeated by Quade:

Systems analysis should try to create as well as to eliminate alternatives. The invention of new alternatives can be much more valuable than exhaustive comparison of given alternatives, none of which may be very satisfactory. The job of the systems analyst is thus not only analysis but also design. His analysis should suggest new alternatives or changes in given ones that will make the preferred system or operation more satisfactory.[21]

Reflecting on their experience as analysts in the Department of Defense, Enthoven and Smith tell us:

Relatively unhampered by tradition or institutional restraints, free from the need to build consensus, without a predetermined position to sell, and without the need to be good soldiers, these analysts could more easily ask the hard questions and pose genuine alternatives, arriving at a recommendation via a more rational and objective process. They were not constrained to defer to rank, age, experience, or chain of command. They had the time to think about important long-range policy problems and the room for imagination, initiative, and fresh thinking. They were comparatively free to gore sacred cows.[22]

I do not quite remember the same halcyon atmosphere of reflective tranquillity. Even if the DOD was like that in the sixties, it is no longer like that; and Enthoven's and Smith's description would certainly not apply to the rest of the federal bureaucracy. Actually their description, if applied elsewhere in the bureaucracy, would be accurate if negatively stated. Most policy analysts are not free from institutional restraints, sometimes do have something to sell, and are not able to gore sacred cows.

20. Charles J. Hitch and Roland N. McKean, *The Economics of Defense in the Nuclear Age* (Cambridge, Mass.: Harvard University Press, 1960), pp. 118–19.
21. E. S. Quade, ed., *Analysis for Military Decisions*, R-387-PR (Santa Monica: Rand Corporation, 1964), p. 319.
22. Enthoven and Smith, *How Much Is Enough?* p. 99.

Theoretically, the policy analyst could be an innovative force in the government, but it should not surprise any student of problem solving that policy analysts search for alternatives in the area of the present solution and that many studies consider only the present program with slight variations. There are examples, of course, of intelligent analysts thinking up creative and novel alternatives by freeing themselves of current solutions and constraints. They may do so by looking at the problem in a future time horizon or by forcing themselves to answer the question: "Can I think of the problem in a totally different way?" On balance, however, one would probably be wrong in assuming that analysis by itself can generate social innovations. Operating under organizational and personal constraints, such as arbitrary deadlines for their products, many analysts see their jobs as evaluating or justifying alternatives that are already in the literature and have been much discussed. In other words, the analyst is very much a processor of other people's alternatives.

The more experience, knowledge, and security an analyst has, however, the more he can afford to explore the novel. The experienced analyst with extensive substantive background in a policy area does not have to resort as much to reducing the range of alternatives as an aid to calculation. In the defense policy area, there are experienced analysts who can recombine with subtlety the components of a problem in such a way as to produce new alternatives. In the domestic policy area, however, analytical conditions are different. First, for many areas the analyst does not know much.[23] Second, there are a plethora of bright ideas floating around, and their consequences have yet to be explored. Finally, the analyst knows that the farther out he goes, the harder it will be to get people to listen to him; so he explores the obvious alternatives and cuts his problem-solving costs.

Whether an alternative is creative is very much a subjective business in which some analysts believe they have been creative and others do not. Obviously, it is not a simple matter to design, to innovate, or to invent. As one analyst said, "the difficult thing is always to try to think of something new, something really clever." A

23. For an example of how the lack of data interfered with evaluation efforts, see Milbrey Wallin McLaughlin, *Evaluation and Reform: The Elementary and Secondary Education Act of 1965, Title I,* R-1292-RC (Santa Monica: Rand Corporation, January 1974).

Department of Labor analyst, for example, does not see his work as innovative: "None of our research represents a knowledge break-through. The best we can do is study the related knowledge and attempt to discern a trend or to act on what appears to be an appropriate alternative. The results are rarely novel and seldom answer more than a specific problem." A politician tells us that it is foolish to believe that analysis involves a full consideration of alternatives. "Those who start by defining the problem take too long. We usually begin with an alternative which we then try to justify."

One analyst's boss wanted her to present new alternatives, but she found this difficult to do because the policy issues were narrow and the constraints, such as organizational rules and structure, were many and not easily changed. As she said, "most of us feel that we have already considered the alternatives we are presenting, previously, and if you have already considered the alternatives and one by one discarded them, it is difficult to present them as alternatives. To us, in most cases, the decision is obvious." In another agency, the drive for organizational consensus, for "completed staff work," drives out alternatives. Nevertheless, it is the job of the analyst to examine alternatives. At HEW an advisory council for a team studying the delivery of health services wanted the team to study only neighborhood health centers. A co-director of the team, however, felt that studying only one alternative was ridiculous, and that the team should also look at upgrading the outpatient care delivered by hospitals. One thing led to another, and the team was able to address the broader problem of group practice versus fee-for-service or individual practice.

Even if the analyst has a fertile mind, there will still be some cognitive limit on the number of alternatives that can be analyzed. At some point in the analysis, the number of alternatives must be reduced so that the consequences of the remaining alternatives can be fully explored. Since the menu of possible policy alternatives is quite large, choosing, not only designing, is critical. And it should be clear that the analyst is not always free to make the choice without constraints. In addition to the alternatives he likes, he must also analyze alternatives preferred by his client and his friends or by the client's opposition. For example, analysts at the Department of Labor were working on a study for the Domestic Council and wanted to concentrate on the allocation of resources in a few localities of greatest need. However, they recognized that congressional interest might encourage a more even allocation among localities, so they also explored alternative degrees of concentration.

Assessing Constraints

A central dampener of the creative urges of the analyst is his perception of politics. Many analysts incorporate into their working style a norm of exclusion. These analysts are likely to exclude from their consideration what their client does not want to hear: "You don't forward unpleasant alternatives, because once you get shot down, then you should learn not to do it again." Such analysts become sensitive to the boss's political environment and act accordingly. A Treasury Department analyst tells us how to determine what the traffic will bear:

If we were considering a major change in the tax treatment of oil companies abroad, we must consider the fact that the oil companies are an important lobby in Washington. I'd be certain before I began my analysis to become familiar with their position regarding the alternatives. Before I would propose alternatives to the assistant secretary, I would attempt to exclude alternatives they would oppose strongly. As for alternatives that oil lobbyists would oppose moderately or where their position is unclear, I would include the alternatives but would probably not spend a great deal of time researching them. There is no sense working extensively on alternatives that will probably be rejected out of hand.

No analyst has to be a creative genius, but at a minimum he should develop sufficient understanding of the problem and sufficient information to provide the policymaker with a range of options. It may be a service to a client to present the infeasible alternative. Unfortunately, the desire to do only what is acceptable can defeat the informational purpose of analysis.

One analyst, for example, expected an increased demand for rural housing. Believing that open-ended analysis, where the problem is studied in detail, is too time consuming and rarely suggests new alternatives, he concentrated on developing a proposal for a contractor that would focus on feasible recommendations. In rejecting an open-ended analysis, he said, "We have a whole roomful of such studies and no one ever reads them." Instead his study would document the need for rural housing, evaluate existing housing supply systems, and recommend minor alterations in present subsidy programs. By concentrating on improving present programs, he believed, it would be easier to gain congressional approval. His political judgment may have been correct, but one wonders about the utility of a two-year contractual effort that at best would support a preconceived policy direction and at worst would gather data on the wrong problem.

Not all analysts defer to the political judgment of their colleagues or superiors. Alice M. Rivlin noted that HEW analysts continued to work on an income maintenance proposal that did not "have the full blessing of the Secretary of HEW, Wilbur J. Cohen. Cohen was already committed to his bold proposal for federalizing the existing welfare system. He believed coverage should be extended to the working poor in the long run but he did not believe such an extension was politically feasible in the short run. Cohen thought Congress would be far more receptive to such improvements as a federal floor under benefits."[24] Despite Cohen's misgivings about opposition from labor unions and Congress, the analysts went ahead to explore the consequences of covering the working poor. One result was that Cohen pursued his policies without the aid of the analysts, and the analysts had no political representative to carry their ideas.

HEW analysts exhibited greater political sensitivity when they were designing alternatives for student aid programs for education. They avoided structuring the program only for poor and lower-income families. Hoping to avoid opposition and to garner some political support, they included medium-income families in the design of alternative grant and aid programs. Similarly, HEW analysts also played around with the design of income maintenance programs in order to avoid a very expensive program and to hurt as few states as possible. This was done by varying the marginal tax rate and the income level (for example, Nixon's Family Assistance Plan used a 50 percent marginal tax rate and $1,600 for a family of four).

One analyst sees his battle with bureaucratic constraints as a point of departure when he says, "Any alternative that opposes that which the bureaucrat wants to do is creative." Such analysts are likely to confuse novelty with creativity. In rejecting a detailed analysis of a bureaucratic policy inclination, they may miss an

24. Alice M. Rivlin, *Systematic Thinking for Social Action* (Washington, D.C.: Brookings Institution, 1971), pp. 26–27.

opportunity to build on and reshape that inclination. Instead they may suggest a novel, but poorly analyzed, idea. For example, if some people like to eat only potatoes and cake, why not simply put protein in their potatoes and cake to improve their diets? A good idea that may not get far, because it conflicts with bureaucratic notions of educating the citizen about proper nutrition.

Sometimes the novel idea gets accepted, not because of analysis, but because the analyst is in the right place at the right time. At HEW an analyst who was interested in using steam cars as a way of cutting down air pollution was able to insert a multi-million-dollar research and development program into the budget. The rush to clean up the environment was like a vacuum cleaner sweeping up available policy ideas.

Creative Timing

The innovative analyst need not create the alternative but rather seize on an already developed idea whose time, he knows, has come. While it may be that we are living in a period of rapid change and growth in knowledge, many policy ideas have been around for a long time. They can be found in the heads of field personnel and in journals and magazines. Some are gathering dust in a forgotten study; others have been resurrected in distant countries. In each administration it takes some sensitive person to pick up the discarded and make it into a new and dramatic policy initiative. If the analyst suggests group health practice or expanding health insurance, he may be relying on a Chinese notion of paying the doctor when well and not when sick. If the analyst suggests a tax on pollutants or paying police by the amount of reduction in crime, he will be relying on notions that have been discussed by economists for years. Revenue sharing, educational vouchers, and the family assistance plan were all previously created policies that went ignored until someone finally said the time is right; we should try.

Evans and Novak, for example, tell us how Moynihan realized that the prospects for welfare reform had shifted. Robert Finch had just read a paper on welfare revision that he had inherited from the HEW bureaucracy:

. . . Three Cabinet members present—Mitchell, Stans, and Romney —missed the point entirely and failed to recognize Finch's paper as a direct contradiction of Nixon's campaign pledge against income-maintenance plans. . . .

As a veteran bureaucratic tactician, Moynihan decided the best ploy was to treat the income-maintenance proposals in Finch's paper as routine, everyday ideas that ought to shock nobody. . . .

. . . In a flash of intuition, Moynihan realized that the frame of reference on welfare had shifted dramatically leftward.[25]

Thus it was that Moynihan became an advocate for the family assistance plan. Much of the content of the policy had been worked out by the previous administration, but it would be Moynihan that would make FAP part of the Nixon administration.[26]

Policy analysts can incubate new directions, holding on to an idea until such time as it makes programmatic sense. Sometimes the opportunity comes in a matter of months. One summer, analysts from Treasury, the Internal Revenue Service, and the Joint Committee on Internal Revenue Taxation of Congress met to discuss possible changes in tax laws. One proposal, developed by IRS and Treasury, would have modified the income tax withholding structure for individual taxpayers. All the analysts at the meeting agreed that the withholding structure was inequitable. Analysts for the joint committee thought that a change was "not particularly pressing but something we should bring to the committee's attention at some point." In the fall, the Nixon administration proposed changes in the tax structure and the committee analyst resurrected the withholding proposal for the committee's attention.[27] Thus, the timing of raising an alternative may be as important as creating it.

PROBLEM DOCUMENTATION

If one observes an analyst at work, the distinction between definition and documentation evaporates. Studies are reformulated.

25. Rowland Evans, Jr. and Robert D. Novak, *Nixon in the White House: The Frustration of Power* (New York: Random House, Vintage Books, 1972), pp. 225–26.

26. See Daniel P. Moynihan, *The Politics of a Guaranteed Income: The Nixon Administration and the Family Assistance Plan* (New York: Random House, 1973), pp. 113–228.

27. For further insight into congressional tax analysts, see John F. Manley, *The Politics of Finance: The House Committee on Ways and Means* (Boston: Little, Brown and Co., 1970), pp. 307–19, 342–52.

Alternatives are just as likely to be thought of at the end of a study as at the beginning. Assumptions are tested and shifted. Moreover, policy objectives are modified as measurements provide new insights. Because of the overlap, one wonders why analysts even make the distinction between definition and documentation. Documentation does involve more number juggling and the application of techniques and tools than problem definition does. Yet problem documentation is mostly an extension, a refinement, of the analyst's initial conceptualization.

HEURISTICS AND TRICKS OF THE TRADE

When analysts are asked about their rules of thumb or tricks of the trade, they are usually puzzled. Some respond on the basis of their professional training and cognitive style and think of techniques such as rate-of-return analysis. Others respond in terms of their working style and point out strategies of getting information and knowing people: "Don't antagonize program people." "Call the good guys in the field." But the most common response is to deny (by not answering) that such aids to calculation exist. Analysis, after all, is an activity that exposes, that brings to light the implications of one action or another. To admit that a part of analysis may involve judgments, some of which may be mechanical, is antithetical to the basic ideology of analysis. Rules of thumb are, after all, the province of the rest of the bureaucracy, while analysis makes claim to some sort of scientific posture. Nevertheless, given the uncertainty involved in analyzing problems of public policy, analysts have to use rules of thumb, factors, and judgments. Every trade has its tricks and tools, and policy analysis is no exception. Without pretending that a couple of pages can cover the range of tricks and tools, let us consider a few used in solving problems.

Policy analysts, like most of us, develop individual working styles. Some of them, therefore, work better in the morning than in the afternoon. Others cannot work in the office and do their "serious" writing at home. A common injunction is to read a lot. The analyst has the usual problem of keeping on top of new developments, but he also has the more severe problem of having to be an instant expert as his assignments shift. So if you have a strong stomach, you can read in the car pool, as one analyst does, on the trip to and from work. Another analyst just reads tables and only glances at the text.

An analyst has to be a ferret if he is to get the information and data to do his job. Just sending a memo to a bureau requesting some information seldom works, because there are too many ways such requests can be ignored. Instead, as one analyst put it, "you have to have rapport with the program people." One central problem with developing such informants or contacts is that it is hard to maintain them over time. When the analytical office and the program people, for example, have a major policy dispute, rapport evaporates. The analyst is often in the position of balancing present and future informational needs.

Of course, there is a great deal of routine but useful information that is easy to get. For instance, many reports in the federal government soon assume a new identity and become known by the color of their cover—as the blue book or the green book. My tactic in getting such material was to appear at the relevant office, make believe that I worked there, and ask a secretary for a copy of the latest red book. Most of the time this procedure worked—except once when I was handed a telephone book.[28]

Despite an image of technical sophistication—Monte Carlo, linear programming, queuing theory—much policy analysis proceeds in a fairly simple and straightforward way.[29] "Technically sophisticated analysis," an analyst explains, "has only limited value in dealing with complex policy issues. It is the analyst's disciplined approach to problems rather than his technical skills that makes him successful." If an analysis calls for a computer simulation or an

28. For an excellent discussion of the tactics of gathering information, see Eugene Bardach, "Gathering Data for Policy Research," *Urban Analysis* 2 (1974): 117–44.

29. The Monte Carlo method is a "device for developing a more prolonged series of experiences than would be economical through direct observation, when the variability of quantities is thought to be of a random character, within specified limits and under a given probability distribution" (Chester R. Wasson, *Understanding Quantitative Analysis* [New York: Appleton-Century-Crofts, 1969], p. 218). Linear programming is "a method for calculating the best allocation mix of scarce resources in any situation in which the important relationships, cost and otherwise, are either approximately linear in form, or can be transformed into linear expressions" (p. 170). Queuing theory is a method of "balancing out the costs associated with the buildup of a waiting line . . . with the costs of reducing the length of the waiting line" (p. 172).

extensive survey, it is likely to be handled by a contractor. Because of time constraints, inadequate data, and the difficulty of communicating to clients, analysts avoid "fine tuning" and their tricks of the trade are mostly maxims:

> Check the data.
> Arithmetic goes a long way.
> Be roughly right rather than precisely wrong.
> Force numbers into the problem.
> Pick tools to fit the time available.[30]

Here is one typical procedure for getting started: (1) identify objectives in terms of output of program and expected effect on clientele or environment; (2) develop a simple model of the program costs to show how money is allocated and what it buys; (3) search for simple output measures to quantify the effect of the program; (4) pick out strong, obvious relationships that lead to policy conclusions. It looks simple, but it isn't. We have already discussed objectives, but what about costs and output measures? Most policy analysts rely, probably too much, on money costs.[31]

MEASURING COSTS

Usually costs are expressed in terms of dollars, but they can also be cast in terms of other resources, such as manpower and equipment. Most people would think that cost information should be easy to get—and actually there is an abundance of it, but it seldom fits the needs of the analyst. One can easily find out the costs of medical personnel by looking at a hospital payroll, but it is another matter to have the payroll computed for a policy alternative the analyst is exploring. It is often impossible to determine from such accounting reports what the people are doing, because they are likely to be listed by organization and not by activity. Even cost accounting may not help, because policy alternatives are not always consistent with cost centers. Since the policy analyst deals in

30. Enthoven and Smith discuss these maxims as premises of systems analysis (see *How Much Is Enough?* pp. 65–69). The same maxims are also cited by analysts who have had little connection with defense policy, which probably reflects an inheritance from systems analysis and the Rand Corporation.

31. In many cases money costs do not adequately reflect "real" costs (i.e., opportunity costs) and they seldom reflect external costs.

examining present programs with a view to future policy, he is in the business of estimating specific future costs, not just copying down whatever costs are listed on some ledger. Despite advances in accounting and management information systems, the information is usually not in the form relevant to a decision-making problem. It was gathered for some past decision or for some other purpose, such as preserving honesty. I can recall going to an air force depot to determine maintenance costs for aircraft. It was easy to find out what it cost to repair and overhaul parts, but it was next to impossible to relate parts to particular kinds of aircraft and usage rates. The depot worried about its job of repairing parts and not about which aircraft received the parts. Indeed, the recipients were not "charged" at all, because they had turned in an old part for a new or repaired one. Gatherers of cost information and policy analysts are really not in the same business. They do not even talk the same language. Let me show you what I mean.

A number of years ago I was trying to dredge out of an air force expense report some statistical relations that could be used for Rand studies. When some staff men at the Pentagon found out that I was actually trying to use their report, they were delighted. It turned out that this report, which was filled out by air force units around the world, had not been used by anybody and I was the first person who had showed any interest in it. The result was that I got an invitation to visit the air force's accounting center in Denver to see if there were any other reports the air force had processed that might prove useful. After the usual polite introductions and tour, I lectured on the business I was in—how we compared weapon systems and force units to aid policymakers. I stressed the importance of generating information by program, force unit, or weapons system. There were a few moments of silence. My hosts were wondering which report, out of the hundreds they handled, to show me. Finally, a senior officer said, "Well, we have the milk subsidy report." This report identified the money spent on milk for children living on air force installations. It was quite apparent that my hosts, military and civilian alike, did not understand me or the informational requirements for analysis. I might as well have been visiting Mars.

Most policy analysts know that "costing is a major part of an analyst's job." Once the analyst also learns that costs have to be fabricated, sometimes out of thin air, he is on the path to the appropriate level of skepticism. He will spend time checking and comparing estimates. As one analyst told me, "You can't trust cost experts."

MEASURING BENEFITS

The problems of costs are nothing when compared with the problems of measuring benefits. How can you tell whether the output of a program meets the objectives if you don't know what the objectives are? One analyst solves this problem by asking the people who are running the program: "How do you know if you are doing better?" In education, for instance, the likely response will revolve around the importance of quality education and of doing "what's good for the children." After some probing, it may be possible to get a better idea of what improvement in education might mean.

Such discussions are exercises in frustration, and so the analyst will fall back on traditional measures, such as amount of future income generated by higher education, percentage of poverty gap closed, number of lives saved, or crimes reduced. It is a skillful business to select measures appropriate to the problem. In transportation problems, for example, a common measure is cost per ton mile; but in problems where time is an important factor, the measure is inadequate: one needs a measure or a method that reflects whether an item is delivered overnight or takes three months.

A policy can have a single benefit amenable to many methods of measurement, but it also can have many benefits with many different measures. Some analysts will try to reduce such complexity by converting the different measures to a common denominator, such as dollars. Other analysts think such a practice is wrong and try to preserve the complexity for the client, so that he can be the one to make the decision. If there are only minor differences in the measures and they all push toward the same recommendation, then the client probably will be able to make up his mind. But when there are many measures and the measures are quite different from one another—where getting more of one benefit means getting less of another—the client will wonder what he needs an analyst for. In such cases, the analyst will have to be concerned about communication and not just measurement (see chapter 7),[32] and he will resort to such techniques as normalizing his results. In an HEW study of maternal and child health, for example, the analysts presented their work in terms of a community of 50,000 people. In this way it was easier to grasp the effects and costs of various programs.[33]

DEVICES FOR COPING WITH UNCERTAINTY

No problem-solving activity that I am aware of operates under conditions of perfect information. Therefore, it is entirely appropriate for an intelligent analyst to use what devices he can manufacture for coping with uncertainty. For example, if there is no production function in a particular policy area, then the analyst may be quite correct in examining comparisons between different institutional experiences to determine a norm, a standard, or to see in some tenuous way what the relationship is between input and output. At HEW an analyst was working on a study to increase the supply of nurses. He found that 600,000 nurses were not working in their occupation. Not knowing whether this figure was a lot or a little, he looked at other occupations to see what their experiences were and to have something for comparison. In another health study, the analyst looked at other countries in order to compare the number of doctors and hospital beds. Cost estimators know that in

32. The point is that the analyst has to cast the many consequences or impacts of his alternatives in a comparative framework that will be understandable to the client and will facilitate his decision. Rand analysts, for example, "developed a presentation technique called the colored scorecard. It provides the decision-maker with an effective picture of the relative advantages and disadvantages of alternatives systems being compared. The technique presents a column of impacts (each one in its own natural units) for each alternative system being compared. Then, colors are added to indicate each system's ranking for a particular impact: green shows the best value, blue the next best value, orange an inferior value, and red the worst value. These colors are meant to show only the system rankings for a particular impact, not their exact performance; this is shown by the impact values themselves that are visible through the colors." L. G. Chesler and B. F. Goeller, *The Star Methodology for Short-Haul Transportation: Transportation System Impact Assessment*, R-1359-DOT (Santa Monica: Rand Corporation, 1973), p. viii. For other applications of the colored scoreboard technique, see Bruce F. Goeller et al., *San Diego Clean Air Project: Summary Report*, R-1362-SD (Santa Monica: Rand Corporation, 1973), p. 38.

33. U.S. Department of Health, Education, and Welfare, Office of the Assistant Secretary for Program Coordination, *Maternal and Child Health Care Programs* (October 1966), tables 4.4 and 4.5, pp. IV-9 to IV-10.

the long run their estimates will tend to be low, for a variety of exogenous reasons, so there is a tendency to increase the estimate or to round it up. Sensitivity analysis is nothing but an elaborate fudge factor in which the key elements of an analysis are varied to see the effects on the results. You increase or decrease an estimate by 30 percent and hope that it won't make any difference.

Devices, such as sensitivity analysis, do not necessarily make the job easier. They increase the burden of computation. Most of the time the analyst will find himself making many more calculations. He will try to bracket the truth. Without a definite answer, he will resort to ranges, to high and low estimates, and to multiple measures. Using statistical techniques, such as regression analysis, the analyst often finds that he is estimating something that is not within the limits of his data. What does he do? He tries to make the estimate in a number of different ways. He can take last year's number and adjust it, or he can use a different source of data, or he can compute a rough factor from aggregate data (for example, dividing budgetary expenses for real property maintenance by the total value of real property). If the answers come out roughly the same, he feels more comfortable in using them.

Even the great search for a "dominant" alternative makes for more work.[34] If all the alternatives look alike, then there will be no analytical basis for recommendation. In analyses where it is possible to alter ingredients and assumptions, the analyst can make his favorite alternative look bad; then, if it still comes out better than the rest, he not only has something to recommend but can do so more easily. A fortiori is one way to facilitate the comparison and choice of alternatives; break-even analysis is another.[35] They are important tricks for communicating with a client as well, as Kahn and Mann note:

More than any other single thing, the skilled use of a fortiori and break-even analyses separate the professionals from the amateurs. Most analyses should (conceptually) be done in two stages: a first stage to find

34. "We call a system," Quade explains, "which is best in any circumstances a 'sure thing' or 'dominant.' We can seldom find a truly dominant system, but sometimes . . . we can come close." Quade, ed., *Analysis for Military Decisions*, p. 17.

35. Quade explains these methods as follows: "To make an analysis a fortiori, we bend over backward in making the comparisons to 'hurt' the system we think is best and to 'help' the alternative systems. If it then turns out that after we have done this we can still say we prefer the handicapped system, we are in a strengthened position

out what one wants to recommend, and a second stage that generates the kind of information that makes the recommendations convincing even to a hostile and disbelieving, but intelligent audience.[36]

Consider the problem of discount or interest rates. Such rates are used in analysis to correct for the effect of time or time preferences in the calculation of benefits and costs. Most analysts agree that discounting is necessary—without it there would be no way of comparing future choices with present ones. After all, the same benefit probably is worth more today than, say, twenty years from now. The problem comes about in choosing a rate. In a poem, attributed to Kenneth Boulding, we can see the analyst's problem:

> . . . the long term interest rate
> determines any project's fate.
> At two percent the case is clear,
> At three, some sneaking doubts appear;
> At four, it draws its final breath;
> While five percent is certain death.[37]

For years the Army Corps of Engineers and the Bureau of Reclamation had been undertaking projects on the basis of low rates (for example, 3.25 percent), while for years, particularly at the OMB, analysts were arguing for at least a 10 percent rate. In reviewing the situation Gene H. Fisher found a range of rates, from 3 to 15 percent, being recommended or used. He explained the disagreement as follows:

---

to make recommendations. Sometimes we cannot do this. . . . In this case, we might try a *break-even* analysis: We decide what assumptions must be made about important values in order to make the performance of the two systems essentially the same. Then we can simply ask people to judge whether these assumptions are optimistic or pessimistic." Quade, ed., *Analysis for Military Decisions*, p. 173.

36. H. Kahn and I. Mann, *Techniques of Systems Analysis*, RM-1829 (Santa Monica: Rand Corporation, 3 December 1956), cited in Quade, ed., *Analysis for Military Decisions*, p. 173. Italics in the original omitted.

37. Hirshleifer and his colleagues, for example, in examining water resource project allocations, point to a similar conflict: "It is not often realized how sensitive efficiency calculations are to the rate of interest or discount assumed. Since in water supply projects the bulk of the expenses are normally incurred early in the history of the development, while benefits are stretched over a relatively long period, a low interest rate makes projects look good, while a high interest rate makes them appear bad." See Jack Hirshleifer, James C. De Haven, and Jerome W. Milliman, *Water Supply: Economics, Technology, and Policy* (Chicago: University of Chicago Press, 1960), pp. 160, 114–74.

In spite of the considerable amount of discussion of the subject, however, a substantial degree of difference of opinion *seems to exist* among the experts. We underline the phrase "seems to exist," because in many of the discussions it is not always clear whether the rate of discount being considered is confined to time preference only, or to time preference plus a supplemental rate for risk or uncertainty.[38]

Fisher in his discussion went on to argue that "analysts should not worry too much about the discount rate because in most long-range planning in the *military* realm the ranking of the alternatives is likely to be insensitive to the time preference discount rate over a relevant range of rate assumptions."[39] William A. Niskanen, in reviewing Fisher's book, felt differently: "The book is irresponsibly agnostic about the appropriate discount rate. . . . Both the Department of Defense and OMB have recently endorsed the use of a 10 percent rate for choices of whether to approve a specific governmental activity, and this position . . . deserves support until a good case is made to the contrary."[40]

OMB's position for the higher rates was not based on the Fisher distinction between rates that include uncertainty and those that do not. OMB had another rationale for its position which, without getting into the complexities, was based on what was happening with investments in the private sector. The argument over which rate, in any event, was not confined just to technicians and experts. For example, a senior official of OMB argued about rates with Secretary of the Treasury John B. Connally. OMB wanted a 10 percent rate and Connally wanted a 5 percent rate. Then, according to a former OMB analyst, Connally suggested a "Texas compromise," and thus they settled on a 7 percent rate. The compromise, which was restricted to the water resource area, then was reported in the *Washington Post*.[41] By 1974 the compromise was shoved aside when Congress passed a law resulting in a 5⅞ percent discount rate.[42] OMB still held to the 10 percent rate for nonwater resource projects.

38. Gene H. Fisher, *Cost Considerations in Systems Analysis*, Rand Report R-490-ASD (New York: American Elsevier Publishing Company, 1971), p. 227.
39. *Ibid.*, p. 228.
40. William A. Niskanen, book review of Gene H. Fisher's *Cost Considerations in Systems Analysis*, in *Policy Sciences* 5 (1974): 238.
41. *Washington Post*, 3 January 1972, p. A1.
42. The change in procedures for the Water Resources Council due to Section 80 of the Water Resources Redevelopment Act of 1974, Public Law 93–251, March

Analysts at the receiving end of a 10 percent rate—at AEC, NASA, and Interior, for example—realized that with such a rate their agencies would not be able to initiate many projects. As one NASA analyst said, "With the discount rate that high, you either have a damn good project or you're really interested in it enough to spend the time reworking the figures." Another analyst, at Interior, agreed with the superiority of a 10 percent rate for judging "economic efficiency" but at the same time pointed out to his client that the agency has other objectives that cannot be quantified, such as the stabilization of farm communities and the maintenance of the family farm. Since "we are responsible for criteria other than economic efficiency, it is appropriate to use a lower discount rate." At NASA, to satisfy OMB's "greed for analysis," analysts were continually restudying the space shuttle system. Evidently the agency was sufficiently interested in the outcome to make a number of studies: "We have so many studies of space shuttles that we don't know which to believe. When the time for the decision comes, we'll just grab one of them and use it. . . . We just can't continue to drop boosters in the ocean."

The analyst without a program to protect, as in OMB, has no problem. He can use the 10 percent rate. But the analyst committed to a program is in a more difficult situation. If he wants to be objective, he can make his computations on the basis of a number of different rates, high and low, and let the policymakers choose from an array of answers. If he is confused about his role, he can argue about the inadequacies of his work and point out all the things he did not consider. If he is dishonest, he can use a 10 percent rate but change his measurements of benefits and costs so

7, 1974, and the stipulation of a 5⅞ percent discount rate is recorded in *Federal Register* 39, no. 158, 14 August 1974, 29242–29243. This is not the first time that Congress has been involved in the technical aspects of analysis. For example, Robert H. Haveman has observed that "Current agency practice in the ex ante estimation of navigation benefits has been determined by direct congressional action in the Department of Transportation Act of 1966. This is the only category of benefits for which Congress has explicitly dictated the definition of benefits and the concepts to be used by agencies in evaluation efforts. Largely because of this intervention, current navigation evaluation procedures deviate more from ideal procedures than in any other project purpose." Robert H. Haveman, *The Economic Performance of Public Investments: An Ex Post Evaluation of Water Resources Investments* (Baltimore: published for Resources for the Future, by Johns Hopkins Press, 1972), pp. 45–46.

that the answer comes out right. Whichever path he chooses, it will mean more computational work.

HELP FROM THE BUREAUCRATIC CONTEXT

If the answer to uncertainty is more work, then analysts have to adjust their working style, and the bureaucratic context of analysis certainly helps. First, bureaucracies set time schedules and work does fill the available time. Whether the work has to be done in a few minutes on the back of an envelope or in a few months, the time constraint determines what can be done. To make the quick estimate, the analyst works by crude analogies and factors. For a longer-term estimate, he may have time to specify and measure and cover a bigger chunk of the problem. One of the first things the analyst learns, however, is to ask for more time—and sometimes he gets it. When President Nixon announced that he was going to submit legislation within thirty days to ease the impact of deseg-regation, a senior HEW analyst complained that the staff needed at least two months. When the thirty days were up, the press asked where the legislation was; the White House's response was that the administration was holding consultations. These "consultations" lasted another thirty days.

Supposedly the overnight job is less accurate than the three-month effort. In any case, the creaky, slow-moving policy process allows for revision, because after a crisis comes correction: "The first stab at an important policy is usually done in a hurry, but we generally have time to redo our work more slowly." In recalling how hard pressed he and his colleagues were in preparing the secretary of the treasury's testimony to Congress on the president's economic policy, an analyst pointed to some inaccuracies and said that, "now that the heat is off, we can rework our estimates for greater accuracy in preparation for the executive session where the decisions are really made."

Second, bureaucracies divide up the analytical work. Here an analyst explains the conditions under which it is sensible to divide up the work:

I suggest that there is a process of multilevel decision making in analysis. For example, I know that the EPA [Environmental Protection Agency] has an analysis effort studying the costs and benefits of environmental standards. . . . In a sense, the analytical job has been divided in a logical way, and the standards serve as the analytical interface. On the other hand, if I did not have knowledge that the environmental standards were being examined, or if I did not have confidence in the competence and objectivity of the analysis group, I should then insist on including an evaluation of the standards themselves in any analysis I did. . . . Multilevel decision making offers an opportunity and a modus operandi for higher and lower level analytical groups to work together in a logical and satisfying way.

With many analysts and many assumptions, the usual skepticism of the individual analyst is put aside in favor of trust and acceptance. A Treasury Department analyst tells us how the division of labor works in the case of estimating the effect of an investment tax credit:

One analyst is responsible for one input (the effect of the credit on the automobile industry); another for another type of input (the effect on steel industry investment); etc., until the problem reaches me. I do not contest these previous assumptions. They are accepted as gospel. For one thing, I usually know the individuals involved and trust their work; but more important, I don't have time to rework other people's estimates. Therefore, the outcome is a composite work and there is very little opportunity for an analyst to skew the results or deliberately influence the decision by strategically selecting assumptions.

The cumulative effect of such acceptance, of course, could lead to an unintended bias in the results, and this leads us to a third point about the bureaucratic context of analysis: the climate of advocacy. We have already discussed supportive analysis and the usefulness of a client's directions; but we have not noted that the general feeling of advocacy, which is part of organized life and the policy process, can reduce the amount of an individual analyst's work. Organizations in the policy process become sponsors of programs. The clients in these organizations are known advocates and proponents, and it is not unusual that analytical activities support them. So far nothing that we would not expect. But what is interesting is the reaction of analysts in other agencies who review and advise on somebody else's program or legislative proposal. Such analysts sense that the proponents of a new bill, for example, have already elaborated on its positive aspects. They will make sure that policymakers understand the full cost implications of the bill, what hot water they might be stepping into. In a sense, these analysts do half of an analysis. Whether the halves of the proponents and their critics add up to a whole analysis is an interesting question to which I do not have the answer.

A climate of advocacy also encourages many estimates for the same thing, a situation that the analyst can take advantage of. Imagine the problem of estimating gross national product (GNP). Everybody is in the act: the Council of Economic Advisers, the Department of Treasury, the Office of Management and Budget.[43] From the Federal Reserve Board to Wall Street, wherever there is an economist, there will be a forecast. For fiscal year 1970/71, the agreement on the estimate of GNP had been reached by the staff of the various agencies; but as the estimate went up the ladder, political leaders chose a more optimistic one as a basis for anticipating federal revenues. As a senior Treasury analyst explained the situation:

One ought to talk about economic forecasting as objective and technical. But a forecast cannot be separated from a program decision. . . . The administration was using the forecast as synonymous with its program. Because its economic program was prosperity it could not publish the accurate estimate of GNP. My prejudice of course at the time was simply to turn the forecasters loose and treat the estimation of the GNP as a purely technical matter. Maybe I am too chicken and it is a tough question, but at the time the administration was determined and there was little you could do short of resigning.

The analytical staff of the Joint Committee on Internal Revenue Taxation of Congress is also required to forecast GNP. Usually the staff consults with four to five economists, who submit their estimates. In a week, two committee analysts gather what other estimates they can—for example, from members of the administration—and by looking over everybody else's estimates they make their own forecast. The analysts feel that their estimate is usually quite accurate because it is based on the judgments of other experts and is made later. In the case of the estimate for 1970–71, aware of the political motivation behind the administration's optimistic estimate, they were able to discount that estimate as politics and at the same time use it to box in their own estimate.

---

43. For a detailed account of the actors and procedures, see Lawrence C. Pierce, *The Politics of Fiscal Policy Formation* (Pacific Palisades, Calif.: Goodyear Publishing Co., 1971), pp. 38–84.

CONCLUSION

Considering how difficult it is to solve policy problems, analysts ought to be pleased that some of their work is handled directly or indirectly by politicians. Of course it is frustrating to do a study, come out with a solid recommendation, and find that it goes nowhere. In Detroit, for example, analysts did a study on fireboats at least three times. Each time they came out with the same result. They really did have a dominant alternative. It did pay to replace a steam-powered boat with two small diesel boats because of considerable savings in personnel costs. The union, however, did not want to lose three firemen; and since the union contributed to the mayor's campaign fund, the study died.[44]

I see no reason to be depressed by such a negative example. After all, politicians often come up with policy ideas that are as good as most; and if they want to skip the analyst and his problem-definition stage, why not? On the other hand, if the analyst does not want to be ignored, he cannot ignore politics. And as we have seen in this chapter, he doesn't, particularly in his selection of objectives and design of alternatives. He uses his knowledge of politics as an aid to solving problems. Whether his political knowledge and sensitivity are adequate for the job is another matter.

One suspects that the use of political knowledge, however, is fairly similar to the use of technical and substantive knowledge. Both rely on the analyst's cognitive style and his ability to make shaky judgments in the solving of problems. As one analyst puts it, "Well, you have to take data that are less than perfect and form judgments and then use them. You have to ask yourself whether you're losing a lot by not being too careful, and to make these a priori judgments you have to know a great deal about the subject and see whether you can get away with it when your work is below par." When making these judgments, we expect that the analyst knows when to keep to certain standards and also when to slough them off in order to be able to perform. While the scientist in a university enjoys the luxury of being able to insist on approaching perfection, the analyst in an operating bureaucracy knows only that

44. For a discussion of this event, see Richard Lehne and Donald M. Fisk, "The Impact of Urban Policy Analysis," *Urban Affairs Quarterly* 10 (December 1974): 121–22.

he must perform. As part of his working style the analyst operates on the premise that the information he will provide to his client is better than no information at all.

Obviously, it is impossible in only one chapter to describe how analysts work on problems. Defining the problem, analysts very correctly say, is the most significant stage in reaching for solutions. As an extension to problem selection, problem definition is an essential political choice, for it means that some policy alternatives will get attention and others will be ignored. Practically speaking, a badly formulated problem is never really solved. It will resist solution when it is too open and not properly cut down to size. It will succumb to an obvious, but erroneous, solution when it is too closed and its assumptions have not been examined. But conceptual blinders in terms of a cognitive style have to be put on; otherwise the burden of calculation will be immense. Knowing a policy area, using one's professional background, reading, talking to beneficiaries, and listening to clients can help in defining problems.

At some point the analyst will put aside other people's perceptions of the problem and insert his own objectives and definition. He will break the problem down into its components, into variables and constants. He will piece together alternatives and examine their consequences. Building on what and whom he knows, he will look at the current alternatives, but he will hope to find something new. Almost without noticing it, he will be in the problem documentation stage, reducing and juggling numbers, using techniques he learned in school and rules of thumb he learned on the job. If he spends too much time polishing his numbers, the political system around him will come up with a solution before he does. The bureaucratic context of analysis, however, does prevent a total eclipse of the analyst, because, if it does nothing else, at least it sets a time schedule which encourages him to produce when the clients wish to consume. That there are disadvantages as well as advantages to the bureaucratic context of analysis will become evident in the next chapter. That there are inadequacies in the analyst's data, knowledge, and theory as a basis for advice, as well as in his political judgment, will be further explored in chapter 8.

5

The Bureaucratic Context

One of the imperatives of solving problems is knowing how to organize to solve them. At the beginning of this book I pointed briefly to the importance of understanding the analyst's organizational situation, and throughout subsequent chapters I sketched in parts of this situation and its consequences. Now it is time to focus directly on the bureaucratic context of analysis and on the ways in which this context affects the production of analysis and the analyst.

In referring to the "bureaucracy" I have sometimes simply meant the executive branch of our federal government. At other times I have meant a complex, large, formal organization, built on paper in the shape of a pyramid and composed of levels and boxes—a place of routine, rules, impersonality, and specialization. The executive branch is composed of many such formal organizations. It is a bureaucracy made up of bureaucracies. Probably its analysts are not much different from analysts in other complex, large-scale organizations, such as state and local governments or, for that matter, private corporations.

In the bureaucracy, as in many other situations, one does not usually do analysis by oneself. Bureaucratic policy analysis involves help and hindrance from others. Other members of the analyst's organization will set goals which can support or undermine his work. They control important resources such as information, access to computers, and not-so-trivial items such as office space, desks, and telephones. They possess the institutional memory; they know about present programs and buried skeletons. Therefore, the analyst must quickly learn about his organization. It is not enough to get on top of policy problems; he must also get on top of organizational dynamics.

Understanding the dynamics of the bureaucratic context involves answering a number of questions: Where is analysis done? Who competes with the analyst in the business of giving advice? How do the choice of names, the claiming of organizational territory, and other bureaucratic tactics affect the analyst and analysis? How is analysis itself organized?

Theoretically, an organization can liberate or inhibit and waste the energy of its members.[1] The good organization supposedly liberates sufficient energy for its members to accomplish the tasks they set for each other. In contrast, the bad organization strangles and diverts the energy of its members to unproductive and pathological behavior. In the sense of freeing energy the bureaucratic context is both good and bad, but usually when we think of bureaucracy we think of pathology. "Bureaucratic" for many of us is a pejorative term. And with good reason, as Victor A. Thompson has observed:

Personal behavior patterns are frequently encountered which exaggerate the characteristic qualities of bureaucratic organization. Within bureaucracy we often find excessive aloofness, ritualistic attachment to routines and procedures, and resistance to change; and associated with these behavior patterns is a petty insistence upon rights of authority and status. From the standpoint of organizational goal accomplishment, these personal behavior patterns are pathological because they do not advance organizational goals.[2]

In this chapter, we will see that some policy analysts in the late sixties and early seventies had succumbed to the pathology of their bureaucratic colleagues. Part of the explanation for this stems from their marginal status in the bureaucracy. Generally, bureaucracies give more status, prestige, and resources to the holders of positions in the hierarchy than to the staff persons and specialists who work

1. Chris Argyris, *Integrating the Individual and the Organization* (New York: John Wiley and Sons, 1964), pp. 3–7, 20–34.
2. Victor A. Thompson, *Modern Organization: A General Theory* (New York: Alfred A. Knopf, 1961), pp. 152–53.

for the position holders. The policy analyst, like other staff specialists, does not direct hundreds of bureaucrats in the management of million-dollar programs. He does not have a constituency to support him when he is in trouble; and like the staff person who relies on the holder of a position, the analyst is dependent on his client.

To exacerbate the usual marginal status of staff personnel, the policy analyst's role was not well known, accepted, or defined. When the data for this book was gathered, most practicing policy analysts had not graduated from schools of policy analysis; and unlike accountants, lawyers, and civil engineers, their profession was just emerging. "To occupy a position not fully accepted by significant others in the organization," according to Thompson, "tends to make one isolated, a minority in a hostile world. This kind of insecurity may result from a new specialty not yet fully accredited and accepted."[3] In the federal government of the late sixties and early seventies, the policy analyst was just beginning to be recognized, and the bureaucracy had been less than generous in its distribution of rewards and status to him. Thus, it was understandable why analysts attended, for example, to jurisdictional tactics just like other bureaucrats.

Despite the energy loss deriving from pathological behavior, the bureaucratic context does much to liberate the analyst's energy. It helps to divide up analytical work so that it is manageable and can be done within a time constraint. It expedites. It provides an organization flexible enough to respond to policy problems as they emerge. It puts the policy analyst on teams and task forces to work on short-range problems, and at the same time it also allows the analyst in a somewhat permanent unit to anticipate long-range informational needs.

To see the interaction between analysis and its bureaucratic context, we will first examine a temporary task force that worked on special revenue sharing for transportation. Then we will move from the temporary to the permanent bureaucracy, to the formal and regular organization which provides the permanent positions to be used for temporary tasks. Throughout we will be concerned about the strengths and weaknesses of the bureaucratic context, whether permanent or temporary.

3. *Ibid.*, p. 156.

TEMPORARY TASKS

When President Nixon, on January 22, 1971, announced in his state of the union address that revenue sharing would be one of the primary efforts of his administration, bureaucrats and politicians were surprised by the inclusion of special revenue sharing.[4] General revenue sharing was an old idea which had been pushed by Walter W. Heller and Joseph A. Pechman in the previous Democratic administrations. Its time had come, but special revenue sharing was a new wrinkle. Throughout the history of intergovernmental fiscal relations, the tension between giving money freely and tying strings to it had been resolved by a growing number of categorical grants. Thus, for the president to suggest that 130 categorical grants be consolidated into six special revenue sharing programs, from which funds would be automatically allocated by formula, must have been a shock to federal officials, particularly those who had spent their careers figuring out ways of spreading the federal largess.

The six programs—law enforcement, manpower, urban community development, rural community development, transportation, and education—were chosen by the White House on the basis of the interest in grant consolidation that had been demonstrated previously by various departments. Secretary of Transportation John A. Volpe, for example, "had been advocating a balanced transportation system and a merged transportation trust fund."[5] On March 18, the president asked Congress to consolidate 23 grant programs into a single program for special revenue sharing for transportation. A month later the proposed Transportation Revenue Sharing Act of 1971 (S. 1693) was referred to the Senate Committee on Commerce. As it turned out, the bill was not enacted; but the way in which it was developed can still teach us something about the bureaucratic context of analysis and, particularly, how a task force of analysts was organized and functioned.

THE TASK FORCE: SHARING ANALYSTS

In the short interval between the president's statement of intention and the delivery of the proposed legislation, a number of

4. For general background, see *National Journal* 3, no. 14 (3 April 1971): 703–39; and no. 15 (10 April 1971): 761–807.
5. *National Journal* 3, no. 14 (3 April 1971): 714.

analysts and their clients were involved. There was no single decision maker or client. As a participant in the policy process, each organization had its own set of clients and analysts who interacted and compromised. Not considering the various interest groups and Congress, these organizations included the Domestic Council, OMB, the Department of Transportation (DOT), and DOT's component administrations such as the Federal Aviation Administration and the Federal Highway Administration.

Starting from the top, there were the staff men of the Domestic Council, Edwin L. Harper and Raymond J. Waldmann, who worked for Executive Director John D. Ehrlichman and, of course, President Nixon. At OMB there were at least three analysts and examiners, who reported to Assistant Director Donald B. Rice, who in turn worked for George P. Shultz, the director of OMB. Deputy Under Secretary John P. Olsson was in charge of the DOT effort. Working for Secretary of Transportation John A. Volpe, but reporting to OMB, he had to wear two hats during the work on revenue sharing. DOT's Office of Budget and Office of Planning and Program Review reported to him. His director of budget, Walter Boehner, had considerable experience in government, having worked as an analyst for the Federal Aviation Administration and OMB, so it was natural that he was appointed the secretary of the department's task force on special revenue sharing. Boehner was essentially the chief analyst while Olsson was his political client. It was up to Boehner to figure out not only what had to be done but who would do it within DOT.

OMB was supposedly responsible for formulating the various special revenue sharing proposals. Ehrlichman, however, had suggested that task forces be set up in each federal department as a way of gaining support and cooperation from within the departments. OMB was to oversee the operation; OMB personnel attended the meetings of the DOT task force and appeared "open minded," but its people still saw DOT's role as advisory. Yet rather than being in charge, it appears that OMB was in the middle between the White House and DOT. In any event, Rice of OMB asked Secretary Volpe to convene a task force in late January 1971.

Before Boehner could convene a task force, he had to get a better idea of what it would do. OMB had sent to DOT a two-page memorandum outlining some basic questions (for example, What sort of balance should obtain between allocations to state and local agencies? Should a portion of the funds remain at the federal level?). OMB's idea was to stimulate the development of issues in order to start getting some decisions. Boehner, however, was still trying to define the problem. He called some of his analysts together to brainstorm, and from that session came a paper entitled "Proposed Disposition of Present Grant Controls under Revenue Sharing Programs." Then he called a meeting of various central analysts and representatives of top-level offices to discuss the paper. As one of the analysts put it, this informal group "tried to identify the parameters within which the task force would operate. Before constructing the formulae to apply to programs . . ., we first had to study the needs which the Department of Transportation must meet and get a better idea of the concepts of revenue sharing." The informal group had a number of concerns, such as the need for planning—"Why pour money down the drain if local officials haven't done the planning?"—and Olsson raised these concerns with OMB.

Having gained a general conception of what the task force was supposed to do—form legislation and determine the amount of money that would go into special revenue sharing for transportation—Boehner had to choose its members. Besides making sure that he included various analysts and representatives from the central staff, such as the general counsel and the assistant secretary for environment and urban systems, the critical problem was to choose representatives from DOT's administration. Boehner decided on high-level program planners or program analysts, people who would be able to see the broad picture as well as the problems of their own organizations. He also sought participants who, in addition to having a substantive understanding of programs, had an ability to analyze and solve problems. In retrospective praise of them he said, "They knew the problems, so they were able to solve them better than any number of unknowledgeable analysts. Yet they were able to separate themselves from specifics to work at a general plan." Well, not quite. Many of them would not separate themselves from the interests of their administrations. Instead of being co-opted into supporting revenue sharing, many of the task force members saw revenue sharing as coming from the top down, and they acted as representatives of their administrations. One of these representatives described his role as "protesting here and there, trying to work out pitfalls, yet attempting to stay within the spirit of the program. We were fairly stubborn—as stubborn as we could be—but because of that we were able to get some concessions."

At the first meeting of the task force, Olsson, Rice, and another OMB analyst explained the various constraints that would be placed on special revenue sharing; for example, there would be no matching requirements. However, the OMB personnel thought that the meeting had not provided enough understanding about revenue sharing. Moreover, they felt that the policy decisions they presented had not made much of an impression, because they "came across as simply our ideas on the subject." After the briefing Boehner told the task force members, "Now you know as much as I do." He instructed them to go back and think about special revenue sharing and how it applied to their program areas. The members came to the next meeting armed with issue papers that discussed their administrations' problems. Boehner took these issue papers and delegated the task of reading them and identifying overall problems to three of the central analysts on the task force. These common problems were then sorted into general categories to be discussed by members of the task force. The work was divided among the members to deal with the allocation formula, safety standards, planning requirements, budget and funding, and administrative procedures. For each of these problems, the members produced yet more issue papers and discussed them at the task force's nearly daily meetings.

Here, then, was the essence of bureaucratic problem-solving life. Analytical work has to be divided. No single person can do the whole job. No single person knows enough about the problem or about how to handle it. Work has to be chopped up and then pulled back together by the use of loosely ruled teams, groups, or task forces. Since many small, detailed policy decisions have to be made, and since every issue is multifaceted, the use of written communication is essential. The writing of memoranda is not merely a protective bureaucratic reflex. Memoranda on policy issues focus discussion, try to simplify the complex, and push for particular decisions (see chapter 7).

While the task force was busy writing issue papers, a number of policymakers were making decisions that would be converted into legislation. This collective client (see chapter 6) was made up of Harper and Waldmann of the Domestic Council, Rice and another analyst from OMB, and Olsson from DOT. Most of these clients had daily contact with each other, but they did not always share the same policy preferences. The urban mass transportation representatives, for example, requested that urban mass transportation money be separated from other money allocated under the transportation special revenue sharing fund. But OMB felt that, if this concession were allowed, the highway representatives, FAA representatives, and other members of the task force would similarly press for separate allocations within the special revenue sharing fund. Therefore, OMB disallowed the exception. Olsson then sent a memo appealing OMB's decision to Waldmann, who discussed the matter with Ehrlichman. The White House then decided the issue in favor of a separate fund for urban mass transportation. On another occasion, Olsson approached Rice privately with regard to allowing another exception. Rice spoke with Harper privately. Harper replied that he would defer to Rice's judgment on the issue. Rice wanted to maintain the closest possible conformity to the early constraints set forth by the White House, so he denied Olsson's request. Olsson then approached Volpe and convinced him of the need for the exception. Volpe appealed directly to the president and won the concession. Volpe had several such sessions with the president, winning some and losing some. FAA, for example, had convinced Volpe that its airport money should be excluded from the special revenue sharing program, but the president did not agree and Volpe's appeal was rejected.

Olsson, as the man in the middle, not only had to resolve those issues with actors outside of DOT but also had to ensure that the task force stayed on track. Because of the task force's exclusion from the decision making of the policymakers and because of the pace of activity, the general atmosphere of secrecy, and the lack of feedback, Olsson was not particularly liked by the members of the task force. "The guy's just not too swift," one analyst remarked. "He drove us all up the walls. He made the transit people mad, but the highway people didn't mind. The safety people wanted government control of funds; the airport people wanted control by the airport authorities. No one got what they wanted, nor did anyone feel that Olsson was even listening." Another analyst expressed his frustration with this criticism: "Olsson kept telling me my papers were stimulating, but he doesn't understand local government."

An analyst who worked directly for Olsson has a different viewpoint. In defense of Olsson, he felt that the task force members did not understand Olsson's position, nor were their own products always useful. Their client was not Olsson but the organizations they represented. Their issue papers were often an expression of organizational preferences. As evidence of the inadequacy of the issue papers, he reported that one analyst was instructed to rewrite his paper four times. The issue papers were not always as organized and clear as they might have been if there had been more time. Sometimes they were too technical and complex, a "mass of unorganized information," but they gave Olsson a "feel of the range of alternatives involved." Sometimes the "feel" was inadequate, as one of his assistants reports: "When we would ask for new alternatives, we kept getting back answers that were the same thing that existed before revenue sharing. They just could not believe that it was possible to change their programs, even though, I think, they believed they were trying to make the conversion. We had to go back through their reports to sift out what actually was essential to preserve."

The issue papers had to be "boiled down to pick out the gut issues" for final decision making. Whether the task force knew it or not, Olsson was the consumer of its issue papers. Over the period of the study he made extractions from the issue papers and then explained the central issues briefly in memoranda to Secretary Volpe. He sent Volpe about six such memoranda. In addition, he gave him one formal briefing. Olsson's superiors left him alone because "he knew what they wanted to come out of the task force."

His assistant describes the process of Olsson's interaction with individual members of the task force as follows: "The analyst would start and then produce something that was not 100 percent but was the best he could do. Olsson likes details and therefore would review the work carefully. Then he would go back to the analyst with questions before he made his decision. If the analyst did not like the decision, he [the analyst] would scream, and Olsson would look at the problem again and possibly change his decision." But once decisions were made there was not enough time to inform the entire task force. As it turned out, the final legislation was written by Olsson and DOT's lawyers with OMB's participation; the task force was not consulted.

TIME CONSTRAINTS

No doubt searching for information has its costs, and the costs should not exceed the benefits gained from the information. No doubt the researcher should stop when he feels he has gotten enough information. But analysts, as searchers for information, seldom are satisfied; instead, they keep working, raising issues and pushing preferences up to the last bell, up to and sometimes a bit beyond the time limit their organization has set. To meet the White House's mid-March deadline for legislation, DOT's task force had about a month to develop its program. Although the White House kept pressing them to complete the job, the analysts worked a few weeks beyond the deadline.

Whether the one-month constraint gave them enough time to do the job cannot be determined. In any event, the analyst usually sees his allowed time as inadequate. Not all problems can be anticipated and prepared for, so having only several weeks or months to work on complex issues inevitably results in frustration. One analyst on the task force wanted to read a three-foot-high stack of material on revenue sharing, prepared by a foundation, but reported that "we didn't have time to read it; we were working fourteen hours a day and on weekends just to get our specific job done." Another member's major complaint about the task force was that "not a damned bit of stuff had been done in the department before the president announced the program. It was very hectic. We worked a lot at night and every weekend for two months."

Why didn't DOT get started earlier? In November 1970 Volpe attended several meetings in which he was informed that revenue sharing would offset the department's categorical grants and that the president would propose it in January. Given the White House's desire for secrecy and many other things to worry about, Volpe was hardly in a position to alert his staff. Senior OMB officials who were asked by the White House in late December to determine which programs should be merged into special revenue sharing and to assess the impact of special revenue sharing on reorganization plans were equally stymied. They could not talk to their counterparts in DOT and its various administrations to convince them of the urgency of the issue and the likelihood of an immediate decision. But even after the president announced his revenue sharing proposal, DOT officials dragged their feet. One bureaucratic reaction to uncertainty is to wait and do nothing, and of course it does take some time to organize. OMB officials who were responsible for coordinating the detailed transportation proposal were not happy with DOT's effort at organizing: "We started off late and were always behind. The task force should have been operating at least in late January, but it was hindered in getting started by a battle within the Department of Transportation over who would be included on the task force. They also stalled while waiting for more guidance on the issue of revenue sharing from OMB or the Domestic Council. People just don't want to make decisions until they're forced to make them."

Although a time constraint helps define what *can* be done, it also has a number of unfavorable consequences. A tight time constraint discourages extensive participation and the building of consensus, and it reduces the frequency of policy feedback from clients. The analysts on the task force did not have enough time to consult their clients and had to act as if they knew what their respective organizational positions might be. Wheel spinning and unnecessary work occurred. Opportunities to convert the participants to the idea of revenue sharing were lost. Decisions once made were reversed, with resulting embarrassment. As one OMB analyst explained, "Both the task force members and we were put in awkward positions by our inability to discuss decisions with our superiors. On a couple of occasions I was embarrassed and possibly discredited by being overruled. We were moving blindly on the basis of our best judgment, and some of our decisions therefore were overruled when appealed by Volpe to Ehrlichman or the president."

DIRECTION IS NOT DEFINITION

The president had directed that special revenue sharing legislation be sent to Congress. It was up to Donald B. Rice, assistant director of OMB, and Edwin L. Harper and Raymond J. Waldmann, as Domestic Council staff, to see that the president got what he wanted. Their job was to sit on DOT and ensure commonality with other special revenue sharing proposals. There were certain policy components that had to be adhered to. For example, in addition to the elimination of matching requirements, money was to be distributed by formula; and recipients were to get at least what they had been getting under previous categorical programs (a *hold-harmless* provision).

OMB had prepared a "prayer book" containing questions and answers on revenue sharing for the task force. According to the secretary of the task force, however, it was "hard getting people to think in terms of the president's philosophy. Each time we found ourselves disagreeing with the philosophy of the program, we would return to the prayer book and see if we could get back on the track." But it was hard to stay on the track because, while a president may direct that a study be done, he is in no position to define it. There were more questions to be answered than analysts. If money was to be distributed by formula, then by which formula? If grants were to be consolidated, then which grants? If money was to be given, then to whom and under what conditions? On what basis should hold-harmless be measured—by last year's grants, or by a five-year average, or by a future year's grants? Issue after issue had to be resolved, and the resolution was often accomplished within a climate of advocacy. Staff from OMB and the Domestic Council spoke for the president; task force leaders spoke for the task force and for the secretary of transportation; and task force members represented their administrations.

Knowing who somebody worked for was not always a clear indicator of position and political alignment. Consider the problem of determining the allocation formula for urban mass transportation. Everybody agreed that the formula should be simple so that it could be understood by Congress. OMB was concerned about the hold-harmless provision. Olsson, as head of the task force, was interested in determining future demands for funds and reconciling them with past allocations. DOT central analysts and representatives of the administrations were looking for measures that would reflect transportation needs.

Yet there was bound to be disagreement over who had the greater need. The analyst from the Urban Mass Transportation Administration initially proposed that 95 or 90 percent of the urban mass transportation funds be allocated to 33 metropolitan areas of 1,000,000 population or more. The remaining 5 or 10 percent would be left for areas or cities of smaller size. OMB analysts and several of DOT's central analysts agreed that the formula should favor urban rather than rural construction. The Federal Highway Administration disagreed; it wanted to send more money to smaller areas and so proposed a 70/30 ratio. Conflict also broke out over what constituted a metropolitan area. If a large area was defined by 250,000 instead of 1,000,000 people, then the funds would be more widely spread around the country. Olsson, perhaps more politically attuned and concerned about appearances, thought it would be appropriate to have the same per capita assistance for both small and large cities. He thought the 95/5 ratio was a "red flag," as it appeared to be too favorable to the large metropolitan areas. The mass transportation people countered by pointing out that farm subsidies benefit rural areas. Olsson nevertheless insisted that the analysts explore smaller populations and lower ratios. Some formulas had as little as 50 to 60 percent going to the large areas. One such formula would have given a small midwestern city enough money to replace its entire bus fleet every year. Finally, the analysts told Olsson that the original 95/5 ratio was best suited to the urban mass transportation program.

There was little experience to go on. The Urban Mass Transportation Administration had not been in business for many years, and most of its grants had been made on a project by project basis. Without sufficient experience to have developed norms of equitable distribution or data to predict where demands might come from, the bureaucrats were adrift in a sea of personal preferences. In consultation with the administrator of the Urban Mass Transportation Administration and the assistant secretary for environment and urban systems, Olsson decided on a formula that allocated 80 percent of the funds to metropolitan areas with populations of 500,000 and over and 20 percent to the smaller areas. Volpe agreed, but OMB did not. While OMB agreed with Olsson that 20 percent should go to the smaller areas so that their cities could fund bus systems, it insisted that the size of a metropolitan area be 1,000,000, thereby favoring the large urban areas. The final bill, then, followed the 80/20 percent split, with 1,000,000 being the dividing line between large and small. In addition, every state was guaranteed at least $250,000, so that Alaska, Idaho, North and South Dakota, Vermont, and Wyoming would not be disappointed.

Determining the allocation formula for the general transportation element of the revenue sharing package was not easy either. The funds had been declining, and it was hard to meet the hold-harmless constraint. Nevertheless, there was a spirit of cooperation between OMB and the DOT central analysts in designing the formula. Most of the work was done within DOT because it had larger computers than OMB. The analysts would experiment by choosing different factors and applying different weights, such as 25 percent based on the state percentage of total U.S. population. Urban population, the area of a state, and postal route mileage were other factors. An OMB participant described it as "analytically great fun. We started with a zero base and were able to build from practically nothing. The formula was a great analytical challenge. It took well over a thousand computer runs before we were able to produce something with which we were satisfied."

DEFENDER OF THE FAITH

The task force members "had great difficulty in really believing that local decisions are better than those made at the federal level." Special revenue sharing attacked them where they lived. It promised to cut some of the strings of national purpose as exemplified in terms of standards. Standards, ubiquitous as they are, are usually defended by bureaucrats, and the analysts on the task force were no exception. Furthermore, even if they had wanted to cut free of the standards, they could not. There were standards on civil rights, planning, environment, safety, engineering, minimum wages, and relocation assistance that could not be ignored, no matter what the rhetoric of revenue sharing said. Olsson had explained to the task force that it need not worry about auditing controls, safety standards, or labor and civil rights provisions; but as the analysts said, "The FAA, Highway Administration and Highway Safety kept coming back and saying that we couldn't give carte blanche authority to the local officials and that we must add specific requirements to ensure minimum safety and uniformity of standards."

The bureaucratic analyst soon takes on the mentality of his agency. He cannot escape the preferences of his organization; and soon, rather than remaining a skeptical generalist, he, like other bureaucrats, becomes a defender of the faith. In the name of explaining the complexities of his agency's program, he seeks to preserve prevailing methods of operation. Each task force representative, therefore, made every effort to retain aspects of old programs in the new one. FAA, for example, wanted to "preserve uniformity and adequate safety standards in the national airport systems" by including specific regulations in the new revenue sharing legislation. In order to conform to the philosophy of revenue sharing, the secretary of the task force encouraged FAA to review its legal authority for the enforcement of safety standards. Once it was found that FAA had an independent basis for such enforcement, the issue was resolved. Nevertheless, the secretary of the task force had his problems because none of the representatives of the administrations could wear a departmental hat. As he says, "Each of them was protective of his own area. We had to call upon their expertise in each problem, but it was very difficult to get them to pull themselves away from the way they currently operated and see ways to change their program to conform to revenue sharing."

While the agencies were trying to add stipulations, White House and OMB staffmen were trying to eliminate them. Secretary Volpe, for example, wanted to add some standards and incentives to encourage highway beautification. He instructed Olsson to include them but was overruled. The OMB and White House were having a hard enough time keeping out old standards without adding a relatively new one, such as beautification.

Sometimes it pays to be a defender of the faith. Although matters may appear to be closed, with enough pushing and stubbornness the bureaucrat can get his way, or at least part of it. Right from the start, the White House informed DOT that it would not be able to impose planning requirements on a project. There would be no project approval or review of plans by DOT. "The task force," a member pointed out, "could define the process by which money would be received by local entities, but we could not include in that process a strong arm for the federal government." The representatives of the DOT administrations particularly were unhappy about this erosion of DOT's planning authority. Their administrators made numerous trips to Volpe to point out the dangers inherent in the situation. What would happen to the national transportation or airport system? Commenting on the FAA representative, an OMB analyst said, "He fought us all the way. He wanted to preserve a national airport system that doesn't in reality exist."

For the analysts from the administrations, planning was not some sort of empty ritual. It was the guts of the enterprise. Transportation projects had a long lead time, with many years between paper plans and actual construction; to see a project through to completion required "maintenance of effort," or adequate resources planned for and allocated through time. It went against the professional grain to allow state and local recipients to start and stop projects at will. At one point the task force even voted to require a state planning process as a prerequisite for passing funds to the local level, but the vote was overruled by Olsson. OMB and the White House were also stubborn. There was no "system" to protect. Maintenance of state and local effort was not required. Recipients would not be required to follow a plan; they would get their money by formula without prior federal approval of projects.

All was not lost. Apparently, a slight wedge could be driven into the White House position. It was possible to use decisions made in the other areas of special revenue sharing as possible points of compromise. When DOT's task force members learned that the law enforcement proposal included planning requirements, they began to look for ways to insert some planning into their own proposal. One device was to give the secretary of transportation discretionary funds which he could use to encourage state and local officials to do some comprehensive planning. As one analyst put it, "if you do good planning, we'll sweeten the pot." OMB and the White House resisted the idea, but task force members kept pushing inside DOT to get it accepted.

The hold-harmless provisions came to the rescue of the advocates of planning. Recipients were not supposed to lose money. But an analyst who had been working on various allocation formulas thought it might not be possible to design a formula that would be entirely harmless. So he suggested that discretionary funds be used to meet the hold-harmless requirement in cases where the formula did not work. At the same time, the task force member from the Urban Mass Transportation Administration was pushing for a "consortium-of-governments" provision for metropolitan areas. A consortium implied a certain amount of coordination between governments, which is another way of ensuring some measure of planning. As it turned out, the White House finally relented, mainly because of DOT's inability to meet the hold-harmless requirement, and allowed the secretary to have 10 percent (about $200 million) of general transportation shared revenues at his disposal. According to S.1693:

The remaining 10 per centum shall be available for commitment by the Secretary at his discretion, except that if a consortium of governments shall be the recipient of shared revenues . . ., the Secretary shall make additional commitments to that consortium equal to 10 per centum of the shared revenues. . . . In addition, the Secretary may commit these funds to recipients at his discretion for any transportation activity he deems appropriate, but shall give priority to assisting recipients in developing and implementing comprehensive transportation plans, establishing consortia of governments in metropolitan areas having powers to implement comprehensive transportation plans for the various jurisdictions comprising the consortia.[6]

The final bill had a number of other provisions dealing with planning. While the bureaucrats would no longer be able to approve and to fund on the basis of plans, they had not lost the entire battle. The mass transportation analyst summed up the victory of the consortium-of-governments provision: "Most of the other departments wanted this but didn't get it. We held out longer and succeeded. It was a big win."

Given the pressure of time, it is a wonder that the task force members were not at each other's throats. Conflict was mitigated by some of the members not treating the activity seriously. Why go through a lot of infighting if the bill would not get through Congress? Other members felt that they had something to gain by their participation. Upon return to their administrations they would be the experts on revenue sharing, the explainers to the uninitiated. And, indeed, their knowledge was put to use; for example, the secretary of transportation asked one of the analysts to draft responses to letters from mayors who were concerned about the impact of the proposed legislation on their cities. Moreover, analysts know that the ability to make an input does not stop when the deadline of a study is reached. The analyst from the Urban Mass Transportation Administration, for instance, felt that the mass transit fund would be adequate for older cities with existing transportation systems (for example, New York and Chicago), but that cities wanting to initiate a new system would be in trouble. Outlining the problem by calling attention to the specific needs of Atlanta, Georgia, he sent a six-page report in June to the secretary, who in turn sent it on to OMB. One purpose of his report was "to keep the secretary from saying these things—to stop him from promising Atlanta huge amounts of money that will not

6. U.S. Congress, Senate, S.1693, 92d Cong., 1st sess., 1971, pp. 8–9.

be forthcoming." The bureaucratic policy analyst with staying power has many opportunities to be a defender of the faith.

ANALYSIS AS ORGANIZATIONAL WASTE

Every organization wastes some of the energy of its members in performing its various tasks. Temporary organizations, such as the revenue sharing task force, are no exception. In the process of designing legislation, its members also produced analytical waste—analysis, information, or advice that was not used. It would be surprising if this were not the case, given the conditions under which temporary problem-solving organizations work. The combination of the arbitrary deadline, the lack of consensus on the definition of the problem, and an inadequate base of experience and knowledge produced false starts and wasted efforts. Moreover, the conflicts of the permanent bureaucracy were transferred to the temporary organization. With their multiple clients, the members of the task force were bound to stray sometimes from the president's target; some of their memos and issue papers were self-serving and thus ultimately discarded or abused. The product of analysis in this sort of situation does not represent the one best alternative. Instead, it reflects the diverse preferences of policymakers and, as a counter in the bargaining game, can easily be dispensed with or ignored.

Was the analytical waste a product of bureaucratic pathology? For the most part, I think not. After all, the task force did do its task: it produced a legislative proposal. If it had not, if it had been hung up on jurisdictional and status questions, then the behavior of its members would be pathological. As long as tasks are performed when needed and with a little efficiency, analytical waste should be viewed as an expected part of the policy process. Thus, the persistent analyst, with preferences of his own, should be prepared to redo many studies and write many memos; neither he nor his organization will get their way without paying the price of analytical waste.

Having explored an example of the frequently used temporary context for conducting analysis, let us now look at the permanent organizational context.

PERMANENT POSITIONS

WHERE ARE THE ANALYSTS?

One problem in discussing the organization of policy analysis is that it is not a simple matter to locate the analysts. Some of my hard-nosed friends, who equate analysis with economics and systems analysis, insist that there are only a handful of "real" analysts in the government. Moreover, they claim that during the Nixon administration it was hard to find Republican analysts. No doubt partisanship affects the demand for different types of advice, but it does not necessarily affect the demand for policy analysts. By the middle seventies the 800 analysts in 16 domestic agencies who were analyzed in the late sixties must have grown exponentially, if not in quality then at least in quantity.[7] There must be thousands of policy analysts. So where are they?

If the world were as rational as we could wish, policy analysts would be working under the title of policy analyst and in offices of policy analysis. But such is not the case. Analysts go by a variety of titles or classifications.[8] They also work in a variety of shops. Scan this March 1971 list of "program evaluation and planning officers" used by the evaluation shop of OMB:

Agency	*Title*
Agriculture	Director of Agricultural Economics
	Director of Program Evaluation and Planning Staff
Commerce	Special Assistant to the Secretary for Policy Development
	Assistant Secretary for Administration
Defense	Assistant Secretary of Defense (Systems Analysis)
	Assistant Secretary (Comptroller)

---

7. See Keith E. Marvin and Andrew M. Rouse, "The Status of PPB in Federal Agencies: A Comparative Perspective," in *Public Expenditures and Policy Analysis*, ed. Robert H. Haveman and Julius Margolis (Chicago: Markham Publishing Co., 1970), p. 453.

8. See Dr. Augustus B. Turnbull III, *The PPB Systems Analyst: Skills and Training Requirements* (report prepared for the U.S. Civil Service Commission, Bureau of Training, August 1969), p. 3.

Agency (continued)	*Title* (continued)
Health, Education, and Welfare	Assistant Secretary for Planning and Evaluation Deputy Assistant Secretary for Evaluation and Monitoring Deputy Assistant Secretary for Program Systems
Housing and Urban Development	Deputy Under Secretary for Policy Analysis and Program Evaluation
Interior	Director, Office of Program Analysis
Justice	Assistant Attorney General for Administration
Labor	Assistant Secretary for Policy, Evaluation, and Research Deputy Assistant Secretary for Policy, Evaluation, and Research
Post Office	Assistant Postmaster General for Planning, Marketing, and Systems Analysis
State	Deputy Assistant Secretary for Budget and Finance
Transportation	Deputy Under Secretary Director, Office of Planning and Program Review
Treasury	Assistant Secretary for Administration Director, Office of Planning and Program Evaluation
International Development	Deputy Assistant Administrator for Program and Policy
Atomic Energy	Director, Division of Program Analysis
Central Intelligence	Director of Planning, Programming, and Budgeting
Civil Service	Executive Director Director, Office of Management Analysis and Audits

Agency (continued)	*Title* (continued)
General Services Administration	Assistant Administrator for Administration Director of Program and Policy Planning
National Aeronautics and Space Administration	Assistant Administrator for Administration
National Science Foundation	Division Director of Science Resources and Policy Studies Head, Office of Budget, Programming, and Planning Analysis
Office of Economic Opportunity	Assistant Director for Planning, Research, and Evaluation
Office of Management and Budget	Assistant Director for Evaluation
Peace Corps	Director of Program and Training Evaluation
Small Business Administration	Assistant Administrator for Planning, Research, and Analysis
U.S. Information Agency	Chief of Evaluation and Analysis
Veterans Administration	Chairman, Administrator's Advisory Council.

Some minor bureaucratic pathology can be discerned from what is on and what is not on the list. First, the list was out of date, because the federal bureaucracy is constantly shuffling offices and people. One analytical chief, for example, upon returning from a 40-day sick leave, found that his planning office had been transferred to someone else. He had been promoted, and we found him in a plush office wondering what had happened. Instead of trying to solve intractable problems, we reorganize. We will see that analytical units themselves also play the great organization-chart game. One could argue that such movement in the bureaucracy makes for efficiency and adaptation. One thing is certain: such movement makes it hard to evaluate and locate policy analysts.

Second, notice how infrequently the word "policy" is used in a title. Each title implies an office behind it. Where are the offices whose central concern is policy? For the 25 agencies, I count seven instances of the use of the word "policy" and only one instance of "policy analysis." Before the reader accuses me of having gotten the wrong list, be assured that no matter how tightly policy analysis is defined, many of the offices on the list do policy analysis. The point is that policy analysis goes on under a variety of protective umbrellas, such as the following:

Administration	Information	Programs,
Analysis	systems/services	programming
Analysis and audits	Operations	Program analysis
Budget, budgeting	analysis/research	Program
Evaluation	Plans, planning	development
Finance	Policy	Program systems
	Policy analysis	Research, statistics
	Policy development	Systems analysis

The designation "policy analysis" is just catching on. The field is new, after all, and what is new is also risky. Thus, the infrequent use of "policy" may reflect an anxiety-ridden desire of many bureaucratic analysts to appear politically neutral, a minor widget in the great machinery of government. Some analysts sound like a civics textbook: the determination of policy is up to the president and Congress, to the interplay of interests and representatives. No doubt some analysts simply hide their policy activities behind suitable technical names. Some do not hide at all. Others are convinced that they have nothing to do with policy but only with the efficiency of policies chosen by others. The head of one shop of analysts, for example, claimed that his office was involved not in policy analysis but only in internal resource allocation. He down-played his position in influencing "policy decisions." He saw himself as a "staff man, an advisor looking over the shoulder of the operating man." In the department there were people who dealt in "cosmic policy"—those policies affecting the department's functions and its relationships to other entities in the environment. This planning and evaluation office, however, dealt with "operational analysis," with the efficiency of internal operations.

In my experience, internal operational analysis and external policy analysis overlap, if not on paper then in practice. Watching war games and riding in an armored personnel carrier as an operations analyst provided me with a basis for analyzing new concepts of mobility for army units, such as an air assault division. Moreover, the administration and operation of "cosmic" policies involve policies in their own right. Without maintenance policies, the airplanes would not take off; and without safety policies, nuclear reactors could kill us all.

Which brings me to a third but not pathological feature of the list: its incompleteness. The list represents only the tip of an iceberg. It omits, for instance, many independent agencies. Did you know that the National Foundation of the Arts and the Humanities had an Office of Planning and Analysis? I never found out what it did, but it was there. The Federal Power Commission is also missing, yet its Office of Economics used econometric models for purposes of price regulation.[9] My point is not to criticize OMB's list (which obviously was created for OMB's purposes) but to point out the pervasiveness of activities involving policy analysis. Organizationally speaking, the list has to be extended vertically and horizontally.

HOW TO ORGANIZE

Even when we stay close to the top of a major department, there will be a number of analytical units, each dealing with a chunk of the policy turf. Treasury is a good example of a department whose policy area is complex enough to support a division of labor without the analysts tripping over each other's feet. At the time of my research, there were at least four assistant secretaries who had analytical units reporting to them. Consider the Office of Tax Analysis, which reported to the assistant secretary for tax policy. It had over 20 professionals, who were organized by various taxes (for example, excise taxpayers, business, revenue estimating, and aggregate economic forecasting). The four analysts on the business taxation staff concentrated their efforts on defining tax preferences for commodities such as oil, real estate, timber, and hard minerals.

9. See Joe L. Steele, *The Use of Econometric Models by Federal Regulatory Agencies* (Lexington, Mass.: Heath Lexington Books, 1971).

The forecasters were usually involved with the "troika" (OMB, Council of Economic Advisers, and Treasury) but also were studying the effect of wage freezes on price levels. The revenue estimators worried about the effect on revenue of changes in the tax law.

On the other side of the organization chart in Treasury was the Office of Debt Analysis, which reported to the assistant secretary for economic policy. It had a staff of about 30, half of them clerks and half professionals. Each year the office reviewed approximately 300 legislative proposals, about one-third of the bills coming to the department. The other two-thirds went to the other analytical units, such as the Office of Tax Analysis.

When they were not reviewing bills, the analysts in the Office of Debt Analysis organized studies. The analyst chairing a study had two important levers to use in pursuing the objectives of his client: the choice of committee members and the writing of the final report. The Export-Import Bank, for example, was interested in establishing a credit facility. The secretary of the treasury was not keen on the idea and asked the office to study the idea and submit a report. The analyst in charge convened an interagency committee composed of representatives from OMB, the Department of Commerce, Treasury, and the Export-Import Bank. How does the analyst know whom to invite? First, it depends on the purpose of the committee, which in this case was probably to find fault and data to support the secretary's objections.[10] Second, substance, or the "nature of the subject," indicates who will be interested. Third, it is wise to be liberal with invitations, as there is more risk in appearing to exclude an interested party.

Analytical units have been organized on paper by substance or function, or a mix of the two. When substance is used, work is divided by policy area, such as health or education. Functional organization usually involves some activity that cuts across policy areas. A straightforward example is an information systems unit that provides computer support to other units. Frequently, analytical units will take on functional form because their organizers believe it is possible to divide work by type of advice, such as

10. Aaron Wildavsky tells us that "it is an error to assume that the only purpose of committees is to make decisions." For a short list of other purposes, see his *The Revolt against the Masses: And Other Essays on Politics and Public Policy* (New York: Basic Books, 1971), pp. 388–89.

evaluation, planning, coordination, or analysis. At the time of my research, OEO's Office of Planning, Research, and Evaluation followed this functional form; it had research, evaluation, planning, program analysis, and information service units. Within each unit there were subject-matter specialists, on housing or income maintenance, for example. Within the Office of Education's Office of Program Planning and Evaluation, about 30 professionals were substantively divided up, for the most part, by the level of school; for example, there was an Elementary and Secondary Programs Division and a Post-secondary and Special Education Programs Division. Supposedly, each division did some planning, evaluation of issues, and program analysis.

Which way is better, substance or function? Neither organizational theorists nor clients can make up their minds on this question. Consider the central analytical unit of HEW. Each time it would get a new assistant secretary, its organization would change. Over time the office was organized by function, then by substance, then by function, and then, as of 1972 (see chart 3), by a mix, supplemented by some units doing quasi-analytical activities (for instance, the Office of Special Concerns). With its many boxes on paper, the 1972 organization seems to have been cumbersome; but one hopes it was effective, since analysts from different boxes did work together. Of course, there were jurisdictional problems—there always will be. For example, the program systems people were developing agency planning procedures which the health analysts felt were silly and an interference with their work.

No matter how one organizes on paper, it is vital that the arrangements be loose. Most analysts at one time or another are on loan to somebody else. The formal organizational chart of permanent positions is for external relations, a sign of bureaucratic territory. Internally, analysts should know and usually do know that they must be flexible enough to be able to respond to opportunities and changes in demand. Since, as I have said, much analysis is performed by teams, committees, and task forces, it is important to have a place to come from and go back to. The formal permanent organization, as a steward of the steady state, is such a place. It is those boxes on the organizational chart that provide the manpower to make bureaucracy adaptive to changes in its environment to the point where the apostles of the "matrix" form of

CHART 3. Central Analytical Unit at HEW in 1972

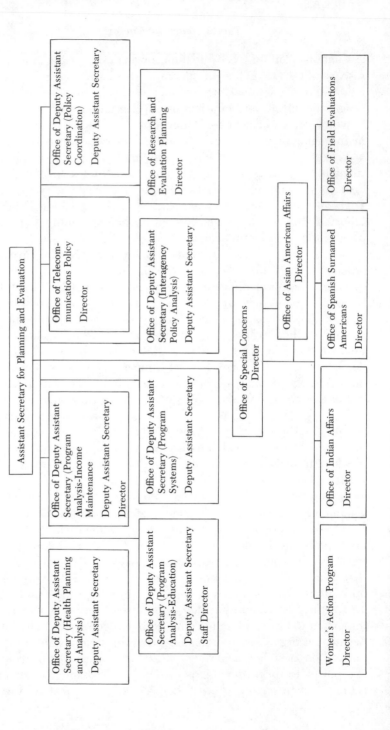

organization would never imagine. Thus, the boundaries around boxes cannot be taken too seriously if analysts are to do their jobs.

LET GEORGE DO IT

Sometimes a chart with many boxes indicates a shallowness in analytical capability. Since everybody is a deputy assistant secretary, a chief, there are no foot soldiers to do the work. Each box contains only a handful of analysts, so that when there is a big job to do, there is hardly anyone there to do it. Another indicator of shallowness is when one of the analysts reports that there is "no time to do research" and that the analyst "must know how to manipulate people and contract for research," or that the analyst "needs experience in research management." Looking at the paper organization alone, it is hard to ascertain the depth of analytical capability. At NIH, for example, an analytical office had 30 professionals assigned to it. On inspection, there were only two people who conceivably could have been doing policy analysis studies.

One consequence of a small or shallow analytical unit is that the analyst soon believes in letting George do it. Indeed, some units see their primary function as getting somebody else to do it. Rather than *let* George do it, one *gets* George to do it. I found that at the General Services Administration (GSA), the central analytical office of seven professionals felt very dependent on the analytical staff of the various services that made up the administration.[11] Whether a problem was analyzed depended to a large extent on whether the analysts could convince the staff of the services to undertake it. As the head of the central office remarked, "We cannot pursue anything in too much detail without the services' cooperation. The climate varies among the services, some aggressive, others conservative, and some of them just plain stuffy."

The idea behind letting George do it is to get the credit without the work. This is the essence of coordination, and some analysts who are politicians become quite good at it. Consider the analyst who worked for Secretary of Commerce Maurice H. Stans. When Stans became secretary, he decided to terminate a state technical assistance program that gave advice (from engineering to account-

---

11. GSA was composed mainly of five component services: the Federal Supply Service, the Property Management and Disposal Service, the Public Buildings Service, the Transportation and Communications Service, and the National Archives and Record Service.

ing) to local businessmen in impoverished areas. Congressional reaction caused Stans to reconsider his decision, and he asked an analyst to propose a new program that would avoid the problems of the previous one. The analyst superficially investigated the assistance program and identified the kinds of problems with which Stans was concerned. Then he contacted the assistant secretary in charge of science and technology and got him to take on responsibility for designing a new program. He offered his help but avoided long-term involvement. He explained that all the staff members in his office operated in a similar manner because long-term involvement was too time-consuming.

FIND A HOSPITABLE HOST

The organization of a department affects the organization of analysis. Sometimes we expect too much of policy analysis, as if it could cure organizational sickness. In a situation of excessive decentralization, for example, we think that setting up a central analytical unit will make everything all right. But usually everything is not all right, because the unit itself becomes a victim. Whatever the particular sickness is—a hostile environment, recruiting troubles, lack of leadership, fragmented and autonomous bureaus, size and complexity—a policy analysis unit by itself cannot do much and instead succumbs to the same problems. The policy analysis unit will be a reflection of its host organization.

The image of an analytical unit spreads throughout the analytical corps. Units get reputations for doing good or bad work. Such reputations are ephemeral—those that obtained while I was doing my research have probably changed—but they are useful to look at in trying to understand the organizational effect on analytical units. In the Department of Interior, for example, an analytical unit was set up in the 1960s. It had a reputation for doing work lacking in substance and quality. No doubt there are many explanations for this bad reputation, but one of them is organizational. The analytical unit was placed at the top in Interior, but Interior is recognized as a loose confederation of bureaus. One supposes that its leaders thought that, with a central office and an overall "planning system," they could pull the strands together. Such was not the case, because the degree of autonomy of the bureaus encouraged the decentralization of analysis. Since the bureaus were free to do as they saw fit, they produced supportive analysis as needed while the central office refined meaningless procedures. GSA has had its problems too; because of its unglamorous work, it has had difficulty attracting quality staff. At HEW, the quality of the work has varied with the secretary and the person in charge of the unit.

Some units do not reflect the image of their hosts because they probably never had an organizational host to begin with. For a variety of reasons, they are stuck into an organizational home but really do not belong there. After a while the organization discovers that it has a unit that does not do much for it, eats up resources and slots, and also proves embarrassing on occasion. Take the Technical Analysis Division (TAD) of the National Bureau of Standards, U.S. Department of Commerce. Created in January 1965, it started out with a staff of 12, and by June 1970 the staff had grown to 120. Concentrating on systems analysis and operations research, TAD's high-quality staff provided technical assistance and performed studies for a variety of federal, state, and local clients. Essentially it operated as a contractor, because 90 percent of its work was supported by clients outside the National Bureau of Standards.[12] Not doing much work for its host, NBS, and competing with private consulting firms, TAD became a target. Complaints went to the White House and to the secretary level about the inconsistency of a Republican administration encouraging government at the expense of private enterprise. TAD's director tried to defend his operation by pointing out the disadvantages of private consultants, but to no avail. After a review of TAD's performance, its director was encouraged to leave his job and TAD's scope and staff were reduced.

Another example is provided by the Evaluation Division of OMB. Although much smaller than TAD, it also had an uncertain role with its host, OMB. For the most part, its high-quality analysts were loosely assigned to policy areas to raise the quality of analysis and to encourage its production throughout the government. One of them particularly tried to spread the analytical word to state and local officials. But within OMB the analysts found it hard to win friends. Their influence was limited to "kibitzing and inserting analysis during the review of a department budget by the deputy director and director of OMB." As one analyst told me, "We can

12. U.S. Department of Commerce, National Bureau of Standards, Technical Analysis Division, *Project Summaries, 1967–1969* (Washington, D.C., n.d.), p. 1.

raise issues with the deputy director, but in the end we usually
have to rely on the examiners for success." The examiners understood the agencies and their budgets and saw little need for the
analysts. As another analyst put it, "We are still trying to establish
our role, and they [the examiners] do not believe they need our
advice." Moreover, the analysts were not sympathetic to the
requirements of the examiner role: "We have accused them [the
examiners] of being in bed with the agencies." Unable to make
peace with the examiners or to find clients for the work it wanted to
do, the division was eliminated in June 1972, after a decade of
frustration, when its director left the federal service.

WHAT'S IN A NAME?

In the bureaucratic struggle for jurisdiction and status, names
take on particular importance. The name of a policy analysis unit is
a signal to the bureaucracy of intent and regard. The name reveals
the areas in which the unit intends to work and confirms that this
intent has the blessing of the boss. Most units operate under the
title of the Office of ———, with the usual shredding into
divisions and branches. Since many bureaucrats believe that power
increases with the level of the hierarchy, which office the unit is in
is quite important. Supposedly, it makes a difference whether it
works in the office of the secretary, or under secretary, or assistant
secretary, or deputy assistant secretary. I suspect that the difference is more important to the bureaucrats and analysts than to the
secretary. He can reach down to the bottom of his agency for a
policy analyst if he wants one. The bureaucrats, having less first-
hand knowledge of the analytical unit, look to name and location as
a sign of potential influence. Analysts know that bureaucrats are
calibrating them, so they also worry about their name and location.

Consider the recent history of analysis in the Defense Department. In the early 1960s, analysis was housed in the comptroller's
shop, but Secretary of Defense Robert S. McNamara dealt directly
with the analytical office. Time passed and the reputation of the
Office of Systems Analysis spread, and the unit became more
visible. As tangible evidence of its security and influence, the office
was placed under an assistant secretary of defense for systems
analysis. For the most part, the players did not change during this
period; Alain C. Enthoven still ran the shop of analysts. The
change in name and location, however, made it clear to the

external world that analysis was important and that an analyst reported directly to the secretary of defense.

By the end of the decade and with a change of administration, the Office of Systems Analysis began to run into trouble. In 1973 the trouble was reported in the *Wall Street Journal:* "In decline for many years, the office suffered a major blow yesterday. Defense Secretary Elliot Richardson announced that the office was being 'redesignated' the Office of Defense Program Analysis and Evaluation, and will be headed in the immediate future by a 'director' rather than by an assistant secretary."[13] Once again the formal organizational chart had caught up with informal relationships of influence, but this time in the opposite direction, toward a reduction in influence. Such a fall from grace concerns the analyst because it will make it harder for him to get information and do the job of overall defense analysis. "The fear of one systems analyst," according to the *Journal,* "is that the downgrading of the office will 'give all kinds of wrong signals to the military,' indicating to them that they will now be freer to follow their instincts and parochial service interests in weapons and force planning." No doubt the signal had gone out a number of years earlier, in 1969 when the role of the analytical unit was reduced to "that of a passive commentator."[14]

Changes in name not only reflect previous organizational action but also state future intentions. When an analyst took over the Evaluation Branch of OEO's Office of Planning, Research, and Evaluation, she added "analysis" to the name so that the staff would be empowered to make program recommendations beyond the scope of existing field operations.

A person who is not sympathetic to bureaucratic folkways will not appreciate how much significance is placed on a change of name. The effect of a new mandate is created, whether or not the unit delivers on its intentions. In several different locations in the Department of Agriculture, analysts reported that their role was increasing in importance in the department. The evidence for the increase was a name change of a unit of the Forest Service, from the Office of Program Planning and Special Projects to the Office of

13. *Wall Street Journal,* 12 April 1973, p. 8.

14. Alain C. Enthoven and K. Wayne Smith, *How Much Is Enough? Shaping the Defense Program, 1961–1969* (New York: Harper and Row, 1971), pp. 333–34.

Program and Policy Analysis. According to the analyst who directed the office, he, the chief of the Forest Service, and the chief's deputy believed that the change was necessary so that there would be "more policy analysis . . . within the Forest Service." Moreover, the change in name would demonstrate to the divisions and to field personnel that the office was capable of doing policy analysis. Besides these advertising gains, it seems that the change in name also legitimated the office's role in the budgetary process, a role that had been called into question particularly when the office had disagreed with the Division of Timber.[15]

Another reason for changing the name of an analytical unit is to avoid past bureaucratic antagonisms. Believing that a new name may produce a new image, a senior analyst in the Department of Agriculture sought to change the name of the unit he directed from the Planning, Evaluation, and Programming Staff to the Office of Planning and Evaluation. The PEP Staff, as it was called, had developed a reputation for antagonism and a lack of tact—for being "a bunch of McNamara whiz kids." The senior analyst argued to his boss, the under secretary, that the PEP Staff was identified with program budgeting (PPBS) and that, while the Nixon administration embraced many of the same concepts of rational decision making, PPBS was a creation of the previous administration. The change in name was promulgated in a memorandum from the secretary of agriculture (secretary's Memorandum No. 1728: "Planning and Budgetary System," 28 April 1971). Here is the relevant excerpt:

The Office of Planning and Evaluation (formerly the PEP Staff), reporting to the Under Secretary, will coordinate and conduct special analytic studies, review and help prepare the Program and Financial Plan, analyze the effectiveness of programs designed to achieve major Department objectives, and provide staff assistance to the Program and Budget Review Committee. The Director of the Office of Planning and Evaluation will work in close cooperation with the agencies and staff offices of the Department, especially with the Office of Budget and Finance and the Office of Management Improvement.

15. Name changers can be subtle and devious: In order to avoid bureaucratic resistance and expand his territory without a formal change, one California state official told me that he was using what he called the "drip method": he was slowly changing the name of his office by signing his letters with the new name and also by putting the new name on the business cards of his analysts.

If we compare this excerpt with the relevant paragraph from the superseded memorandum, we will see that the change is cosmetic. Other than a change in whom the analytical unit reported to, the unit's function and work, at least on paper, were almost exactly the same. Here is the paragraph from the superseded memorandum (secretary's Memorandum No. 1675: "Planning-Programming-Budgeting System," 20 December 1969):

The Planning, Evaluation, and Programming Staff, reporting to the Director of Agricultural Economics, will coordinate and conduct special analytic studies, review and help prepare the Program and Financial Plan, analyze the effectiveness of programs designed to achieve major Department objectives, and provide staff assistance to the Program and Budget Review Committee. The Director of the PEP Staff will work in close cooperation with the agencies and staff offices of the Department. The work of the PEP Staff will be carefully coordinated with the work of the Office of Budget and Finance.

Whether the change in name actually reduced bureaucratic anxieties is an open question. It did not for the senior analyst, who still worried about the name change because old-time bureaucrats might interpret it as signifying "a change in our function"; for example, for the bureaucrat an "office" carries greater weight than a "staff."

Sometimes signals from name changes are confusing and bureaucrats cannot tell whether there has been an increase or decrease in turf and responsibility. Imagine the HUD analyst who increased his influence with his client, an assistant secretary for community planning and management, but at the same time lost some of his functions. As director of the Office of Plans, Programs, and Evaluation, he had run one of the oldest program budgeting shops in HUD. The virus of reorganization hit, and his budget and data systems functions were transferred to the bailiwick of another assistant secretary. In line with HUD's general efforts at decentralization, his office's evaluation function was shipped to the regions. Rather than conducting an evaluation, the office would mainly design procedures for evaluation along with carrying out its other responsibilities. Redesignated the Office of Policy and Program Development, it was intended to be the assistant secretary's main advisory unit, a kind of quick-response think tank. Thus, its 22 professionals were loosely assigned to projects in order to "maintain maximum flexibility to fight brush fires for the assistant secretary."

STAKE YOUR CLAIM

If the analysts in HUD's Office of Policy and Program Development were unhappy about losing a few functions, they need not have been. Their boss was on the lookout for more. He followed urban and housing legislation as it proceeded through Congress and "could see that urban growth would be the thing in the coming years." Wanting "to get into it," during a HUD reorganization he suggested to his client, Assistant Secretary Samuel C. Jackson, that an urban growth unit be assigned to his office. As his deputy explained, "We approached the assistant secretary and staked our claim." The assistant secretary, receptive to the idea, established the Division of Urban Growth Policy within the Office of Policy and Program Development. A central reason for including "policy" in the office's new name was to stress the staff's interest in urban growth policy.

Grabbing for the new turf had an immediate payoff, because the legislation required that the president submit a report on urban growth: "We just created the division and let Jackson suggest to Secretary Romney that we be assigned the task of drafting the report." The analyst who was nominally in charge of the division believed that, given the office's loose organization, his division was not particularly distinct from the rest of its units. But having the division on paper was important in order to get the assignment within HUD and to get the White House to give HUD the major role. According to the analyst, the existence of the division showed the staff of the Domestic Council that HUD had the capability to proceed in the preparation of the report.

The production of the first draft of the urban growth report provides an interesting lesson in organization. One would think that the preparation of a policy report would be a simple and straightforward activity, but then one would not be familiar with the Byzantine ways of the federal executive branch. A task force of the Domestic Council, made up of cabinet-level officials, was charged with drafting the urban growth report. Although the task force involved other agencies, such as HEW and Agriculture, it was the secretary of HUD, George Romney, who was in charge. And because the task force seldom met—there were something like two meetings in half a year—the person who actually directed the various staff was a member of the staff of the Domestic Council.

I have never understood why organizational charts go up and down with rectangles when most organizational relationships are triangular. In this case, we have the staff man of the Domestic Council, Secretary Romney, and the HUD analysts. For example, the analysts prepared an outline of the report and submitted it to the White House staff man. He made some minor changes and then submitted it to the Romney task force, which accepted it. Now it was time to do the report; but the White House staff man, busy coordinating other projects, often did not have time to discuss various policy issues with the HUD analysts. Since the report was a "major push" of the office and everybody's reputation was at stake, the analysts did not like these delays. Therefore, they appealed to their boss, Assistant Secretary Jackson, who in turn appealed to Secretary Romney, who in turn told the White House staff man to spend more time on the report.

The lure of White House involvement is that it provides "the potential of putting forth light on the subject or of presenting a new idea with the real possibility that it will be accepted." But there are also disadvantages. The HUD analyst who was doing most of the writing of the report, for instance, wanted to produce something with a "minimum of rhetoric and a picture of the issues balanced between points of view." He hoped to present the alternatives and their consequences clearly, so that action would follow. The White House staff man, however, had his own ideas. He strongly suggested a particular style and content which, according to the analyst, would make the report "rhetorical, one-sided, and nonobjective."

Well, one cannot have everything; the analysts may not have liked what they were writing, but at least they had staked their claim in an area that would require their services for many years to come, since the president was required to issue periodic reports on urban growth.

CONFLICT AND COMPETITION

Establishing an analytical unit in an organization is bound to cause conflict. As with the traditional problems of staff and line, the managers and operators of governmental programs perceive the analysts as a threat to their programs. Part of this perception is due to the location of the analytical unit, which, at least on paper, is close to the head of the agency. Part is due to the identification of analysts with budgeting. Many analytical units were at one time part of a budget shop or at least sought alliances with budget men for additional leverage. Even when the formal relationships with budgeting are terminated, the image lingers on—the analyst is a person who asks "cold-blooded questions to cut the budget." Thus analysts, like budget men, are "worms-in-the-woodwork," but usually they do not have the advantages that budget men enjoy: many analysts have not had enough time on the job to develop the contacts and accommodations that allow budget men to perform.

This conflict between analyst and operator is nothing new. The conflict among the staff and between analytical units is more interesting. Staff are usually competing with each other for the attention of the client. Such competition can lead either to improving the quality of work and advice or to diminishing it. Recall the OEO study of suburbanization discussed in chapter 3. There were two competing analytical units: Planning, Research, and Evaluation (PR&E) and the Office of Program Development (OPD). The actual distinction between the units was murky, but the analysts agreed on stereotypes. An OPD analyst described PR&E as "that bunch of pipe-smoking types," while a PR&E analyst said that other parts of OEO considered PR&E as those "high-paid, pipe-smoking intellectuals who contribute nothing to the poor." Another PR&E analyst agreed with this description but felt that it applied generally to OEO. He explained, "The administration is changing OEO into a research and evaluation unit for the White House. Because of this, we've lost the operating arm of OEO which was really involved with helping our client. We're now getting an influx of very high-level academic people but . . . we've lost some very dedicated people, and I think the agency has lost a commitment to the poor."

"OPD thinks up what might work and tries it—we are the thinkers, they are the doers," a PR&E analyst said. An OPD analyst agreed: "We are known as the crude ones academically; we feel we are stronger in developing programs than PR&E." While PR&E considered OPD too operationally oriented, OPD considered PR&E too research-oriented.

OPD's people were considered "unanalytical." They had a broad social science orientation and relied on knowledge of social problems rather than technical skill. PR&E was heavily staffed with economists and mathematicians who were skilled in techniques of analysis that could be applied to a variety of subjects.

Supposedly OPD was in the demonstration business and undertook projects "to identify bugs in the program before it was expanded nationwide." PR&E, besides doing in-house research, was in the experimentation business. The difference between demonstration and experimentation is a bit elusive. Both offices, for example, were conducting research in day care. OPD searched the nation for exemplary centers, studied them, and offered case studies which private organizations and the government could use in designing day-care centers. PR&E, instead, reviewed the literature and might sponsor two or three centers, evaluating the components of success.

In order to build a bridge to OPD, one PR&E analyst took drastic action. In past meetings with OPD he used to smoke his pipe, but "this only reinforced their image of us as distant intellectuals. The image was wrong, so I no longer smoke my pipe in the presence of the OPD staff. Every little bit helps." Nevertheless, the basis for a working relationship—albeit a slightly hostile one—was there because both offices needed each other. If OPD had the ideas, then PR&E had the resources with which to follow through. OPD, for example, initiated educational vouchers as a pilot project. After some internal struggle, the project was reassigned to PR&E. OPD's analysts viewed such outcomes with mixed feelings. On the one hand they suffered a sense of failure when PR&E "picked up the ball." On the other hand they realized that without PR&E the project probably would not have been completed.

There are a number of reasons for PR&E's victories in the bureaucratic wars. The problems the office took on were fairly specific and were not as tied to implementation and action as OPD's demonstrations were. PR&E was less likely to step on people's feet. In any event, PR&E built a history of demonstrable results. According to an OPD analyst, the key resource PR&E had was its director, John O. Wilson, "one of the golden boys of the administration." Evidently "people trusted Wilson's view of research." OPD was not as fortunate; it had been "headed by nothing but a series of political hacks." The people in OPD felt that "in any contest PR&E would walk off with all the marbles." OPD had had "three directors in a year, and each one seemed to be worse than the previous one. PR&E . . . had one director during the entire Nixon administration."

The conflict between the two units seemed somewhat beneficial to OEO. Policy ideas were generated and there was a blending of capabilities. One unit's deficiencies were made up for by the other's strengths. Moreover, there was a formal mechanism for resolving conflict, a project selection committee that decided which research OEO should conduct and sponsor. The two units were encouraged to work together, and they did. Not all internal staff conflicts are as beneficial.

HUD, a massive and unwieldy department in 1970 and 1971, had a dubious reputation for its analytical products. There were many reasons for this reputation, some stemming from the origins of the department's various components and some related to its complex of political constituencies. A central reason could be traced back to the bureaucratic context of analysis. With operations decentralized to the field and the Washington staff reorganized, policy analysis was fragmented and dispersed.

At least on paper, HUD was paying attention to policy analysis. To my knowledge, it was the only federal agency that had a deputy under secretary for policy analysis and program evaluation. His office had a big job:

The Deputy Under Secretary for Policy Analysis and Program Evaluation advises the Secretary and the Under Secretary with respect to program formulation and evaluation; makes comprehensive studies and analyses of developments, trends, and problems relating to national housing and community development goals and makes recommendations for changes in program policies and objectives; designs or directs the design of data systems to serve the needs of the Department; conducts economic analyses; assembles and evaluates statistical data for Department use; and provides functional supervision for the Secretary with regard to the performance of these functions throughout the Department.[16]

With such a big job, one wonders why the office was so small; it contained 6 professionals, while HEW's central analytical unit had over 100. Besides fighting fires for the secretary, the office reviewed the analyses of other HUD shops. Most of HUD's analysts

16. Office of the Federal Register, National Archives and Records Service, General Services Administration, *United States Government Organization Manual, 1971/72* (Washington, D.C., 1 July 1971), p. 352.

were spread throughout the department. The operating units in the regions and areas were expected to conduct their own evaluations, and there were policy analysis units assigned to the various assistant secretaries. The assistant secretary for housing management, for example, had an Office of Program Development, which was composed of a Program Planning and Evaluation Division and a Program Statistics Division. It had a staff of over 50, many of whom performed clerical chores in the Statistics Division.

Conceptually, such a decentralization of policy analysis can have advantages and disadvantages. Having access to data and exposure to operating problems certainly is an advantage. A primary disadvantage, even in the best of decentralized situations, is that the analysts will be working on smaller, more compartmentalized problems. With analysts spread out and refining individual programs, there is less capability for comparing programs and for analyzing alternative departmental policies. The logic of decentralization pushes toward a situation in which the field operator or manager is his own analyst, which can make sense for smaller, project-type organizations in which central control and direction are of little consequence.

HUD, however, was not such a small organization. It did require some measure of central policy direction and control, and its central analytical office was not staffed adequately to meet the need for department-wide advice. Nor were the analytical units working for the various assistant secretaries always able to fill in the gaps. The reorganization of HUD had left areas of disputed territory and uncertainty over jurisdiction. Analysts spent their talents not only in grabbing territory for themselves but also in backing their clients, the assistant secretaries, in their jurisdictional squabbles.

Consider the conflict between Floyd H. Hyde, assistant secretary for community development, and Samuel C. Jackson, assistant secretary for community planning and management. Community Development supervised a number of HUD's operating programs, such as model cities and urban renewal. Community Planning and Management was involved in the "software" parts of programs, such as providing planning and management assistance and grants. The conflict came about because it was not always clear where planning stopped and operating began. For example, Jackson felt that the development of criteria for selecting water and sewer projects was in his area, but so did Hyde. The result was that analysts on both sides worked on developing criteria. Competition among clients, if it does nothing else, creates a demand for analysis.

Within Community Development there was competition for analytical territory. The Office of Policy and Resource Development contained four divisions: the Policy Development Division, the Evaluation Division, the Resource Utilization Division, and the Program Regulations-Development Division. Lacking a director of the office for a period of time, the division directors were used to reporting directly to Hyde. Each of them was vying for Hyde's attention, so it was not unusual for each to describe his own shop as "the key division within the Office of Policy and Resource Development" or to claim that, "when it comes right down to it, we make 80 percent of the policy in this division."

Were there any differences in the mission of each division? It is hard to tell, but one of the directors explained that the four divisions were created to represent the sequential steps in the process of formulating policy, as follows:

Stage	*Unit*
1. Problem identification	field operations
2. Investigation of problem	Evaluation Division
3. Analysis of findings	Policy Development Division
4. Alteration of regulations	Program Regulations-Development Division
5. Notification and cooperation with other agencies	Resource Utilization Division
6. Change in action at local level	field operations

This description fits the Regulation and Utilization divisions but does not clarify the role of the Evaluation and Policy Development divisions. It is between these latter two divisions that competition was keen and not necessarily productive. Some observers saw Development as "philosophical" and Evaluation as "operationally oriented." Whatever the difference between the units, it is clear that they were using different tactics to survive.

The director of policy development was relying on his personal relationship to Assistant Secretary Hyde. The office gossip was that the director had done a good job for Hyde when the assistant secretary was in charge of the model cities program. At the time the director was a GS-15 hoping to become a GS-16. Since he could not be promoted without becoming a division director, a separate Policy Development Division was created when HUD was reorganized. The director himself confirmed his personal relationship to Hyde:

Loss of turf is not a danger for us because of my long-term relationship with Hyde. Our relationship extends far beyond normal work assignment. I can afford to allow another office's name to appear on a document because our office is important to Hyde in many other informal ways. If I don't agree with the results of analysis carried out by another branch, though, it will not pass. Floyd and I have a long-standing rapport from our work together in the model cities program. This degree of rapport is not shared by the other directors.

The director of evaluation was trying to impress Hyde by a tactic of bureaucratic imperialism. His division was trying to build an image of action, an image of a unit deserving of "meaty" assignments on current issues. For example, the division knew that unless it did something Policy Development would get the assignment to draft a new funding procedure because of its director's friendship with Hyde. An analyst from Evaluation described what happened: "We were very interested in the project and so worked hard and quickly to get something down on paper first. . . . To get the assignment, we tried to associate the new funding procedure with evaluation. If we could get evaluation attached to it, we could stake our claim." Staff from both divisions were involved in this area, but the Evaluation analysts saw their role as increasing when their division was asked by Hyde to draft his speech on the subject.

Members of the Evaluation Division referred to Policy Development as "redundant" or concluded that "in the end, Policy Development will be eliminated as a separate function." Who was really winning in this bureaucratic and pathological struggle? If size is a criterion, Evaluation was. It had a staff of over 20 professionals, while Development had only about 6. Policy Development had had some turnover, and vacant positions had been downgraded and not filled. One analyst who had a choice of joining either unit chose Evaluation, because "with all the reshuffling going on, we're all concerned about our own survival in the organization. The Policy Development staff is a group of floating special assistants dependent on the personal whims of Hyde."

One indicator of Policy Development's diminished strength was its work on HUD's planned variation program. In this program, which involved some 20 cities, HUD was attempting to allow the cities greater discretion in the use of funds and was providing additional funds for city-wide implementation of plans and for increasing the management capacity of local executives. In short, in the name of local flexibility, planned variation relaxed some of the constraints of categorical grants. In any event, Hyde assigned the project to Policy Development. The analyst in Policy Development, not having any staff, decided on a decentralized method for organizing the work. For example, Evaluation would be responsible for developing a mechanism for reporting on a city's use of HUD's money, and the Regulation Division would eliminate unnecessary federal regulations which go along with categorical grants. All four divisions were assigned a piece of the pie. But the project did not proceed as planned. Each division wanted the whole pie; there was competition for larger roles and an overlapping of responsibility.

The division directors failed to appoint individuals to carry out the specific responsibilities for accomplishing each division's share of the work. Instead, each director acted as if he were in charge of the whole job. The analyst reported that when it was necessary to determine progress on an aspect of the project, he was unable to identify who in each division to ask for information. When he called a meeting to discuss the planned variation project, the composition of the group varied with the subject. There was no consistency in the personnel working on the project. The analyst felt helpless in reestablishing control over the project. He wished he had used a task-force approach, with definite assignments of representatives from the various divisions.

CONCLUSION

What, then, have we learned about the bureaucratic context? We have seen that both a permanent and a temporary context influence analytical activities. The permanent context provides a home base for assignment to temporary tasks. It provides a place of departure for the staffing of numerous ad hoc analytical organizations. Like a bank lending out money, the steady-state bureaucracy lends out analysts to meet pressing analytical challenges. Yet unproductive conflicts, bureaucratic pathologies, and analytical waste exist in either context.

The permanent context is depicted in organizational charts and manuals, but we have learned not to trust them. Evidently, analysts operate under a variety of labels, and the names of their organizational homes are chosen for momentary bureaucratic advantage. Despite the camouflage, we are left with a strong impression of the shallowness of analytical capability, of the prevalence of more chiefs than Indians, and of competition for territory rather than concern for analytical tasks.

Now, competition in giving advice can be a good thing if good advice is given. The policy analysis business is not so cut and dried that duplication of analytical units and overlapping assignments are necessarily wasteful. Such redundancy, however, is not always creative.[17] Excessive fragmentation of analytical activity coupled with ambiguous territorial assignments and nourished by feelings of marginal status and ambition, diverts the energy of the bureaucratic policy analyst. In extreme situations, the goal of providing reliable and accurate advice is displaced by the goal of aggrandizement. According to Anthony Downs, "aggrandizement is defined as increasing the amount of power, income, and prestige attached to a given position."[18] Such aggrandizement, staking one's claim, can drive out competitors to the point where "winning" the assignment causes a losing situation for the organization and client.

Clients, the secretaries and assistant secretaries, who bemoan their analysts' display of ambition rather than advice have only themselves to blame. It is the client who creates and maintains organizational arrangements, and both client and analyst live with the consequences. If the White House sets up an organization to get the support of other policymakers, as it did in the case of the revenue sharing task force, it should not be surprised that it has also encouraged a situation of multiple loyalties and clients. If the

17. For the advantages of redundancy, see Martin Landau, "Redundancy, Rationality, and the Problem of Duplication and Overlap," *Public Administration Review* 29 (July-August 1969): 346–58.

18. Anthony Downs, *Inside Bureaucracy* (Boston: Little, Brown and Co., 1966), pp. 93–95.

organization is sick, then analysis will also be sick. If everything is up for grabs, then the analyst will become a grabber. If the name of the game is credit without work, then the analyst will become proficient in getting George to do it.

Despite its pathologies, the bureaucratic context does have advantages and strengths. Besides helping adapt government to changing circumstances, the bureaucracy is skilled at dividing up the work and communicating its results. Fortunately, its analysts have learned to live with severe time constraints and still provide a measure of expertise. Considering the complexity of modern governance, these talents should not be deprecated. Although the organization of analysis is imperfect, it is still intrinsic to the solving of public policy problems.

6

Clients

Clients are policymakers. They hold the offices of prestige and power. Analysts, it should be clear by now, do not have an independent base of power, although they do have political resources, such as their expertise. What power they do have is derived from their relationships to specific clients. This relationship between client and analyst is one of many, because each client has a cluster of advisors. One interesting question, then, is: How do analysts differ from other advisors in their relationship to their clients?

To make matters simple, let us suppose that the client has three types of advisors: staff cronies, program managers, and policy analysts. The program manager works for the client but is also independent because he runs a bureau or an agency, and some program managers are policymakers in that they do not need the client to get access to the policymaking process. At the other extreme is the staff crony, who, like the policy analyst, seldom has an independent base of power. The crony provides social support, answers the client's mail, and does what is asked of him in exchange for friendship and access to policymaking. While the crony is close to the client, the program manager and client are likely to have a distant relationship, since the program manager has a jurisdiction to defend and a constituency to look after. When the crony and program manager advise the client, their advice may be sound; but their relationships with the client will influence its acceptance. As an example, consider the situation in which the client is suspicious of both advisors. His crony is too close to him to have an independent perspective on the policy problem. His program manager is too independent of him to be trusted to view the policy problem from the client's perspective. In this situation we see the special tension of the client-analyst relationship. The policy analyst must be so dependent on the client that the client believes that the analyst understands him and his particular situation. At the same time, the analyst must be so independent of the client that his advice appears to be fresh, unfettered, and objective.

Sometimes my students upset me when they say they do not need a client because they intend to work for the public interest. Now if someone knows what the public interest is and wants to pursue or work in the name of it, I certainly cannot object. But pursuing the public interest is quite different from working for it. One cannot hand over a report or memo or any other piece of analysis to the public interest. Without clients, who would eagerly reach for that table of numbers or bit of wisdom that analysts can provide? Without clients, who would need analysts?

Besides being receivers of analytical goodies, clients are useful. They help solve problems. They are good sources of intelligence themselves. They may know how to select problems and perhaps even define them. In exchange for their analysts' services, they say to the rest of the bureaucratic world: These analysts are OK; they do respectable work. But clients are not mere legitimators; they are the analyst's levers for influencing public policy. Short of running for office, how else can the analyst get his ideas across? The best way to see one's ideas used is to give them to somebody who knows how to use ideas. Just who the clients are and what they want is the subject of this chapter.[1]

WHO IS THE CLIENT?

One aspect of policy analysis in its bureaucratic context is that the analyst's client is not the same as the client of other professionals.

---

1. One caveat: This chapter focuses largely on the analyst's rather than the client's view. I hope to pursue the perspectives of clients in a future work.

The physician, for example, serves patients, and these patients, the beneficiaries of his skills, are his clients. At the federal level, however, policy analysts serve clients who are the users, and not usually the beneficiaries, of their work. Beneficiaries are more likely to be treated by the analyst as a statistical expression, as benefits, such as a reduction in infant mortality rates. Unlike the advocate-planner who works for a local community, the federal policy analyst is distant from the feelings and desires of those whom he ultimately serves. Field trips and data from experiments cannot set quite the same expectations as working directly for somebody. The beneficiaries, the targets of analysis, are taken into account in the design of policies; and they certainly are a political force that can facilitate or deter the implementation of a policy analysis, but only occasionally are they actually clients.

Over his career the analyst will have many clients and many masters to serve. He works within an extended family of clients which is complex and changes over time. When he is a broker of knowledge or advances himself or his own ideas, he serves and works for himself. He may actually feel that he is his own client. Once he knows something about a policy problem, for example, it is natural for him to have a viewpoint and to become an advocate. If the client has no goals and wants to be told what to do, it is likely that the analyst will depart from a textbook stance and tell him. Not content with being a catalyst, the analyst will play decision maker through his dummy client. Some analysts, particularly technicians, see themselves as working for the research and professional community. Other analysts have an inflated conception of their mission: the president is their boss, not the man at the next desk. A policy analysis, moreover, can have many audiences and any one of them can become a client.

"He's the man you work for," one analyst responds. "He's the man who tells you to proceed with the project or approves your analytical recommendations." He is the chief analyst and his bureaucratic client. But after some reflection, this answer proves too simple. For example, it ignores analysts on a committee assignment, who work for the chairman or for the few strong people on the committee. "And this does not mean," another analyst points out, "that you don't also take care of the other people who are your clients or in some way your constituents. You do take care of legislators and anticipate the president's problems."

CLIENT-ANALYST RELATIONSHIPS: INTENTIONS AND INTERACTIONS

The difference between "take care of" and "work for" escapes me. Obviously, some distinctions are being made here. Instead of asking who the client is, suppose we ask what he does? A client either sets the analytical agenda, or uses the analyst, or uses the analyst's work. By this definition—despite the fact that most analysts see their immediate boss, the assistant secretary or secretary, as their client—virtually any actor involved in the making of policy can turn out to be a client. A congressman, the president, an agency, a committee, a lobbyist, a citizen—all conceivably can be clients. Any one of them potentially can ask the analyst to do something or can use what he does. Some are unaware, unwilling, and unintended clients. Others are quite the opposite; that is, they are quite consciously the clients of analysts, while it is the analysts themselves who lack intention and are unaware. In short, what the client does—who he is—depends on mutual intentions and interaction.

Let me explain. Neither client nor analyst exists by himself. When clients are identified, social relationships between client and analysts are also specified. Depending on the social proximity between the client and analyst, the frequency of interaction will vary. But this interaction is also based on the intentions of both the client and the analyst. The client, for example, may intend to use the analyst's work, whereas the analyst, say a technician, couldn't care less; indeed, if he had known of the client's intentions, he would never have done the work to begin with. Assuming that the frequency of interaction will vary with these intentions—that is, the more the analyst wants to work for a client and the more that client wants that analyst's work, the greater the frequency of interaction—we can identify four main types of client-analyst relationships. These are summarized in table 2.

The designation of the type of relationship also provides a convenient way of referring to clients; thus, there are immediate, peripheral, remote, and future clients. For example, the immediate relationship occurs when the analyst in the bureaucracy works on a request from his immediate client, the secretary. The client expects an answer and the analyst intends to give him one. At the other extreme, where the analyst is working on something with no particular client in mind and in fact where there is no serious client looking for his work, there is no present interaction;

TABLE 2: Client-Analyst Relationships

Does Client Intend to Use Analyst or His Analysis?	Does Analyst Intend for Client to Use Him or His Analysis?	Frequency of Interaction	Relationship Type
1. Yes	Yes	High	Immediate
2. Yes	No	Low-High	Peripheral
3. No	Yes	Low	Remote
4. No	No	None	Future

any relationship that might exist will be in the future, with some future client. In the immediate relationship, one would expect a high degree of contact and communication—perhaps even trust —in selecting, defining, and solving policy problems. In the peripheral and remote relationships, the frequency of interaction depends on the client. A stubborn peripheral client with a foot-dragging analyst can still create a situation of high interaction —remember the daily meetings of DOT's revenue sharing task force. On the other hand, a willing analyst with a disinterested and remote client is not likely to hear his petition answered. Let us explore a number of examples to illustrate the classification.

Recall the analyst who worked for the Urban Mass Transportation Administration. Shortly after the revenue sharing program was announced, Senator Harrison A. Williams, Jr. of New Jersey, a Democrat, contacted Secretary Volpe for information. After a procedure downward through the chain of command, the analyst was assigned to meet with the senator, who refers to himself as "the daddy of mass transit." The half-hour meeting with Senator Williams was important to the analyst, for, as he explained, "it doesn't matter whether the man is Republican or Democrat, we help our friends." Theoretically, the analyst was in a difficult situation because he was working for three clients with perhaps divergent interests: his immediate superior, the administrator of the Urban Mass Transportation agency; the head of the department's revenue sharing task force, Deputy Under Secretary John P. Olsson; and Senator Williams and his staff. In the particular situation, however, of meeting with an agency sup-porter, Senator Williams, the analyst was open and candid and treated the senator as his immediate client. Although the analyst basically favored the block-grant approach which was a feature of the president's program, he did point out to the senator the "difficulty of getting resources by formula allocation to places where needs are greatest." The senator wanted information and the analyst was happy to provide it.

The analyst is also used by and uses the lobbyist, a peripheral client. An analyst at HUD's Federal Insurance Administration, for example, meets frequently with representatives from the insurance industry to get their viewpoint. They are quite helpful in informing him about which policy recommendations would be favorably received by the White House. The lobbyist in a peripheral relationship is helpful because he wants to use the analyst. Explaining the process, the HUD analyst said, "We get together often with these representatives. They may drop the name of someone with whom they have spoken in, say, the Department of Labor, and describe that person's feeling on a particular issue. If we are interested in pursuing it, we will then call that person in the Department of Labor and talk more with him."

These peripheral clients do not order the analyst to do anything; rather, they subtly influence him by planting an idea in his head. When another HUD analyst was on a field trip to design an evaluation of neighborhood facility centers, a number of local actors approached him and complained about HUD regulations which required a center to serve a variety of purposes. Some citizens wanted a single-purpose center—say, for recreation—and the analyst commented, "We will try to get more data on this and see if we can build a case to get that policy changed."[2]

Analysts are often clients. For example, from time to time OMB analysts from the evaluation office have been the peripheral clients of agency analysts. Because OMB analysts have seen themselves as upholders of standards of analysis, their role as client has not always been subtle; indeed, sometimes it has been openly acrimonious, causing conflict in their interactions within OMB and with the particular agency. A case in point is that of the OMB

---

2. The Neighborhood Facilities Program was authorized by Section 703 of the 1968 Housing and Urban Development Act. It provided grants to help local public bodies finance the development of neighborhood centers to serve the health, educational, social, and recreational needs of low and moderate income communities; see *Neighborhood Facilities: A Study of Operating Facilities*, U.S. Department of Housing and Urban Development (Washington, D.C., December 1973), p. 3.

analyst who wanted the General Services Administration (GSA) to study changing its accounting system so that direct comparisons between GSA's activities and the private sector could be made. The costs of GSA's maintenance of buildings, for example, could then be compared with the private sector's cost. Each year OMB and GSA agree on issues to be studied for the coming year, and issues that might embarrass the agency are not usually chosen. OMB's budget examiners and GSA agreed that the accounting issue should not be studied; accordingly, the examiners prepared a letter to GSA identifying the issues for 1968/69 but omitting the accounting study. The OMB analyst, who had argued with the examiners for several years over this issue, was as determined as ever that GSA would study it. So he wrote his own version of the issue letter, including in it the accounting study. Both letters arrived on the desk of the director of OMB, and, in the words of the analyst, "the director was forced to choose between the examiners' innocuous letter and mine. He could not dodge the issue." OMB's director signed the analyst's letter, thus ordering a study that GSA vehemently did not want to do. One suspects that any study that GSA analysts will do on this subject will satisfy their immediate agency clients rather than their peripheral OMB clients.

The number of potential peripheral clients is quite large. The reason, simply, is that once the analyst commits his information to paper, that information takes on an independent existence. Any reader of a policy analysis can become a client if he chooses to use the information. Indeed, the same policy report can be used by opposing sides in the policy process. Who the analyst's immediate or peripheral client is, then, seems to be a function of which side the analyst wants to win. Consider the situation of Dr. W. Edward Cushen and his staff from the Technical Analysis Division (TAD) of the National Bureau of Standards after they had completed a study of the criminal activity of defendants not in jail but awaiting trial. During Senate hearings on a Department of Justice proposal for preventive detention, TAD's study became an issue.[3] Each side claimed that the study supported its position. We can see this

3. The proposal would have authorized the legal pretrial detention of certain "dangerous" defendants. It was offered by the Nixon administration in response to increasing crime rates, trial delays, and a decreasing reliance on money bail; see the *Congressional Quarterly Weekly*, 19 October 1969, p. 2019.

clearly in formal statements which are part of the record. First, the Department of Justice:

The National Institute of Law Enforcement and Criminal Justice of the Law Enforcement Assistance Administration has released a study by the National Bureau of Standards on pretrial recidivism. The Department of Justice notes that this study strongly documents the need for the Administration's legislative proposal for pretrial detention of dangerous criminal defendants.[4]

Then, Senator Sam J. Ervin, Jr., chairman of the subcommittee that was holding the hearings and a strong opponent of preventive detention:

I am pleased that the Law Enforcement Assistance Administration of the Department of Justice has released its study on bail reform and the operation of Washington's criminal courts. This study was commissioned by the Department of Justice many months ago, after the Department had proposed its preventive detention legislation. The study promises to be the first thorough statistical analysis of the operation of the criminal courts of Washington. It should be extremely helpful to the Congress in evaluating the pleas of necessity which have been presented on behalf of preventive detention. . . .

It is to the credit of the Law Enforcement Assistance Administration that it continued the study until completion and then released it, despite the fact that it proves to be very damaging to the Department of Justice's case for preventive detention.

I regret that before this study was released the Department tried to slip its preventive detention proposal through Congress by hiding it under a misleading title of the District of Columbia Crime Bill. This extraordinary approach toward the legislative process suggests to me that the Department had advance warning that its own study would not support the claims it has made on behalf of preventive detention.[5]

Putting aside the dig at the administration's legislative strategy, it is quite clear that the participants were drawing very different conclusions from the same report. To be more exact, the participants had drawn their conclusions before reading the report. Senator Ervin, as a defender of constitutional rights, believed that preventive detention was in conflict with the Fifth, Sixth, and Eighth amendments. John Mitchell, attorney general, saw the proposal as part of a broader administration policy to get tough on

4. U.S., Congress, Senate, Committee on the Judiciary, *Preventive Detention Hearings* before the Subcommittee on Constitutional Rights, 91st Cong., 2d sess., 1970, p. 1194.

5. *Ibid.*, p. 1195.

crime and had actually submitted a preventive detention bill to Congress before commissioning the TAD study. At the hearings the objectives of both sides were simple. Senator Ervin, for the record, would use the TAD study to show that recidivism rates were low, that is, that only a small percentage of defendants were involved in criminal activity while out on bail and awaiting trial. The Department of Justice's spokesman, Deputy Attorney General Richard G. Kleindienst, while not trying to discredit the TAD report, which his department had paid for, would try to interpret the figures in such a way as to show that the rate of recidivism was quite high and that, therefore, preventive detention was required. As an example, here is some of the testimony:

Senator ERVIN. Well you certainly couldn't afford to imprison 94 innocent people to get the six out of a hundred that are convicted of some crime while released on bail? . . .

The only scientific study that I have ever heard of in respect to the District of Columbia is the one which the Department of Justice commissioned LEAA to do through the Bureau of Standards.

Mr. KLEINDIENST. That could possibly be true, Senator . . . .

Senator ERVIN. And they came to the conclusion there that—I interpret the report to show that of those who were arrested for violent crimes, only 5 percent committed another violent crime while on bail.

Mr. KLEINDIENST. No, I don't believe that is correct, Senator. I would like to comment on the National Bureau of Standards study, because here again is a situation where you have some statistical information, but like all statistics, if they are not carefully examined, you have to wonder what their relevancy is.

To begin with, that study did not and was not commissioned to study all crime. Perhaps half of the crime that existed was not reported at that time. . . . About one-third of the sample defendants were not released from jail. If you consider the criminals excluded from the study, then the recidivism rate would be more like 40 percent.

We feel that these statistics in the National Bureau of Standards report support our bill because we feel that the study suggests a true recidivism rate approaching 40 percent.[6]

To complete the record, Senator Ervin called in Dr. Cushen and his analysts to testify:

Senator ERVIN. In other words, would it be accurate for me to say that with respect to the hard data that is indisputable data?

Mr. CUSHEN. Yes.

Senator ERVIN. Or as nearly indisputable as—

6. *Ibid.*, p. 92.

Mr. CUSHEN. As indisputable as you can get.

Senator ERVIN. Data to be collected in the field of this kind which indicated a rearrest rate of 7 percent for felonies and rearrest rate of 5 percent for violent crimes and rearrest rate of 6 percent for dangerous crimes from those in the sample who had been initially charged for similar crimes.

Mr. CUSHEN. Yes.

Senator ERVIN. The 40-percent figure is a figure which is based, not upon hard data, but upon the application of standard statistical procedures in this field?

Mr. CUSHEN. I think it is based on pretty good judgment. It is certainly not based on our numbers. . . .

Senator ERVIN. . . . I want to commend the excellence of your study. . . . It is the first scientific study that sheds any light whatsoever on this subject.

Mr. CUSHEN. We are quite grateful to you, sir, and we are looking forward to opportunities whereby this particular profession can really be of increased value.[7]

A few years after the hearings, Dr. Cushen delivered a lecture in which he cited the TAD criminal justice study as a success.[8] It had taken a year to do and had cost the Justice Department about $180,000. John Mitchell had not found the answers to his liking, but Sam Ervin had. Ervin had become the analyst's immediate client, while the original client, the Department of Justice, had slipped to peripheral status.

Now let's look at remote clients. Central coordinating bodies, such as the Domestic Council, are often remote clients, particularly when busy policymakers turn over their jobs to zealous but uninformed staff men. Consider the situation when President Nixon thought it would be a good idea for the federal government to give some relief to local property taxpayers. Perhaps the government could adopt a value-added tax and take on some of the burden of financing local schools.[9] It was an interesting idea, and the Domestic Council set to work on it. After about a month of activity within the White House, Domestic Council staffers broke

7. *Ibid.*, pp. 137–38.

8. It was not such a success from the perspective of what happened afterward to TAD and Cushen himself, its director; see chapter 5.

9. A value-added tax is a form of sales tax which is collected at each stage of the manufacturing process in proportion to the value added at that stage. For an introduction to the problem and its political context, see Frank V. Fowlkes, "Economic Report/Administration Leans to Value-Added Tax to Help Solve National Fiscal Crises," *National Journal* 4, no. 6 (5 February 1972): 210–19.

down the problem and assigned pieces to various agencies, such as HEW, OMB, the Council of Economic Advisors, the Department of the Treasury, and the Advisory Commission on School Finance (which had been appointed a few years before the president got interested in property tax relief and had been working in the general area). While Treasury had been collecting information on value-added taxation since World War II, when the tax had been proposed to finance the war, it had no information on the property tax because it was a local tax. Yet the various analysts had to be concerned about the property tax; after all, the proposal was a property tax relief measure. At HEW, for example, the analysts wanted to improve the level of school fiscal support and the equality of the distribution of funds, but they could not escape property tax issues. Upon investigation, they found that there was no simple per-pupil formula for distributing tax relief. States had quite different uses of the property tax, and the incidence of tax was not consistent with a per-pupil distribution formula. If such a formula were used, there would be "random windfalls." Their conclusion was that the president would not be able to relieve the property tax as he wanted to. But when they tried to communicate the results of their work to the staff of the Domestic Council, they got nowhere. The staff, composed of a lawyer, a political scientist, and two military lieutenants, either did not understand or did not want to understand. The president had wanted property tax relief and the analysts had the temerity to suggest that it might not be possible. In isolation these remote clients, the staff of the Domestic Council, wrote their own proposal and ignored the advice of the HEW analysts. As the 1972 election time neared, the value-added tax proposal evaporated, because "no one proposes a new tax in an election year."[10]

Many long-term studies or investments in analytical capability are for future clients. The future is the great comforter of wounded egos. Besides, we do know that today's discarded notions become the policies of the future. The important thing is to preserve the policy notion in some sort of record. Take the case of an HEW analyst who was working during a presidential transition. His work on educational loan banks had been converted into the language of

10. A former OMB analyst believes the proposal died at least six months before the election because of the lack of political support and opposition from agencies such as OMB.

legislation; but without a president to sponsor it, the proposal was gathering dust. Then a senator's office called the analyst and asked for some legislation on educational loan banks. So he got his proposal out of the files and sent it to the senator, who then submitted it to Congress as a bill. The analyst thinks he must have been the only one to read the bill, because nothing happened. But at least he had put his proposal into the record for some future client. The senator, as a kind of publisher, was not the analyst's client. There was no interaction between the two of them. They were both playing a game for the future.

If the analyst sticks with it, the future has a way of working itself around to the present. In the 1960s, for example, a Treasury analyst was interested in the costs of various federal credit mechanisms. Toward the end of his term, President Johnson had proposed extending credit by having an urban development bank. Then President Nixon was interested in a federal bank for financing. By 1971, the analyst was busy using his work on credit mechanisms in drafting speeches for the secretary of treasury. It does not always take much for a future client to become an immediate client.

INFORMAL AND FORMAL CLIENTS

Part of the difficulty in locating the analyst's clients is that on paper he works for somebody but in fact he works for someone else. This is routinely the case where analysts have close ties to the staff of congressional committees or where a congressman dominates a particular policy area. The Treasury Department provides examples of both situations. Consider the analysts who work for its Office of Tax Analysis. Their formal clients are the director of the office and his boss, the assistant secretary for tax policy. Their informal clients are the staff of the Joint Committee on Internal Revenue Taxation. Bureaucratic analysts routinely exchange revenue estimates and information on the consequences of various proposed changes in taxation with congressional analysts, and such exchanges can be in the interest of both clients.

When it comes to money matters, Congressman Wilbur D. Mills, former chairman of the House Committee on Ways and Means, set the agenda for many analysts. No doubt if he asked for assistance from the bureaucracy, he got it. But he did not have to ask. If he was interested in a proposal, Treasury analysts would examine it if for no other reason than to offer some alternatives that would achieve the same objective with less loss in revenue. Mills, for example, suggested that persons with incomes below national poverty levels be exempt from income taxation. Treasury analysts were sympathetic with the objective and had tried before to accomplish it, so one of them worked out what combination of deductions and exemptions would be best. The figures for the various alternatives were then pulled together for the secretary's testimony to Congress.

If one took snapshots of the policy analyst in action, the actor who is in more pictures with him than anyone else is probably his client. When an OMB analyst has more contact with White House staffers than with OMB examiners or directors, it is likely that he is working for the White House rather than OMB. Nor is it so unusual for an analyst to view the director of his office as an unnecessary step in the policy process, as the person who "just passes on the recommendations without change." In such cases, the analyst will be in contact with the person who receives these recommendations. An agency analyst assigned to work on a project for the Domestic Council will actually find himself working for a secondary tier of clients, one composed of assistant secretaries and White House staff. Or an analyst may find that he is co-opted by the people he is investigating. As one analyst put it, "We reflect the operating people because we must work with field program people daily." Thus, in proximity to the formal client there is the informal client. Who the analyst writes for, gets guidance from, and gives advice to is a surer clue for identifying the client than the formality of assignment.

As the policy process chugs along, informal clients displace formal clients. The analyst starts out working for the head of his office. After a while, he is called in to brief a deputy assistant secretary or a staff assistant to the secretary. Soon, if the idea flies, he will have greater contact with the department's general counsel, and then he will be writing supporting pieces for congressional testimony and explanations for congressmen and citizens. Of course, nothing operates that simply in the bureaucracy; the displacement process is actually more convoluted, with many stops and starts and interruptions. Where it is simple, one suspects that displacement is one of the privileges of rank: a request from the White House somehow has more weight than what the boss asked you to do yesterday.

THE COLLECTIVE CLIENT

Since analysts are often loaned to interagency teams, they wear a number of hats. They have to be loyal to their agency if for no other reason than to ensure that they have a home to return to when the committee's work is completed. At the same time, they have to be responsive to the committee's various members and to its mission. The analyst working for multiple clients is bound to feel some conflict, but he also enjoys advantages. A committee can be a site for the building of consensus. While it can happen that a study is completed without laying the proper groundwork—which is like hitting the interested parties with a cold fish—the analyst who is able to take into account the various viewpoints of the committee members may be able to achieve acceptance for his work as it progresses.

Recall the analyst who was working for a presidential advisory committee on school desegregation. He and his colleagues would report to the committee, get advice, and then go back to their office to work things out. At the committee meetings there was an opportunity to communicate differences. When Donald Rumsfeld, director of OEO, for example, suggested using an OEO poverty line as a guideline for distributing funds, the analysts were able to point out some disadvantages, such as a lack of statistical information, to such an approach. For their part, the committee members were able to inform the analysts of the objective of pushing more money to the South, an important political consideration that might not have occurred to the analysts if they had been working in their usual isolation.

Sometimes the analyst will have severe disagreements with committee members, and in such situations it pays to have clients back at the agency who can resolve the conflict between agency and committee preferences. HEW analysts, for example, wanted to set aside a certain amount of money for compensatory education programs. Committee members Daniel P. Moynihan and George P. Shultz were against such allocations, mainly because of the lack of evidence that such programs work and because of possible overlap with existing federal programs.[11] The HEW analysts still thought that, when funds were concentrated, compensatory education did work; therefore, they went to their boss, HEW Secretary Robert H. Finch. According to one of the analysts, Finch told them, "All right, you prepare your stuff to convince these birds." The analysts came to the next meeting all primed. They sat at the side, and at the table were the various clients. The discussion proceeded around the table, with each of the clients speaking in turn. Shultz argued against compensatory education. Then, when his own turn came, Finch said, "Well compensatory education is all right"—but he did not offer to give the floor to the analysts, who were about to jump out of their skins. At that point John Mitchell, the attorney general, read from the president's message and stated that he was the president's lawyer and that the president's interest must be preserved; therefore, there was no need for further discussion—compensatory education had to be in. Afterward, when Secretary Finch and one of the analysts were driving back to the office, Finch asked him how he liked the outcome. The analyst replied, "Well for a while I didn't, but it turned out all right." Then Finch, with a smile on his face, said, "I guess my phone call to Mitchell helped." From this incident the analyst concluded that "a little bit of power always helps in an analysis."

THE CHIEF ANALYST AS CLIENT

Probably the analyst's most important and immediate client is the chief analyst. Depending on the location of the analytical shop, he may be an assistant secretary, a deputy assistant secretary, or a director. He is the person in charge of an agency's analysts. He is the man in the middle, between his analysts and his clients. He will influence what his staff does and he will usually be in charge of developing analytical procedures for the other shops in the agency.

11. One can understand their reluctance, because the government was already heavily involved with compensatory education programs, such as Title I of ESEA. According to Murphy, Title I of the Elementary and Secondary Education Act of 1965 was "the largest program ever administered by the United States Office of Education (USOE)." It provided financial assistance (in fiscal year 1973, $1.6 billion) "for the schooling of disadvantaged children in urban slums and poor rural areas." See Jerome T. Murphy, "The Education Bureaucracies Implement Novel Policy: The Politics of Title I of ESEA, 1965–72," in *Policy and Politics in America,* ed. Allan P. Sindler (Boston: Little, Brown and Co., 1973), p. 162.

Usually an entrepreneur, he will have both political and analytical skills. Sometimes politicians become chief analysts, but technicians seldom do. The job requires refined communication skills, since the chief analyst must often interpret his analysts' work to technically unsophisticated clients. Of course, the analyst does occasionally work directly with the client—say, with the secretary of a department—but even then the chief analyst will be around to back him up in case he trips over his own words.

In addition to defining and selling the analytical product, the chief analyst plays the important role of insulator. Frequently the client will neither understand nor appreciate analysis. Like other people, in the bureaucracy and out, analysts want to be loved. As one analyst puts it, "A person wants to feel appreciated; a person wants it recognized when he's done a good job, recognized by a person who understands and appreciates his work." Now when the client is not appreciative, the chief analyst can be. When the client asks stupid questions, the chief analyst can make them appear sensible. When the client asks for analysis and more detail to postpone making a decision, the chief analyst can take out the sham quality of the exercise and emphasize its future utility. In short, the chief analyst can insulate his staff from the demoralizing effects of an ignorant but well-meaning superior.

It is not easy for the chief analyst to play insulator, because it is very easy for analysts to become cynical about their work. Cues are abundant. When the shop starts experiencing a high turnover, for example, even the most insensitive analyst will know that he is not appreciated. The quickest cure for such a situation is for the chief analyst to take the offensive. He has to show his analysts that he is capable of getting across his point of view to the client. He has to see that the shop makes an "impact on the program." This is one reason, among many, why the chief analyst is seldom an objective intellectual eunuch but rather an advocate with preferences. Let me show you what I mean by referring to a speech by another analyst.[12]

In 1973 the Department of Interior got a shot in the analytical arm when an experienced and capable analyst moved from HEW to become the department's assistant secretary for policy analysis.

12. The speech, by a federal policy analyst, was made at a conference at the Graduate School of Public Policy, University of California, Berkeley, in October 1973.

One issue the department faced was whether or not to lease public lands in Colorado, Utah, and Wyoming to private companies for extracting oil from shale. Actually, the issue had been studied a number of times over the past decade, but what would the new chief analyst say? Here is an imaginary description of the critical meeting with the secretary of interior:

Sometime next month the secretary will have this same circle of people back into his office, and there will be a little random discussion at the beginning of the meeting about the program, and the secretary will sit back and he will say, "Well, what do you say, shall we dig it?" And he will go around the room, and I would imagine that something like this will happen.

The assistant secretary, for instance, for energy and minerals will say "Yeah, let's dig it, but the only problem with this program is it isn't fat enough for the private companies. We really should subsidize it, Mr. Secretary."

The assistant secretary for land and resources will say, first to himself, "My bureau, the Bureau of Land Management, will manage this leasing operation. My bureau helped design the operation." And then he will say to the secretary, "Yes, Mr. Secretary, let's dig it, and the program as it stands is just fine for digging oil shale."

The assistant secretary for fish and wildlife and parks will be sitting next and he will say, "For Christ's sake, Mr. Secretary, don't dig it. You will foul up the fishing, you will disturb the antelope. Don't dig it." The commissioner of Indian affairs will probably pass.

The assistant secretary for legislation will say, "Mr. Secretary, you will lose more; because of the energy crisis you will lose more points on the Hill by not digging it than you will by digging it."

The assistant secretary for management will say, "Well, Mr. Secretary, I don't really care whether you dig it or not; but if you do, the organizational arrangements for digging it have not been well worked out."

OK, now it has come around to the assistant secretary for policy analysis. Now one thing the assistant secretary for policy analysis could do would be to say, "Well, Mr. Secretary, as you know, I don't take positions on controversial issues. I am here to provide you with analysis and information. Anything you want to know about the possible effects of this program or the alternatives to this program I will be happy to supply you with, but of course I don't contaminate myself by taking positions. I have all these neat guys on my staff who can calculate any elasticity you want." Well, that could be one way he could react, but of course he doesn't. He says, "Mr. Secretary, I favor option two for the following reasons," and he establishes a position of his own.

Now let me point out why he does that. He is in the secretary's office daily to make decisions. What the secretary wants from him is help in making decisions. He wants his opinion on what should be done. He expects his opinion to be backed by analysis; but even if there is no analysis to back it, he must offer an opinion. He is not necessarily a dirty-handed advocate in a situation like this, and the Mr. Clean image of the uncommitted, information-gathering analyst does not apply to a man in this position. It may apply some places, but it does not here. Whether he has any effect on the secretary's decisions really depends fundamentally on his personal standing with the secretary, and he cannot maintain that standing except by repeatedly taking positions.

The chief analyst cannot just preach that analysis should be used; he has to use it.

THE CLIENT'S EXPECTATIONS

What do clients expect of analysts? Some analysts, particularly technicians, do not have the faintest idea. Sheltered by the heads of the analytical shop, such analysts live in a dream world. Their more realistic counterparts, however, are not much better off when it comes to generalizing about the expectations of the client. Everyone agrees that expectations differ with clients, or "the men who are running the show." And most analysts agree that some accommodation to a client's needs is necessary. As one of them says, "I am not interested in forcing my ideas or techniques on my boss. . . . I realize that I must change my style until it meets the inclinations and style of my boss. It is his prerogative to make decisions. I must create the process that meets his needs." We have already discussed the client's need for timely information for decisions and support (see chapter 2). The client also expects the analyst to provide protection and direction.

PROTECTION AND DIRECTION

While his supportive analysis provides protection for a policy, the analyst is also expected to provide more immediate protection for the policymaker. At a minimum, the analyst feels that he should keep his client out of trouble. It stands to reason that, if he protects his client, then he will also protect himself. Clients want to appear knowledgeable, particularly when making an appearance before a congressional committee. If the analyst has done his job, then the client will not find himself taking ridiculous or indefensible positions. Sometimes the analyst protects his client by being his "objective sounding board." Clients like to try out their ideas without getting hurt, and analysts who are good listeners and know when to criticize can be their audience. The client expects the analyst to get out of the building and know what is going on. An out-of-date sounding board is dangerous. Clients do not want to be jeopardized by a study or an analyst. Consider what happened when the Office of Education assigned one evaluation task to an analyst. In order to compare results over time, the analyst suggested that a "Coleman report" type of study be done; but the very idea of doing anything that would revive the negative feelings of school men and their supporters was enough for OE to kill the idea. In this case, the analyst should have known better because of past HEW efforts to restrict the distribution of Coleman's work; James S. Coleman has noted that his report, *Equality of Educational Opportunity*, was suppressed by his client, HEW.[13] In short, the client wants the analyst to keep him out of trouble, not put him into it.

Clients also expect analysts to provide some sense of direction to them as individuals and to their agencies. How much direction is a function of how much the client already knows about where he is going. If he is the kind of client who says "tell me what to do" or "please shoulder the burden for me," the direction can be considerable. At the other extreme, if he is the kind who has strong opinions of his own—who wants to hear various points of view but reserve the decisions for himself—then the analyst will be one voice among many. The analyst may find himself not so much providing direction as ascertaining how to get to a preconceived place. During President Johnson's administration, the decision was made to have a government-subsidized supersonic transport (SST). A number of analysts continued to suggest better alternatives to a complete governmental subsidy of the SST, such as a cooperative arrangement between government and industry, but they got nowhere. If industry would not pay for it and the government wanted an SST, then the question became one of how government should finance it.

In looking for direction, clients all too often seek simple answers to complex problems. They want a table or a scale to tinker with.

13. James S. Coleman, *Policy Research in the Social Sciences* (Morristown, N.J.: General Learning Press, 1972), p. 13. A detailed version of the proposed "Coleman Revisited" evaluation study is contained in Milbrey Wallin McLaughlin, *Evaluation and Reform: The Elementary and Secondary Education Act of 1965, Title I*, R-1292-RC (Santa Monica: Rand Corporation, January 1974), pp. 79–82.

After the "hard facts," they want a "clear-cut solution." The expectation is that analysts should be able to answer the client's questions, but one analyst recalls how different his bosses were in their expectations. His present boss wants a full listing of the pros and cons of an issue. His previous boss, on the other hand, wanted a report that would back up the analyst's recommendation; and when he was not presented with a simple and single recommendation, he would say, "Don't give me this mishmash; I want to know what to do." The client's desire for direction is usually for the short term. He wants the analysis so that he can do something about it before he leaves his office. Clients set up some analytic offices to be nothing but short-term advice mills, while others are given the mission of planning the future configuration of the agency. Often the planning mission is just a device for legitimating the analyst's poking into short-term problems and criticizing other people's visions. The head of a major federal agency, for example, described his expectations of his program planning office and his chief analyst in this way:

We wanted more than anything else to break out of the non-productive, over-simplified type of planning . . . and get someone who could analyze the potential comparative cost-benefits of Federal programs and design evaluations which would really have some usefulness to us. . . .

X knew that politics aren't rational, but he wasn't always able to accept the fact when we would make program decisions because they were good for the President even though there were better alternative programs. But this was no particular problem. My view of his office was that it should be somewhat detached from day to day affairs and able to speak to the rest of the shop independently. X rather liked this ex cathedra posture which I encouraged, but I don't think it won him lots of friends.[14]

Sometimes when the analyst is told to plan the future department, it is just a means for getting him out of the way of more pressing and operational matters. When the client assigns an analyst to provide short-term direction, he knows that the analyst will be under control but also underfoot.

In providing protection or direction, the analyst can preempt the client in making the decision. As we pointed out in chapter 4, the analyst, using his feelings for political feasibility, substitutes his own policy objectives and rules out alternatives in selecting and

14. From a letter available in my files. I have substituted X for the analyst's name.

defining problems. Probably clients would prefer to use their own judgment, political or otherwise. The incentives in the bureaucracy, however, encourage the analyst to anticipate his client's calculations. Ironically, the client establishes these incentives. He contributes to the perception that acceptance of advice is success. It is a subtle business. The analyst, sensing the "environment of decision making," will exclude a recommendation if he does not feel some receptivity on the part of the client. He will not suggest a national strategy when he knows his client has a strong bias for dealing with state governments. The conventional wisdom has it that analysts leave out important qualitative variables in their work. They are supposed to shun the softer, more qualitative, more tactical and strategic dimensions of public policy problems. From his superior vantage point and political sensitivity, the client is supposed to add these dimensions to the policy process. And so he does—except the analyst may have got there before him.

STYLE: EXECUTIVES AND INTELLECTUALS

The style of a client will affect what he expects from his analysts. One prevailing style of clients in the federal government is that of the executive. Such a client, as one analyst described his assistant secretary, is "frightened by any form of intellectual discussion." C. Wright Mills, in describing the chief executives of corporations, caught the essential qualities of executive-clients:

> Among them are those who resent reading a report or a letter longer than one page, such avoidance of words being rather general. They seem somehow suspicious of long-winded speeches, except when they are the speakers, and they do not, of course, have the time. They are very much of the age of the "briefing," of the digest, of the two-paragraph memo. Such reading as they do, they often delegate to others, who clip and summarize for them. They are talkers and listeners rather than readers or writers.[15]

These are impatient men who often are briefed on the run or in the bathroom. They want specific responses and are not shy about expressing their displeasure when they do not get what they want. An analytical office that proceeds with them in an "up-in-the-air academic manner" will soon be out of business. Often they have their own ideas and see no need for analysts to provide them with

15. C. Wright Mills, *The Power Elite* (New York: Oxford University Press, 1959), p. 130.

material. For them, policymaking is mostly politics with perhaps a little analysis.

The intellectual, a client with a completely opposite style, reads and is reflective.[16] Because he enjoys solving problems, he likes the company of analysts and the clarity and order they bring to problems. He likes to define the problem with the analyst, not merely delegate it to him. Only infrequently is the intellectual a former analyst. He may have been a lawyer, statistician, academician, or businessman; but what is crucial is the quality of mind and personality he brings to the job. McNamara is not the only example, as some may think. Here, for instance, is an analyst's positive description of Secretary Elliot L. Richardson, who has been in charge of numerous federal departments:

He is by nature analytical. He is by nature a man who wants to approach problems objectively. He is by nature a man who is perfectly willing to put aside for a time the obvious and sometimes overwhelming political forces that may be pushing him in certain directions in order to think carefully through what the problem is and determine whether or not or how he personally wants to operate, what proposals he wants to make, how he wants to rationalize the positions he wants to take. He's very much willing to do this, and therefore he very much has provided a very strong stimulus to the development of good analytical capabilities, not only in my office but insofar as possible throughout the department.

Some analysts are of the opinion that policy analysis cannot flourish unless the client is more an intellectual than an executive. Thus, according to one, if the client

conceives of problems as being exclusively in the domain of political bargaining and negotiations and conceives of the allocation of resources and the shaping of policies as essentially a process of working out acceptable arrangements with congressional committees and with key congressmen and with key senators and with key governors and mayors—that is, if he sees it essentially as a problem of negotiation, compromise, and not as a problem which has an intellectual input, let alone that intellectual leadership should play a role—then the analytical shop will not have a central role to play in decision making.

The analyst's conclusion about the lack of centrality of the analytical shop is debatable. No doubt the fortunes of a particular shop can

16. In contrast to the executive style, I intend the designation of intellectual to include an openness to ideas; but sometimes there is the "rigid intellectual," a know-it-all who uses his analysts to expand and justify his strongly held policy preferences.

decline, but this does not mean that policy analysis necessarily goes out of business. The client could be getting his policy advice from other analysts. The nature of the advice might change; it might be a bit more oriented, say, to short-term political forces. But what is more likely to happen is that the analysis stays the same, while the mode of communication and interaction with the client changes. In a major department, for example, analysts had been working for a dynamic secretary, an ex-governor and certainly a politician, who was replaced by a more studious person with a background in mathematical statistics. The new secretary reads more and asks more questions. Because of the new secretary's background, the analysts have to be more prepared to answer detailed technical questions on such matters as statistical inference. According to one of the analysts, they do the same analytical work but communicate it differently. In situations where the analyst does not change his style to match a new client, he will be ignored. The point is that the use of analysis is precluded *not* by the politically oriented client but by the analyst who finds it difficult to adjust to or live with such a client. Both executives and intellectuals are political, and it is up to the analyst to demonstrate his usefulness to them.

Calibrating what the secretary of an agency wants or needs is a continuing task for analysts. Most of them will agree that if policy analysis is to be effective, the client must really want analysis. Then, in the next breath they will say, "Well, not everybody is a McNamara or Hitch."[17] This meaning is twofold. First, few clients come to their jobs with a built-in predilection for analysis. As in other staff relationships, confidence must be built between client and analyst. The analyst must learn when and when not to speak, even when he knows something. He has to sell himself as well as a set of techniques. Second, clients do not always understand the limitations of analysis. The client has a mess of complex problems on his agenda, and what he is looking for is help. Unfortunately, the analyst is likely to complicate his life with details that interfere with decisions. The analysis may suggest what not to do rather than

17. Charles J. Hitch, an internationally recognized economist and analyst, was comptroller of the U.S. Department of Defense (DOD) from 1961 to 1965. He was an early proponent of the program budgeting system introduced in DOD during Robert McNamara's tenure as secretary of defense; see Charles J. Hitch and Roland McKean, *The Economics of Defense in the Nuclear Age* (Cambridge, Mass.: Harvard University Press, 1960).

what to do. The resulting frustration for both client and analyst leads to the secret hope of many analysts: one of these days, clients will be analysts.

But this is wishful thinking. Suppose the analyst did have a technically sophisticated client, then what? To save his own time, the client would ask for studies. He would also understand the limitations and nuances of the analytical product. His decisions, however, might not be much different from those of an executive-type client. Somehow, political criteria and nonanalytical information from the White House and Congress would creep into his calculus. If he intends to keep his job, no client can remain an analyst. He takes on the hue and constituency of his agency. He sends grants to strange, undeserving places. He acts just like any other appointed official. He is no longer an analyst.

SHIFTS IN ENVIRONMENT

The environment of policymaking changes, and with it so do the expectations of clients. Under a previous administration, for example, one department's analytical office was content to work for the under secretary, who was an inside man concerned about administration. Then the under secretary was replaced by a more political animal. The chief analyst now found himself in an uncomfortable position. His office was supposed to be "objective," yet all his client wanted was political advice on conducting relations with interest groups. Soon the analytical office was transferred to somebody else, a move that took it some distance from the central decision makers of the department. After a while, the secretary felt that the under secretary should pay more attention to the operating programs of the department and be involved in the budgetary process. Needing a different type of information to perform his new role, the under secretary started to use the analytical shop again, and it soon moved back to his own office.

Of course, sometimes the new broom does not sweep much differently from the old broom. Recalling two assistant secretaries for whom he had worked, one analyst saw both of them as having a good sense of political timing, as looking for and finding openings, and as having contacts and working with the White House. One was less an "academic" than the other; he worried less about the precision of the analysis and techniques than the other, and as a result there was a slight decline in the quality of the work.

Whose presidential administration it is should also make a difference, but what sort of difference is not entirely clear. Many analysts agree that the Nixon administration was much more private than the Johnson administration. There are several schools of thought, however, on the consequences of being private. One school has it that during the Johnson administration, domestic policy issues were discussed publicly, many issues were decided in the public arena, and there was less analysis. Since the Nixon administration was less apt to admit openly that an issue was even being discussed, more analysis was going on. Another school believes that, because Democrats under Johnson controlled both Congress and the White House, the importance and frequency of analysis increased; the party could afford to study policy options openly. In the Nixon administration, without such congressional control, the executive branch did not need analysis; rather, it addressed itself to identifying those elements in policy proposals that would enhance the proposals' chances in Congress. As a member of this school puts it, "Economists are not much help in advising politicians on what will make a problem more popular politically. This type of situation demands justificatory reports, not genuine economic analysis." Still another school believes that the amount of analysis was about the same for both administrations, but that the communication and use of analysis were different. In Johnson's administration a great many policy analysis reports were published for external consumption; in Nixon's, analysis still went on but was quietly slipped into the decision-making process.

Despite the gaps, non sequiturs, and conflicts in these various positions, I suspect that the characteristics of the national administration do affect the demand for and supply of policy analysis. We can dismiss the frequency-of-production questions as trivial. What seems more interesting is the administration's effect on the character of the analysis itself. The Johnson administration, for example, was hungry for policy ideas—as one analyst put it, "they were looking for slogans to sell"—so options, alternatives, and ideas were suggested in various policy analyses. Having inherited many of these "slogans," and with its hands full of other matters, the Nixon administration was not very interested (with a few exceptions) in domestic policy; so its policy analyses were more negative, arguing not to do something. Part of HEW's work on primary and secondary school finance, for instance, urged that the federal government stay out of what was essentially a local matter. Evidently, the HEW analysts felt "a great deal of success," according to one, in that "some new disaster was not hatched." At Interior, a water resource study was based on a Johnson administration objective of ensuring an adequate supply of water. When the Nixon administration came in, cooperation between federal, state, and local governments was to be the keynote. So the analysts had to redo their work to provide incentives for state and local government participation.

As the environment of policymaking changes, new occupants take over old roles. With each new occupant, different expectations are set. The analysts are supposed to adjust, and so is their analysis. Exactly how these shifts alter the character of policy analysis is a research question worth pursuing.

CHOICE

BY THE CLIENT

It is a wonder that anyone listens to the advice of an analyst. He is one among many advisors and, more important, he has no program of his own to operate, no turf from which a client's dependence stems. His client's position is very much like the president's as Sorensen describes it:

In choosing between conflicting advice, the President is also choosing between conflicting advisers, conferring recognition on some while rebuffing others. He will, consequently, take care to pay more attention to the advice of the man who must carry out the decision than the advice of a mere "kibitzer." He will be slow to overrule a Cabinet officer whose pride or prestige have been committed, not only to ease the officer's personal feelings but to maintain his utility and credibility.[18]

There are some clients who take neither analysts nor analysis very seriously, and there is not much the analyst can do about it. Imagine the analyst who was working in an office used as a fallback to handle the overflow of intelligence requests. As he puts it,

Offices such as ours are often displayed as analytical offices and rationalized by the creation of elaborate analytical tools and fancy scientific-sounding labels. To the usual assistant secretary, though, the

18. Theodore C. Sorensen, *Decision-Making in the White House: The Olive Branch or the Arrows* (New York: Columbia University Press, 1963), p. 79.

reason for the existence of the analytical office is to give him a group of right people to keep in reserve for when he really needs them. Normally he can operate on the advice and with the assistance of a few personal staff members. In such interludes the analytical office is allowed to go its own way. When the assistant secretary, though, is pressed in an emergency, the existence of our analytical staff gives him the flexibility to respond.

Why does the client have such discretion to treat his analysts in this cavalier, to-be-used-just-in-case, manner? One answer stems from the fact that the profession of policy analysis is still an emerging one. Its theory and base of knowledge are not so developed as to ensure a monopoly of information for the analyst. Because the policy analyst lacks the compelling authority of the person in a mature profession, such as medicine and law, his client can be more like a customer who is able to shop around for the advice he wants. Certainly the policy analyst is in no position to dictate, like other professionals, "what is good or evil for the client who has no choice but to accede to professional judgment."[19]

Indeed, the client has plenty of choices. If he wants political advice, he can go to the agency's congressional relations staff. If he wants costs, he can call up his budget officer. He can always go outside and hire an expert. One analyst, for instance, recalls that his client, a well-trained economist, was suspicious of a forecast he did on the price of lumber. The client, an under secretary, did not like the choice of coefficients used, so outsiders were called in. Sometimes a new broom comes in with his own built-in set of advisors and ignores the permanent staff. Once a bright Harvard academic came down to Washington to run a major office, bringing with him a number of young and energetic MBAs. The MBAs were given the interesting "intellectual" assignments; the routine assignments went to the permanent staff. After a while the academic wondered why the staff was so hostile and upset with him.

When a new secretary takes over a department he will usually be eager for advice and "ideas on what we can do," but he will not know whom he can trust. This is an opportune time for the analyst

---

19. Ernest Greenwood, "Attributes of a Profession," in *Professionalization*, ed. Howard M. Vollmer and Donald L. Mills (Englewood Cliffs, N.J.: Prentice-Hall, 1966), p. 12. Greenwood distinguishes professionals from nonprofessionals on the basis of a number of attributes, one of which is knowledge-based authority. The nonprofessional has "customers" who are free to choose, whereas the professional has "clients" who "surrendered . . . to professional authority."

to build confidence with the client, yet it is a chance that can easily be missed. A Department of Interior analyst says that when Stewart Udall became secretary, he initially relied on his analysts; but as time passed he became less dependent, learned more about the department's various bureaus, and developed other sources of information within and outside the department. Evidently, Udall decided that he did not want a McNamara-type advisor. As he told the analyst, "I don't want whiz kids; I want whiz kids with a heart. You can't really trade off an Indian child's education with the future of the whooping crane."

One of the problems the analyst encounters in establishing himself with his client is that he and the client may speak different languages. This can happen even in more technically oriented departments. At Treasury, for example, an analyst was trying to improve his writing skills so that he could communicate with his assistant secretary, who is not an economist. Commenting on the decline of his office's influence, he said, "When policy people are unable to understand the advice from the office, they turn to others in the Treasury Department or to outside academic or business people with whom they are familiar. These people generally agree with them initially or simply tell them what they want to hear."

Thus, there are a variety of reasons why the client goes to the competition. He may not want to hurt the feelings of someone he needs. He may not understand or like the advice he hears. He may not trust his analysts. If the client can choose, it is evidence of the analyst's dependence on him. When analysts complain that "no analyst thinks the decision maker pays as much attention to him as he should," it is a sign of the client's superior position in the bureaucratic scheme of things. Competition may or may not result in good advice, but it at least preserves the client's discretion, his ability to choose.

BY THE ANALYST

Some analysts make the mistake of doing the study first and then looking for a client. Imagine the analyst faced with a collective client and conflicting policy objectives. It is all too easy for that analyst to select and work on his own problem. Fine, he may come up with a solution, but he may also find that he has no client for that solution.

Thus, the first analytical problem for any advisor should be to choose his client. Regardless of where he works, there are many clients to work for. Each client provides a particular organizational situation for the conduct of analysis. Since not all clients are policymakers, the analyst has to be careful in making his choice if he wants to make an impact on policy. One cautious analyst, who has learned the hard way, tries to check out a potential client by talking to analysts who have worked in the past for the client. He also talks to the analysts who are currently working for the client but discounts what they have to say. If possible, he even tries to reach the former bosses of the client. When he is interviewed by the client, he tries to ascertain if the client really wants analysis and if it will be possible to develop a productive relationship. With the analyst choosing the client, rather than the other way around, the analyst may have a better chance of getting the type of client and situation he wants.

Probably not many bureaucratic policy analysts do the choosing, nor are they as calculating as Colonel House was in choosing Woodrow Wilson. (House had waited about a decade for the right man to come along, a man who thought as he did and would be a vehicle for getting to power.)[20] Nevertheless, I believe as a minimal criterion, analysts should choose clients who want the type of advice the analyst is prepared to give. One analyst, for example, looks for a client who "is in pain and doesn't know how to get out of pain." His idea is to choose an unsophisticated client who will not second guess him, who wants help, and who believes that the analyst will "make the pain go away." A client with contacts in both academic and political circles is desirable; academic contacts help the analyst with his gathering of policy ideas and knowledge, while political contacts help in the selling of the ideas. Moreover, analysts should look for clients who will be around for several years, not only to be able to do analyses but also to have enough time to establish a working relationship with the client. To this end, analysts should also concern themselves with the style of their prospective clients. The analyst-client relationship is something like a marriage: compatibility is essential.

20. See Alexander L. George and Juliette L. George, *Woodrow Wilson and Colonel House: A Personality Study* (New York: Dover Publications, 1964), pp. 85–112.

SUMMARY

When we talk about analysts and clients, we are talking about relationships. Sometimes these relationships are obscured by formal and informal arrangements, by assignments involving multiple loyalties, and by the analyst assuming that he is his own client. Nevertheless, there is a relationship, part of which is defined by what the client expects from his analyst. Clients do have different styles, but most of them still want some measure of protection and direction from their analysts. Both analyst and client have some choice in selecting each other. The client has many advisors to whom he can listen, and the analyst has many opportunities to pursue, both in and out of the bureaucracy. Thus, the client-analyst relationship is based on mutual choice as well as mutual expectations. We will continue to discuss this relationship in the next chapter by examining how analysts communicate with their clients.

7

Communication

Technicians and inexperienced analysts are often disgusted with the amount of effort expended on communicating, particularly on paper. "This place is just a big paper mill," is a common refrain. "If I had wanted to be a writer, I would have majored in English."

Yet the government could not function if its bureaucrats did not have communication skills. Some portions of the time spent in communicating, no doubt, are exercises in bureaucratic pathology; but most of the time spent in communicating is required for coping with the complexities of administration. What is applicable to the general bureaucrat applies with greater force to policy analysts. To say that the analyst is a writer, as I did in chapter 2, does not begin to indicate the significance that communication plays in his life as an advisor. Writing is an essential skill not only in our federal bureaucracy but in the governments of other countries as well. Heclo and Wildavsky, for example, note its importance for British Treasury officials:

Next to a political nose, and a logical brain, the most important skill of the good Treasury man resides in his fine drafting hand. The concise, coherent and penetrating note is the final expression of all other talents. Political sensitivity may be manifested by drafting statements that allow the minister to meet the problem at hand without getting him into additional difficulties. A logical mind is demonstrated by showing that the various aspects of the Treasury position fit together in a coherent package and, if necessary, that the opposing view does not make sense. The man who can draft a good memorandum takes the burden from his superior, incidentally showing him (as well as anyone else along the line who will read it) how able he really is.[1]

Hence, communication is the primary link between the analyst and his client. But before the analyst communicates, he should be clear about what he is trying to accomplish. It makes a difference whether he wants to communicate only with his client or whether the communication is to reach others and thereby serve the client's purposes. And besides determining who his audience is, the analyst should decide how, what, and when to communicate. These various decisions are interrelated; the form of communication is linked to its substance. The purpose of a communication, moreover, can vary by the stage of the policy process in which it is introduced. A report can be written to achieve support for a policy idea, or it can be written in such a way as to appear neutral but actually promote debate and discussion. With such multiple audiences and purposes, there should be a refined choice of modes of communication. Unfortunately, all too often the analyst chooses a single mode—say, a study report—and expects it to do everything. All too often there is neither communication nor trust between client and analyst—a situation in which either one can victimize the other. The failure of analysts and their advice is due in part to inadequate communication practices.

MODES OF COMMUNICATION

THE FORMAL BRIEFING

A small audience of people are busy smoking and talking with each other. Suddenly a well-dressed but nondescript person approaches a slightly elevated stage at the far end of the room. He turns on the light at the lectern and says, "My name is Harvey Shieldkraut, Jr.; this briefing will take 30 minutes." At this point a color slide projects on the screen the subject of the afternoon's entertainment. So begins one of the most used, widespread, entrenched, but pernicious modes of communication in the federal government.

---

1. Hugh Heclo and Aaron Wildavsky, *The Private Government of Public Money* (Berkeley and Los Angeles: University of California Press, 1974), p. 58.

My first exposure to a formal briefing was when I worked at Rand. The Air Force had asked us to brief them on some of our techniques for costing alternative force structures.[2] I was one of several analysts who pulled the material together for the briefing. Over a period of weeks we worked quite hard selecting examples and sketching charts. After what seemed like an unending series of internal reviews and dry runs, the charts were turned over to the professionals in the art department; when the artists were finished we were ready to go to Washington. I went along as the chart carrier for the analyst who was going to give the briefing. Besides carrying things, my part was quite simple. All I had to do was to pass out some pictures during the briefing. (In retrospect, I think such a practice should be avoided, as it disrupts the flow of communication.)

The briefing room was large enough to accommodate about fifty senior military and civilian officials. In the front row, close to the briefer, were the generals. Since I had no rank at all, I sat in the back with my pictures, awaiting my cue. Everything went smoothly, the jokes at the right time, the examples in proper sequence; after all, we had rehearsed the briefing enough times. So when my cue came, I got up and started passing out the pictures, starting from the back and working my way to the front. Having done my job, I returned to my seat and half listened to the rest of the briefing. Afterwards, at lunch, Rand's Washington office liaison, a man of considerable experience in such matters, congratulated us on the excellent job we had done. I had also done a good job, but with one exception. "In the future," I was told, "always pass exhibits to the generals first and then to the less senior officers."

What lesson can we draw from this example? I learned that I should not sit at the back of the room during a briefing. My experience points out the artificiality and stylized nature of briefings. Usually the audience contains friends and enemies, but you

2. As Fisher explains, "the main purpose of a total force cost model is to estimate the resource impact of proposed alternative total force structures for a given military service. A force structure is a time-phased specification of numbers of force units (such as divisions, carrier task forces, or squadrons) by fiscal year over a period of future years for a selected complete set of weapon and support systems." See Gene H. Fisher, *Cost Considerations in Systems Analysis*, Rand Report R-490-ASD (New York: American Elsevier Publishing Company, 1971), pp. 194–99.

would never know it; the formality of the situation inhibits interaction between analyst and client. Often polite questions are asked and polite answers are given, and the ensuing discussion is ritualistic. In line with this, the analyst must not only know who his audience is but also understand its folkways. Passing out pictures in the wrong sequence may not just be a peccadillo. Suppose the generals were so upset with my breach of etiquette that they turned off and did not listen to the rest of the briefing? The analyst should pay attention to such details if he expects to overcome the limitations of the situation.

Sometimes, no matter how skilled and prepared a briefer is, he will not be able to overcome the situation. A number of years ago I was asked to brief the head of the army, the chief of staff, on what a cost model is.[3] The army's comptroller had been given the assignment originally but his staff was afraid to do it, so he got me instead. This time we arrived with a well-rehearsed briefing using colorful slides with overlays. It was a wonderful opportunity not only to explain to the general why he needed cost models to improve his decision making but actually to sell him on a particular cost model that a crew of analysts and myself had developed over several years. The Defense Department had paid millions of dollars for it; so why shouldn't the army use it? In the briefing room sat the two highest-ranking generals in the U.S. Army, while I stood on a small stage about ten feet away. Behind the screen was my slide-carrying analyst, who placed the slides on the projector at the proper time.

The briefing began but then suddenly stopped. The two generals were discussing the need for more dogs to improve security around army installations. I waited until they were finished and then proceeded. Somehow, I mentioned the word rifle, and the briefing stopped again. The two generals now were talking about how the army needed more rifles. And so a thirty-minute briefing took about an hour and a half. Every few minutes something I would say would trigger a private conversation between the two generals. I thought the briefing was a disaster because it had taken so long and communicated so little, but my sponsors thought otherwise. Indeed, in a short time, I received a commendation for

3. For a discussion of cost models, see Fisher, *Cost Considerations*, pp. 166–200.

my contributions to army cost analysis. No matter, the briefing was still a disaster.

Many formal briefings are a disaster in one way or another because of the difficulty of communicating. Yet zealous staff aides go on wasting the time of their busy superiors by scheduling them. Like elementary school teachers who show film strips and movies to get a moment's peace, they put briefings on the agenda as informational entertainment. With minds distracted and eyes glazed, the people in the audience relax and momentarily escape from more pressing matters. Even when they hear the message they may misunderstand it, because it is a little too simple. The subtleties of a policy problem often have to be omitted in order to get the main points across.

The reader will wonder from this description why analysts bother giving briefings. The answer is simple: clients, their aides, and even the analysts want them. Not only do they provide informational entertainment, but they are used to gather political support and to reach remote clients. Often before the secretary signs off on some policy he will want to be assured that various actors inside and outside the agency have been briefed. The briefing—a kind of traveling road show—is perceived as useful for building consensus for a particular policy. Once the briefing has been assembled, the cost of giving it to another potential supporter is slight; and it is much harder for an opponent to claim that he was not consulted after a decision. Of course, no briefing by itself can guarantee that a consensus will be achieved, but it is a start. If an analyst reaches other analysts and advisors with his briefing, they in turn may be able to reach their clients. Sometimes a briefing is the only way in which the analyst can reach his own client. Such an analyst, as pitchman, has to make the best of it. He is more likely to be listened to if the briefing concerns a policy decision the client cares about. Uncluttered charts, brevity, and not presenting too much also help. But when a policy analysis is complex, filled with cautions and special conditions, the analyst, aware of the inadequacies of briefings, will also distribute a detailed memo or formal report.

THE FORMAL REPORT

Even when an administration wants to conduct its policy business in secret and by memo, enough formal reports are written to keep the Government Printing Office quite busy. Congress requires them; presidential commissions want to write them. Analysts write them for clients and when they are seeking clients to sponsor their ideas. The amazing quantity and variety of formal reports make it difficult to generalize about them. Some are works of art; others look like stapled memos. Sometimes I think that the only difference between a memo and a report is the stock of paper and its cover. The typical report has a soft, colored cover and is bound. It might be called a working paper, progress report, study, or program memorandum, or it might carry a subject title; but whatever it is called, it is still a report. Some reports pay more attention to graphics and bar charts than.others. Some use colored pages to emphasize important parts. Some are thin; others are three to six inches thick. Many share a common organization. After a summary, there will be a section on background, stating the problem and alternatives. Then a section on the approach or methodology and data, followed by some playing with the numbers or analysis. Results or findings come next, then a conclusions section, and finally a recommendations section. Sometimes the report will be organized by subject matter, with each aspect getting its own section. Given the variety of analysts and clients, it is no wonder that there are a variety of reports.

Practically all reports have one thing in common—the attention devoted to the first few pages. Busy clients are not apt to get beyond page 10, so something must be done. Indeed the General Accounting Office includes in its reports an additional perforated page, a "digest," which can be torn out for the convenience of its congressional clients. The analyst can also use a separate letter of transmittal to make his case. But more often than not, the case is made in the one-to-five-page summary. For many readers, the summary is the report. Aware of this fact, analysts are quite careful about what they say in it.

A chief analyst at the Department of Agriculture instructs his staff in writing two-page summaries to "sprinkle them with juicy punch lines that will catch the reader's interest." Of course, it is not always easy to divine what will catch a reader's interest. The chief analyst, for example, wanted to encourage credit assistance for mobile homes, prepared a report with this in mind, and scattered it all over, to HUD, OMB, the Council of Economic Advisers, and various elements of the Department of Agriculture.

The report emphasized "opportunities that the government has thus far passed up" because the chief analyst reasoned that agencies are always looking for ways to expand their activities. Requests for additional copies suggest that agencies were reading the report; "but," as the chief analyst complained, "somehow we just haven't hit the magic word." He expected that if he did not get any serious clients—clients willing to pursue the idea—he would rewrite the summary with juicy new punch lines, emphasize different issues, and then send it out again.

In writing a policy analysis report, two distinct problems emerge. The writer must communicate technical material in non-technical terms and he must also be persuasive. Arthur Okun, former chairman of the Council of Economic Advisers, accurately describes the technical communications problem:

The main communications requirement in many economic policy areas is to put things in a way that is comprehensible to decision makers not familiar with the professional jargon. Young expert Ph.D. economists typically cannot communicate with the President because of the technical way they tend to think and formulate concepts. Half of my time in the council was spent as rewrite man trying to translate good staff material about slopes and elasticities into a form that was meaningful to the President, as well as to the White House staff and agency heads, for the decisions they had to make.[4]

So this should be a rule for most analysts: Don't drag the client into too much technical detail if it can be avoided. Detail is sometimes necessary, of course, depending on the purpose of the report. Yet even when it isn't, many analysts cannot bring themselves to omit it. Some are afraid of criticism by their peers; others just do not know how. Generally, they rely on halfheartedness. To the detailed report they will add a nontechnical chapter for the client who cannot grasp the intricacies of their discipline. Clever chief analysts will write a summary report to go along with the technical report (which then may land up as an appendix), or they may brief the client orally and just use the report as backup, never expecting the client actually to read it. A prevailing habit is to shift the detailed technical material to the back of the report, if not to the appendix.

4. From a discussion in *Computers, Communications, and the Public Interest*, ed. Martin Greenberger (Baltimore and London: Johns Hopkins University Press, 1971), p. 106.

Effective communication, whether written or otherwise, must be carried out in the client's terms. Frances Perkins recalls that President Franklin D. Roosevelt was confused by Keynes, who attempted to explain his economic theories with mathematics and just "left a whole rigamarole of figures." Learning from the failure of others, Perkins knew that FDR liked concrete statements and that it was much easier to get a problem across to him in a report by vividly describing a typical case.[5]

If a client is a technician, then one supposes that a technician's report would do. Analysts, however, might as well realize that not many clients are technicians, so they should get used to writing in terms their client understands. This may mean putting informative titles on tables—titles which indicate the meaning of the data—or it may mean doing without tables and numbers and using words instead. Or, in desperation, it may mean substituting pictures for words or using some combination of the two. In short, as one analyst puts it, "If you can't get your ideas across on paper clearly, precisely, and reflecting what your boss wants, and if you don't take advantage of opportunities for slipping your own agenda into the report, then you are bound to fail in a bureaucracy."

Obviously, not everybody writes clearly and cogently, because agencies continue to emphasize the importance of communication by putting out manuals and handbooks on the subject. Here, for example, is a selection from a HUD handbook entitled "Reporting Evaluation: Strategies and Techniques" (pp. 10–11):

An evaluation report . . . may fail if the writing style is miserable.

Be Concise. Evaluation reports should be concise. Use active verbs instead of the longer, passive forms, and eliminate non-essential adjectives.

Avoid Technical Language. Technical language is rarely used in an evaluation report. If it must be used, the terms should be defined as a layman would understand them.

Create a Balance. Evaluators have a professional responsibility to keep their own biases from distorting evaluative findings. . . . Unemotional reporting will have more impact and is less politically vulnerable than the product of histrionic abandon.

Edit and Proofread. Formal written reports should be edited by someone other than the writer.

5. Frances Perkins, *The Roosevelt I Knew* (New York: Viking Press, 1947), p. 225.

Use Charts and Graphs. Tabulate data or use graphs to present it in compact form. Verbal or written explanations should follow the visual presentation. Charts are not a substitute for interpretations of the data. Complete the analysis so that the decision maker need not study the numbers to form a conclusion.

Reports certainly do not sell themselves, but one should write them as if they did. For an interested client who is anxious for the analyst's report, perhaps persuasion is not a problem. Most clients, however, are not interested, get distracted, and have short attention spans. Accordingly, the writing must be so persuasive, both in substance and style, that the client not only picks up the report to read it but reads it through and even (with a little bit of luck) decides to do something. A little attention to language, pleasing quotations, headings, underlining, and organization can help in getting and keeping the client's interest.

A common practice of many analysts is to develop a central theme, which usually can be taken from the thinking or the hypotheses of the problem-definition stage of analysis. This theme provides a skeleton on which can be added the flesh of the complete argument. The writing is persuasive because it builds to a conclusion in a carefully organized way. Here is one analyst's description of his "effective way" of writing:

You present the facts and analysis in such a way so the reader knows what the problem is, and then he is marched through the analysis to the conclusion. The argument seems to have an internal force and logic, and you can see which direction the analyst went, from A to Z.

The point is clear: conclusions and recommendations must be linked logically to the body of the analysis and its central theme and argument.

This tight linkage between what to do (the policy) and why (the analysis) can be misused, and both clients and analysts who review studies should be aware of this fact of bureaucratic life. A different definition of the problem accompanied by a different set of facts can lead to a different recommendation. The extent of such alteration depends on how much the analyst has become an aggressive advocate willing to sell his wares either for personal advancement or through a conviction that a policy has to be changed. One analyst, for example, told us that he will not push a policy change if he believes that the immediate solution of the problem is not essential. If, however, he believes that the problem is in need of immediate solution and his solution is rejected initially, he "will go back to the drawing board and redesign his recommendation." Because of the multiplicity of facts that may be applied to any description of a problem, redesigning a recommendation may require drawing on a different set of facts. More often than not this analyst has found it difficult to redesign his recommendations without rewriting the description of the problem. In his words, "the facts you select to describe the problem usually lead to a single obvious solution."

As a precaution, reviewers of reports should be wary of the too obvious solution. Alternatives may have been chosen not to be explored seriously but as straw men to be knocked down in the pursuit of a single recommendation. One should question why this particular problem, now, or why these data, assumptions, and analyses rather than others. The tight logical report is required for persuasive communication, but nonsense can also be expressed logically. Therefore, checking for consistency, making sure the pieces fit together, is insufficient; one should be skeptical of the pieces themselves.

Many policy analysts, of course, do not consciously distort their work to sell their wares. On the contrary, they are usually so scrupulous and conscientious that they are in danger of being ignored. One such analyst for years felt that personal judgments and insights about a problem had no place in an objective analysis. Only in the last few years has he realized the importance of including this information in his reports. Now he writes a conclusions section that contains inferences that are directly tied to the analysis; and in a separate section, suitably demarked, he presents his personal insights which are not supported by the analysis itself.

Not all reports contain recommendations. Sometimes no clear policy direction is indicated by an analysis. Sometimes the analyst, not knowing which way the wind is blowing, or just following instructions, will omit recommendations and let the client make up his mind about what he wants to do. Sometimes it is more important to focus on the problem and the way people view it than to worry about specific policy recommendations. Daniel Patrick Moynihan adopted this strategy for his report, *The Negro Family: The Case for National Action*. According to Rainwater and Yancey, Moynihan "had decided not to include recommendations in his report—for fear that all of the attention would go to the recommended programs rather than to the definition of the problem and also that there would be premature budget estimates of the costs of the recommended programs."[6]

Although many analysts may act as if writing a report is an end in itself, it is not. It is an initial step in a process of communication. It may lead to a presidential message, to the passage of legislation, and to revised procedures and regulations. Most analysts are happy if their immediate client uses their work, but they are much happier if the president uses it. For example, here is a paragraph from one of President Nixon's messages:

Recent findings on the two largest such programs are particularly disturbing. We now spend more than $1 billion a year for educational programs run under Title I of the Elementary and Secondary Education Act. Most of these have stressed the teaching of reading, but before-and-after tests suggest that only 19% of the children in such programs improve their reading significantly; 13% appear to fall behind more than expected; and more than two-thirds of the children remain unaffected—that is, they continue to fall behind. In our Headstart program, where so much hope is invested, we find that youngsters enrolled only for the summer achieve almost no gains, and the gains of those in the program for a full year are soon matched by their non-Headstart classmates from similarly poor backgrounds.[7]

The lack of results from compensatory education programs originally had been pointed out by an Office of Education analyst. When interviewed, he proudly pulled from his desk his report, "Evaluation of Title I," and pointed to the paragraph from his summary which the presidential speech writers had used:

An analysis of the reading achievement scores of 155,000 participants in 189 Title I projects during the school year ending in June 1967 indicates that a child who participated in a Title I project had only a 19% chance of a significant achievement gain, a 13% chance of a significant achievement loss, and a 68% chance of no change at all. This sample of observations is not a representative sample of Title I projects. It is, most likely, representative of projects in which there was a higher than average investment in resources. Therefore, more significant achievement gains should be found here than in a more representative sample of Title I projects.

---

6. Lee Rainwater and William L. Yancey, *The Moynihan Report and the Politics of Controversy* (Cambridge, Mass.: M.I.T. Press, 1967), p. 28. The full report is reprinted in the book.

7. Office of the White House Press Secretary, *Message on Education Reform*, to the Congress of the United States, 3 March 1970, p. 5.

Certainly the analyst had successfully communicated his work. The president used his evaluation. Too bad that that use did not result in significant changes in the Title I program. The president could say that "American education is in urgent need for reform,"[8] but that did not mean that reform would be forthcoming.

OTHER MODES

Producing briefings and reports are not the only ways in which policy analysis can be communicated. Much communication is accomplished merely by living in the bureaucracy. The analyst sends out memos. He calls on the phone and says, "What would your reaction be to . . .," or "Look out, this is coming," or "That memo which we sent you is for the record; we don't really mean it." He often just reacts to other people's memos or to his client's scribble on the margin of his own. He attends meetings. In short, he tries to get his oar into the policymaking water in any way he can. Let us consider a few examples.

At HEW there is an informal meeting of the secretary and a few key officials, including a senior analyst. One of the officials is going to testify to Congress on the need for controlling air pollution. Believing in equality, he is going to suggest that similar industries be treated in a similar manner. After some discussion, the senior analyst is able to convince this official that such similar treatment would be a rather expensive way of controlling air pollution, and that local areas should have more discretion in choosing which industries should be controlled. Therefore, the official changes his congressional testimony.

Newcomers to the bureaucracy are sometimes disgruntled at being assigned to write a client's speeches. Yet as an experienced analyst points out, "speech preparation is very important in convincing policy people of the value of new ideas. When the secretary makes a speech he becomes involved in the logic of it, and when he gets a good reaction he comes back for more." A speech can be used in two ways. It can be an endorsement for analytical work already done, or it can bring approval for work to be done.

Experiences in the Department of Labor provide examples of both uses. For a while, some analysts at Labor felt that manpower programs could help in the rehabilitation of criminals. They

8. *Ibid.*, p. 1.

"pushed and pushed" and finally got permission to conduct a limited study. The study showed that a large number of persons who had been charged with criminal offenses were neither in prison nor employed. Perhaps federal hiring practices and statutes were working to the disadvantage of persons with criminal records. When the secretary of labor wanted some ideas for future speeches, the analysts suggested that he talk about the role of manpower programs in reducing crime. The secretary asked the analysts to prepare such a speech, which he gave and for which he received praise from the press and outside groups. The idea of a connection between manpower and rehabilitation was further popularized by the attorney general and the chief justice in their own speeches. As a result there was much more interest at Labor in transforming the idea into practice. Now for the second use of speeches: an assistant secretary, asked to go on national television to discuss the four-day work week, prepared for his appearance with help from the department's analysts. Afterward, these analysts were able to convince their client that an extensive study of the issues raised by a four-day work week be conducted because of popular interest in the subject.

Presidential advisors commit their clients to policies by writing their speeches. Whether the advisor communicates with the president, and the president understands, is another matter. But if the advisor can get the president to make the statement, then that statement is an endorsement of a policy. What is interesting is that analysts, as speech writers, do the same thing; and the commitment of a client, for some, is just as good as direct communication with him.

Besides writing speeches, there are other ways to commit a client and more or less communicate with him. Recall HUD's evaluative work on annual arrangement procedures, discussed in chapter 2. The staff had found the field procedures in confusion. Soon after they reached this conclusion, a member of the evaluation staff happened to be riding in the elevator with Assistant Secretary Floyd H. Hyde. The analyst mentioned to Hyde that the evaluation staff had checked around casually and found that annual arrangement procedures varied between regions, and that there was great confusion in the field. It is reported that Hyde responded with some surprise and replied, "Well, there go my people, I guess. I'd better catch them; I'm their leader." Soon after this encounter, Hyde appointed a task force to develop a memorandum for Secretary Romney's signature; the memorandum would state the approved annual arrangement procedures to promote uniformity between regions. Whether in an elevator or in the hall, analysts will attempt to communicate with their clients.

This HUD task force proceeded, like so many others, with endless meetings and drafts, but one communications tactic is of interest. The analyst who used it calls it "the old draft-discussion trick." Analysts on the task force wanted to get the commitment of both their superiors and the field personnel, so they obtained a key official's approval to send out a draft for discussion. According to the analyst, the official's

authorization to send the draft outside the office will make him more strongly committed to the draft and will be a signal to others that they should prepare to comply with the provision of our draft. After this point, it won't even matter in many ways whether the secretary actually signed it. The regions will accept it as a signal of what is to come and begin to comply before it receives any higher level approval. . . . By getting this paper out to the field quickly, the wording may not be perfect but the decision will be made and we can make revisions as time goes by.[9]

The circulation of draft papers to elites is a common bureaucratic practice. Building consensus and getting feedback are the usual objectives of these "staffing" exercises, and analysts can play several roles in them. One role is that of neutral postmaster. An evaluation study, for example, is sent to an analyst for summarization. He writes a summary and sends it out to the "executive staff," the notables of the agency, for comments. When the comments come back he compiles them and sends them out again, to the same notables. He then gets a second feedback, which he converts into policy recommendations for the secretary to endorse. Whole studies can be written and rewritten by such a process. Each office or elite changes a word here and there, or adds or deletes a paragraph, and the analyst essentially becomes the holder of the master copy.

Another role is that of secret advocate. It makes a difference how one summarizes and compiles. Imagine an analyst on a task force reviewing a draft of a study. He does not like the report and threatens to write a dissenting statement. The leader of the task force, wanting to maintain a consensus, allows the analyst to correct the report. The analyst knows the leader will not accept any statements that directly disagree with the main conclusions, so he sprinkles critical comments and questions throughout the draft. With these comments, strategically placed, he hopes to create doubt about the validity of the study. And so he does, because the study is sent back for further examination. For his diligence, the analyst is put in charge of the new study team.

The bureaucratic norm of consultation is usually criticized for reducing policy to its lowest common denominator. Completed staff work means getting everyone to agree before the boss is approached. Why bother him? We can resolve our own differences. So some watering down is likely. But what is not sufficiently appreciated is that such procedures are also avenues for the expression of dissent. Bureaucratic haggling over words for hours does have a purpose. It can preserve an analytical perspective for future use. It may be the only way left for the analyst to communicate with immediate and remote clients.

The analyst who works closely with a client has other modes of communication. He can write a brief memo and stop a project, for example, because it is inconsistent with presidential or another agency's guidelines. At lunch, when sandwiches have been sent in, he can suggest to his client that a policy be restudied—which is as good as stopping it. He may be responsible for preparing his client for the next meeting on the agenda and for this purpose use a four-to-five-page "Q and A," a question-and-answer sheet. Q and A's are frequently used by bureaucratic analysts to explain in a simple way the various complex features of a policy, or they are used to anticipate some rough questions the client may have to answer at his meeting.

The audience for the communication of policy analysis is not only the analyst's immediate client. Both friends and enemies of the analyst cluster around his client and give advice. They must also be reached. To win a marked departure in policy, the analyst actually writes for a much larger audience than he imagines. One analyst put it this way:

Decision making is by consensus, by vote taking. You have to convince the intelligentsia. You have to convince them that your analysis is credible. It has to be credible to them. It has to be done in such a way that they'll read it and believe it. You keep friends and your competitors informed during the whole process in order to do this. In other words, you don't have to worry just about one decision maker; but in selling your analysis you have to make sure the community that gives advice to the decision makers are up to speed on your work.

Central analysts who have to cope with fairly autonomous bureaus have to do more than just keep the various chiefs informed. Consider an analyst who tried to work, with some frustrations, through the bureaus: Although running the risk that the work would be promotional, he followed a co-optation tactic: "We would make our analysis theirs; we would try and let them take credit for it." But sometimes nothing can satisfy these curmudgeons because of basic policy differences. One of them once told this analyst, "I don't care what your analysis shows, I'll fight it on the Hill."

Nor is the message kept strictly within the bureaucracy. Analysts also go outside. Like their counterparts in the think tanks, they spend time promoting their work.[10] Analysts have gone on television, attended symposiums and professional meetings, given lectures, published articles, and even written books. Sometimes going outside is an act of desperation, a risky response to the bureaucratic client's deaf ear. Sometimes it is part of a sponsored program to spread the word. Often it is a personal device, not always to promote a policy but as a means of self-protection.

Clients, as we saw in chapter 6, want to be protected; well, so do analysts. Publishing in an academic journal can preserve the analyst's credibility among his peers and, some analysts believe, maintain an escape route back to the university. An article can also be influential by indirectly giving ammunition, in terms of data and concepts, to outsiders, such as academics, who are free to criticize. The professional literature, moreover, comes in handy when the analyst is caught in a cross fire between administration and congressional clients. An analyst provides us with an example: "When the congressional committee asked us about these estimates, we evaded their direct questions and suggested that the effect is

10. For a discussion of a think tank's considerable efforts at communication, see Bruce L. R. Smith, "Strategic Expertise and National Security Policy: A Case Study," *Public Policy* 13 (1964): 87–94; or his book, *The Rand Corporation: Case Study of a Nonprofit Advisory Corporation* (Cambridge, Mass.: Harvard University Press, 1966).

explained in X and Y journal articles. If they refer to these articles they will see that the price elasticity of demand for exports is different from the administration's announcement." Too much publishing, however, and the immediate client who wants service can soon feel neglected and believe that the analyst is really working for someone else.

Back in the bureaucratic nest, analysts resort to what may appear to be trivial techniques for protection. One tested device is for the analyst to point out the deficiencies of his own work. Better to do it to yourself than to have it done to you. I know of one analyst who even offered to redo his work on price forecasts if the reader wanted to provide him with a different set of coefficients. An artful line exists between such self-deprecation and nourishing the credibility of one's work. Sometimes a few introductory remarks or sentences can set expectations so that readers will not take a report too seriously. Take the case of the analyst who was assigned to write an evaluation of a training program in a southern city. He conducted the evaluation objectively and found that the program was wholly unwarranted and ineffective. These results would be of no surprise to anyone in the department, he reported, because the awarding of the project to the city was a political payoff. In writing up his investigation, therefore, he opened with a brief history, mentioning that the program's inception "was announced by Secretary ———— and Congressman ———— in 1969." This sort of remark signals to the department the reasons for such an ineffective program and also indicates possible constraints on eliminating it.[11]

COMMUNICATIONS AS A PROCESS

I do not want to leave the impression that all an analyst has to do is write a lucid, compelling report that the client will then read and that suddenly a new policy is established. Communications is just as much a process as policymaking and politics are, which is to say that it is complicated, convoluted, probably lengthy, and with

11. An interest in protection is not confined to analysts in the bureaucracy. A former member of a nonprofit research firm reports that his analytical colleagues would invite comments on their drafts from their enemies, incorporate some minor changes into their revisions, and then display prominently the names of the enemies in the acknowledgment section of the final report. I call this tactic ungrateful co-optation, and I doubt whether it can protect the analyst from attack by a determined enemy.

theoretical stages yet to be discerned. A single, prospective policy decision will involve many modes of communication—meetings, letters, memos, reports, and congressional hearings—and many different analysts and clients. The specific characteristics of the communications process, moreover, seem to depend on the politics of the policy decision. Sometimes communications are truncated, in a crisis atmosphere, in the rush for legislation or a decision. At other times the process of communication is open-ended, with no apparent conclusion in sight. Environmental legislation appeared practically overnight, while aid to education took many years to come to some sort of resolution. One might think that simple, efficiency-type policy decisions involve a short, straightforward process of communication. But even such administrative, mostly internal, matters can drag on for what seems forever. As it turns out, no policy decision is simple.

Consider the General Services Administration's money-saving suggestion to replace government sedans in one year rather than in six years. In a General Accounting Office study that supported GSA's position, it was reported that "Five Government studies during the past 16 years have shown that substantial reductions in operating costs could be achieved by replacing passenger cars before they meet GSA's current replacement standard of 6 years or 60,000 miles."[12] Those five studies were just the tip of the communications iceberg. Besides the GAO study there were many internal studies by GSA and OMB, and there were meetings, memos, letters, and congressional testimony. A GSA chronology (dated April 9, 1971), listing exchanges with OMB/BOB for just the years from 1967 through 1971, runs to nine pages and is filled with notations by letters for GSA individuals (such as A for its administrator). A few seconds of scanning some selected notations provides a sense of the process:

March 30, 1967   BOB to A

                      BOB asked for special study on replacement standards for Federal motor vehicles.

---

12. U.S. Comptroller General, General Accounting Office, *Potential Savings by Replacing Government-Owned Sedans Each Year*, Report to Congress, B-158712, 9 June 1971, p. 1.

April 17, 1967   A to BOB

GSA recommended change replacement to 4 years/50,000 miles, as practical matter, though one-year replacement is optimum from economic standpoint.

July 19, 1967   BOB to A (Reply to A letter 4/7/67)

BOB rejected 4 year/50,0000 replacement because of "tight budgetary situation." Said to defer decision on a change in replacement standards until next year (FY 1970).

GSA was to continue discussions with BOB.

April 12, 1968   BOB to A

BOB requested Special Analytical Study of the replacement standard for the Government fleet of sedans in conjunction with the FY1970 Budget.

July 3, 1968   T and B to A

They transmitted the "Study of Motor Vehicle (Sedan) Replacement Policy," which concluded one-year is best, but requested BOB to authorize a test sale of late model vehicles to verify the theoretical formulae.

July 8, 1968   A to BOB

GSA transmitted the Study to BOB, noting that GSA would continue with 6 year/60,000 miles, awaiting BOB concurrence.

July 24, 1968   Meeting

At BOB request, BG and TP met with BOB, to discuss the study. BOB had technical questions about the Study but not about the methodology of the Test.

October 15, 1968   BOB to A

(a) Concurred in maintaining 6 year/60,000 miles.

(b) BOB requested additional data on automotive industry reactions before proceeding with the test.

(c) Asked for other factors in the updated study such as downtime, market impact, new car price, etc.

Suggested GSA/BOB meetings before GSA began modifications.

April 9, 1969   BOB to A

BOB requested future GSA budget requests include Program Memorandum and Reports. Asked for a Report on Automotive Replacement Policy, among other. Report due BOB September 1, 1969.

January 30, 1970   A to BOB

GSA transmitted the "package" to OMB, and also offered to change regulations.

Spring 1970   BOB had several different questions on the Study—Phase II, which were verbally received and answered.

Back and forth the communications went, keeping busy, at one time or another, at least four different offices and analysts in OMB and a similar number in GSA. Why was there so much analytical communication and no results?

Suspicion is one answer. OMB's analysts did not think much of GSA's analysts or its studies which, in OMB's view, promoted preconceived policies rather than determining policies. One OMB analyst, for example, felt that GSA should have investigated a seven-or-more-year replacement policy. After all, GSA's director of program and policy planning, a central force behind the GSA study, "drives an 18-year-old sedan." According to this analyst, GSA's director "excluded seven or more years as alternatives because of a gut feeling of the negative effect which a longer replacement policy would have on the image of government employees. They thought that government employees would have an even lower status if continually seen by the public driving old-model vehicles." Another analyst severely criticized GSA's 1967 study as "analytically unsound" and "lacking in substance." As he says, "The whole thrust of their study was a graph, completely unsupported by data." Back at GSA, officials agreed that the 1967 study was not "good analysis." It seems that in 1967 GSA's commissioner of the transportation and communications service "loved to draw graphs; he was an old engineer before he joined GSA." GSA's 1970 effort was much better, but the OMB analysts felt that it also had deficiencies. GSA had ignored several important costs, such as the costs of capital for the accelerated replacement policy and the costs of processing a larger volume of purchase and resale transactions. Moreover, GSA had no firm data on what they would get in reselling their cars after one year instead of six. So OMB prepared a "counteranalysis."

At the congressional site, GSA, lacking a political constituency, was not doing much better. GSA officials testified that they could save money. At a hearing on GSA's appropriation, W. L. Johnson, Jr., GSA's assistant administrator for administration, stated, "Mr. Chairman, we have in front of the Bureau of the Budget now, and have had for the last year or so, a study that shows that if the [sedans] were replaced at an earlier time, the Government would actually save money."[13]

But that was about it. There was no surge of congressional support for a one-year replacement standard. Perhaps congressmen, just like other federal officials, were afraid of the public's reaction to bureaucrats riding around in new cars. The question of image had bothered GSA officials, and that is why at one time they had suggested a four-year standard when they believed a one-year policy was superior. The forces shifted temporarily, however, when the GAO report went to Congress, because then OMB Director George P. Shultz was asked to consider establishing a one-year standard.

OMB's response could easily have been predicted. It was to tell a number of people to get out their pencils. When you don't want to do something, you study it. OMB's analysts did not merely update previous work; they changed the methodology and inputs.

13. U.S. Congress, House, Committee on Appropriations, *Independent Offices, General Services Administration, Hearings*, Part 3, 91st Cong., 1st sess., 1969, p. 486.

The result was that the "savings" disappeared. Four days later plus a bright analyst and the job was done.

What I am trying to show is the interaction that goes on in analysis; it is not my purpose to judge the appropriateness of these various studies. Changes in how the problem is defined, such as including the advantages of less "downtime" for new cars (time when the cars cannot be used), can easily change results. What is clear is that OMB did not want to pursue a one-year policy, mainly because of the capital requirements and the uncertainty about any significant savings in the future. It is no small piece of change to replace 37,000 sedans every year, particularly when there are other pressing budgetary priorities. To some extent this is why OMB let GSA conduct a time-consuming market study to determine resale prices of cars less than six years old when similar information could have been gotten from an automobile dealer's blue book. This is why senior OMB officials suggested that GSA should explore leasing. Regardless of the quality of GSA's work, GSA may have been right in accusing OMB of "stalling tactics" and of "raising nitpicking questions."

As far as I know, there are probably still some policy analysts in the bureaucracy who continue to worry about replacing the government's automobiles. Some problems never go away, and that may be why the communicating of policy analysis is often open-ended, to be viewed more as a process than as a single activity between a client and an analyst.

MAKE IT POLITICAL

A recurring theme throughout this book has been the interaction between political and bureaucratic considerations and analytical ones. We have seen that analysts do provide political advice and that they also use their political knowledge in selecting and solving problems. At the communications stage of "objective" or "technical" analysis, political considerations become quite important. After all, the analyst is leaving the nest with his hard-won facts and he does not want to be shot down before he gets a chance to try his wings. Acceptance may be predicated not so much on what he says but on how he says it.

Deletion, or political censoring, is the most common way of making a communication political. Written reports, particularly, have to appear clean, as there is no telling where they may land and who will see them. Reference to "political interference" by a member of the House Appropriations Committee or trouble between a mayor and a local agency are deleted by an analyst who says, "the mention of such cynical political considerations would put them [his clients] in a tizzy." The objective is to put your best case forward without getting into trouble; consequently, much effort is devoted to redrafting to "knock off the rough edges." Consider the analyst at the Department of Agriculture who was working on revenue sharing for OMB; he described his censoring role as follows:

After a while you become accustomed to working with the OMB and anticipating what they want. To pass on reports containing phrases such as "we think the program is lousy" is certainly not to gain the favorable consideration of the Office of Management and Budget or the White House. We tried to eliminate red flags such as that and direct our department's comments toward the best implementation of the revenue sharing program.

A number of civil service chiefs of analytical shops say that, if possible, they avoid "hard political considerations" in their reports to begin with. Such information might include assessments of congressional support, analysis of interest-group reactions, and thoughts on the possible reception of a proposal before an appropriations committee. Usually these chiefs are in a position to review reports from the staffs of other assistant secretaries. These reports often do contain "hard" political information, but the chiefs try to stay away from it. As one of them says, "I don't regard myself as a political expert. The assistant secretaries are expected to know the politics of their agencies. I don't think I should try to second-guess their judgment." Another explains, "My boss can make political recommendations, but I am a civil servant." No doubt experienced analysts, in order to survive, have learned to be careful when it comes to making political judgments. But it is also true that politics is messy; it can disturb the simple elegance of an analytical solution. If the analyst is paid to simplify decision making, why should he look to complicate it?

On the other hand, despite the analyst's inclination to avoid political statements, his instinct to protect his client encourages him to make them. He will do so when he believes the judgments of his client's other advisors are in error or when there are important political considerations to be taken into account when choosing among alternatives. In either case, the communication of political information is likely to be done verbally or sometimes through a memo. In a study of housing subsidies, for example, the problem was how much to give to each family. If less was spread to more families, some less needy families would get subsidies. But spreading the money to more families might have greater political payoff. The formal report simply listed the alternatives and their consequences without any mention of political aspects. The analyst then told his client verbally about a possible trade-off between political attractiveness and economic effectiveness.

Bureaucratic communications embrace three levels of political involvement. On the first level is the analyst, who has a veneer of objectivity. He uses politics in a restricted way—for example, to set the analytical agenda with his client: "First I showed him [the client] that there was some political heat, and then, once I got his attention, I could solve the problem with arguments of equity." He generally avoids political inferences in his writing; and if he does not, it is the second-level analyst, his boss, who will read his report and delete potentially troublesome remarks. The boss will pass on the political intelligence privately, in personal memos to or conversations with his own boss. This higher boss represents the third level of political involvement. Probably an assistant secretary and a political appointee, he is usually in a situation of a client influencing another client. Part of his influence derives from his analytical information, but another part from his efforts at political persuasion. He will be concerned with conveying a policy message in such a way as to increase its acceptance by another political actor. At this level, making it political works by addition. The assistant secretary appeals to the known values and symbols of another person by adding key words and phrases.[14]

Recall the blue-collar-worker memorandum mentioned in chapter 3. In its revision, Jerome M. Rosow, assistant secretary of labor for policy, evaluation, and research, added a number of political appeals to enhance the memorandum's chances for White House

14. As Han Fei Tzu said in about 250 B.C., "On the whole, the difficult thing about persuasion is to know the mind of the person one is trying to persuade and to be able to fit one's words to it." See *Basic Writings of Mo Tzu, Hsün Tzu, and Han Fei Tzu,* trans. Burton Watson (New York and London: Columbia University Press, 1967), pp. 73–79.

attention. Since a useful tactic at the outset is to identify what one
wants to do with what the client is doing or would like to do,
Rosow added a recommendation for higher education for the children of workers, because he knew the White House was already
moving in that direction. Then it was important to have a strong
introduction indicating a large political constituency for the policy
recommendations:

The social and economic status of blue-collar workers has become a
subject of increasing concern in the last few years. Recent reports have
identified the economic insecurity and alienation which whites in this
group have felt. What such reports have failed to note is that there are
some two million minority-group males who are skilled or semi-skilled
blue-collar workers who are full-time members of the work force and who
share many of the same problems as whites in their income class. This
nonwhite group also shares the same concern as white workers for law and
order and other middle-class values. Many have moved from subem-
ployment to low-income entry-level jobs, but they now feel blocked from
further opportunity.[15]

Moreover, the timing of and need for action by the administration
had to be highlighted. Thus, the blue-collar workers' "only
spokesmen seem to be union leaders spearheading the demand for
more money wages. They are overripe for a political response to
the pressing needs they feel so keenly."[16] Finally, an appeal was
made to White House staff using Nixon's own theme of forgotten
Americans:

People in the blue-collar class are less mobile, less organized, and less
capable of using legitimate means to either protect the status quo or
secure changes in their favor. To a considerable extent, they feel like
"forgotten people"—those for whom the government and the society have
limited, if any, direct concern and little visible action.[17]

In short, the worker paid his taxes and did not get his share of
governmental programs, and among his various problems was his
"feeling of being forgotten."

When I talk about what is political in the policy analyst's
communications, I mean to caution both client and would-be
analyst to look at the hidden agenda—at what is hidden behind the
language of a policy analysis. The bureaucratic policy analyst, as a

15. U.S. Department of Labor, Assistant Secretary of Labor for Policy,
Evaluation and Research, "Memorandum for the Secretary: The Problem of the
Blue Collar Worker" (April 1970), p. 1.
16. *Ibid.*, p. 4.   17. *Ibid.*, pp. 7–8.

political actor, can use his communications in any number of ways to serve both personal and collective purposes. Like a lawyer who works for many clients, he can change arguments by highlighting different values. When he feels strongly about a policy, there is very little stopping him from communicating his convictions. As an OEO analyst put it, "Often we find that they [the client, the White House] had not thought about the problem. If you can come in with a well-reasoned argument, there is a chance they might be receptive."

In addition to encouraging acceptance of his or his client's policies, the analyst may have other political objectives in mind. One OMB analyst wants to reduce the controversy he has with the department, so he labels all his reports, regardless of completeness, as drafts, adding on the front page: "This report is not necessarily the opinion of the Office of Management and Budget." Another analyst wrote one of his reports in such a way as to ensure that his department would hold on to its appropriation. While at the Bureau of the Budget, he did a study of the JOBS (Job Opportunities in the Business Sector) program, in which the government subsidized private employers to hire the disadvantaged.[18] His analysis showed that enrollment figures were such that the appropriation should be cut. The Department of Labor resisted and showed that it needed all the money. A few months after this skirmish, the analyst left the Bureau of the Budget and joined the analytical staff of the Department of Labor. By this time, employers were making less use of the JOBS program, and the economy was also depressed. The analyst knew from his previous work that the program was in trouble because of the difficulty of recruiting hard-core unemployed, but this time he was assigned to keep the money within the family. He said, "I realized that my original projections were correct and that the need to

18. Administered by the U.S. Department of Labor (DOL) and the National Alliance of Businessmen, the JOBS program provided technical and monetary assistance for the hiring, retraining, and upgrading of the hard-core unemployed or underemployed. According to DOL's budget for fiscal year 1971, plans called for 130,500 training opportunities (plus 18,300 from the Economic Opportunity Act) to be provided through the JOBS program. In the Department of Labor itself, the JOBS program accounted for over one-third of such training opportunities at a cost (in terms of obligations) of about $340 million; see *The Budget of the United States Government, Appendix, Fiscal Year 1971* (Washington, D.C.: U.S. Government Printing Office, 1970), pp. 655–56.

transfer funds was unrelated to the conditions of the economy. Nevertheless, I used the 'softening of the economy' argument because this argument would justify the transfer of the JOBS funds to another employment-creating program rather than out of the Department of Labor altogether."

THE RISKS

Effective communications can lead to promotion or demotion, to acceptance or rejection of one's ideas, to success or failure. It can also lead to risks, to consequences that were neither intended nor anticipated. When the client finally understands what the analyst has been doing for three months, he may not like it: Imagine the analyst who hands in an elaborate study showing that the best place for a new fire station is next to the White House. Worse yet, the client may not be charitable when he learns that the analyst wants to stop one of his pet programs. Suppose that a stupid policy is proposed and the analyst tries to head it off. He writes a memo to the secretary suggesting a better policy. He keeps arguing against the policy whenever he can. Little does he know that the decision on the policy has already been made and that, while he should have been supporting it or at least keeping quiet, he has been articulately opposing it. What then? If the analyst is a political appointee, he can be fired. If he is a civil servant, he can just be ignored and given nothing to do, which is worse than being fired. Here is an example of an "uncivil servant," taken from an article that contains a number of such horror stories:

Gerard M. Brannon was until recently Director of the Office of Tax Analysis at the Treasury Department. A political appointee of the Democrats, Brannon had contracted with a private Pittsburgh research organization called CONSAD to do economic analysis of the oil depletion allowance. The report (never released) and a separate paper Brannon wrote himself, damned the allowance. Brannon lost his title, part of his function, and had his salary cut. It is standard procedure for a new Administration to replace political appointees of the opposite party with men of their own. In Brannon's case he was kept but demoted to *Associate* Director of the Tax Analysis Office, before anyone else had been found to replace him. The old job is still vacant. Brannon claims that he performs "virtually the same job" and does "substantially the same things" as he did before, but with less pay, prestige and authority. Brannon had been a career civil servant before his elevation and that is what he is again, grateful to have a job and charitably reluctant to charge the Administration with malice.[19]

Indeed there are risks to communicating.

Besides personal risks, there are risks to the organization and its programs. A congressman can always pick up a report and say to the head of the agency, "Look here, this is what your own staff says." Such reports do not even have to be critical of an agency's program to make trouble. An objective, neutrally written report that merely points in a certain direction for allocating resources can be used by other political actors to commit an agency to a certain course or change its programs. An HEW analyst who was working on the Family Assistance Plan did a study which indicated that certain health programs could be eliminated if the level of guaranteed income support was raised. In the hands of the administration, the support level was not raised but the programs were eliminated anyway.

In the pursuit of certain policy objectives, agencies have been known to modify or suppress a report. The work of both inside and outside analysts can suffer such a fate. A study of the supersonic transport (SST), performed by a contractor, showed that our balance-of-payments situation would not be significantly improved as proponents of the plane had argued. The Federal Aviation Administration took the models in the study, reran them to get different conclusions, and at the same time tried to suppress the original study.

Distortion and suppression, while understandable from the agency's and client's protective perspective, are not completely risk-free tactics. First, the analysts who did all the work for the original report become demoralized. Second, the report does not stay suppressed for long; it gets leaked, and the agency suddenly finds itself fighting in a public arena. Third, once the story is leaked the reputation of the agency suffers and its analytical credibility is seriously impaired. Finally, the agency may actually be pursuing an erroneous policy by such tactics. In retrospect, the client would have been better off if he had never asked for the study. But how was he to know that the study would not support his program?

19. David Sanford, "Uncivil Servants," *New Republic,* 16 May 1970, p. 13. For other examples, see Charles Peters and Taylor Branch, *Blowing the Whistle: Dissent in the Public Interest* (New York: Praeger Publishers, 1972).

Once advice is communicated, it has a life of its own. Neither analyst nor client has much say about how it will be used by others, because the bureaucracy is not as good at keeping secrets as some of us believe. The analyst who stamps his memo "administratively privileged" or "confidential" and believes that only his client will read and use it will be disappointed. The bureaucracy is like an old roof—it doesn't leak everywhere, but it does leak.

Consider the experience of John O. Wilson, assistant OEO director for planning, research, and evaluation, the agency's chief analyst, who wrote an internal memo in December 1970 to Frank Carlucci, the newly appointed director of OEO. In the memo he protested a number of OMB's contemplated budget cuts, suggesting alternative allocations, with such politically sensitive remarks as:

> I do not believe that you intend the budget to discredit the Agency.
> Political opposition can be expected from Mayors and Governors.
> I sincerely doubt whether the Agency could survive cuts such as these.
> If the residual OEO is to be merely a bureaucracy engaged in self-liquidation, then I would strongly urge that this not be done through a series of yearly budget reductions.
> If VISTA were terminated, the total additional request would only be $54 million, yet I do not think the Agency can politically eliminate this program. The program would have to be terminated in the context of a much broader governmental reorganization in which case both VISTA and Peace Corps could be eliminated for a total savings of $133 million.

OEO employees, fighting to keep their agency from going under, leaked the memo to the National Vista Alliance, and the alliance made it public. The Washington papers had great fun during this period, because OEO employees were routinely leaking such papers. The *Washington Post* referred to the employees' behavior as "cloak-and-dagger activities." On another occasion similar papers had been mailed, left under a tree in a park, and handed over to reporters as a wrapped Christmas present. In the case of the Wilson memo, "supersecrecy precautions taken by the Nixon administration to debate privately OEO's fate failed because an administrative assistant left a copy of the document in a xerox machine."[20] An OEO employee found the copy and put the alliance into business.

20. *Washington Post*, 18 December 1970, p. A16.

Lest we get too excited about the risks involved in communicating, we should recall that the bane of the analyst's existence is to be ignored. My conversations with many analysts reveal that they are not aware of any misuse of their work, in part because there isn't any and in part because they are not aware of any use at all. I would conjecture that there is less misuse than use—and less use, often, than there should be. How would you feel if you were the HEW analyst who reported that retraining former nurses would not help increase the supply of nurses, and the officials went ahead anyway and set up retraining centers only to learn that there were not enough nurses to retrain?

Almost everything at one time or another has been studied and soon forgotten. That is why the federal government buys so many filing cabinets—to fill them with discarded studies. One such study showed that off-the-street, untrained teachers do as well as, or slightly better than, well-trained teachers in teaching adults basic educational subjects. According to the analyst who found the study by accident, none of the resident governmental experts even recalled the study, and this included the agency that paid for it. The analyst felt that such a finding should have been followed up. (As a "well-trained teacher," I should feel relieved that it wasn't.)

THE IMPORTANCE OF TRUST

Communication is not just passing on information, it can also be used to promote trust and confidence between analyst and client. William Gorham warns us not to "become the trusted advisor, or at least delay the day that you do. If the analyst is any good, this will be hard. If it does happen, he should simply assume the new role and turn over the more detached, analytic function to someone else."[21] Of course, the analyst should not become a gutless confidant, interested solely in affection and in exchanging gossip. But without mutual trust and respect, effective communication may not be possible. If an analyst is going to help or influence his client, he may have to become a trusted advisor.[22] For both analyst and

21. William Gorham, "Getting into the Action," *Policy Sciences* 1 (summer 1970): 176.
22. The importance of an advisor's nourishing the trust and confidence of his prince (our client) has been pointed out through the centuries. More recently Halperin has done so for the field of foreign policy. He puts the "ability to gain the

client, the basis of that trust is much more important than the question of whether the analyst should become a trusted advisor. Just what are the ingredients of such trust and confidence?

Beyond the idiosyncratic chemistry that can exist between client and analyst, there are some essentials about which most analysts agree. To establish the necessary rapport, there must be proximity. A close working relationship means just that. The organizational situation should encourage the client's early involvement and continuous interest in the analysis. Such involvement can be a source of social satisfaction for both participants, but it is also an opportunity for the mutual exchange of information which will facilitate the production of analysis. As one analyst says, "Propinquity is crucial in a bureaucracy. In policy analysis as in love, it is important to be close."

Having similar values is also essential. While a political client and a technical analyst will have plenty to disagree about, they must also share some set of general values. Thus, a secretary of commerce and his analyst will have similar views about private enterprise, or, as during Johnson's administration, a secretary and his analysts will share a concern for improving services to the poor. Of course an analyst has to have the opportunity to show that his values are similar to his client's, and this is not always easy to do. One way is for the analyst to show his client that their working styles are similar. If the client believes in the intrinsic value of hard work, of starting early in the day and finishing late, the analyst should set his alarm clock so as to be able to greet the client when he comes in, and he should get used to eating late dinners. Sounds silly, but such behavior is effective in winning the confidence of a client.

Trust, moreover, is based on mutual dependence. Each participant has something to contribute to the relationship. Successful advisory situations are built on the principle of exchange. The analyst has no monopoly on expertise; the client himself knows things the analyst needs to know. Discussing the complementary relationship he had with one client, an analyst said, "He read my memos as an expert in public finance but would also analyze them

---

confidence of the President" at the top of his list of "personal characteristics" for influencing decisions. See Morton H. Halperin, *Bureaucratic Politics and Foreign Policy* (Washington, D.C.: Brookings Institution, 1974), pp. 219–22. See also Heclo and Wildavsky, *Private Government of Public Money*, pp. 14–21.

as a political appointee and member of the Republican party. He was willing to tell me the political constraints and discuss his reactions openly."

Supplementing proximity, shared values, and mutual dependence, both client and analyst can do a number of things to build a relationship of trust. Once in a while, for example, clients have to praise and credit their analysts. Faceless and anonymous advisors are quite convenient for a client, as we all know; but most advisors will not suffer that situation forever, and some visible sign of appreciation can go a long way. Openness also helps. A client has to be willing to listen, particularly to things that he does not want to hear. Openness goes beyond impatiently listening; it also means battling with the analyst, engaging what is said. Here, for instance, is an analyst's description of one of his best clients: "He would ask good questions. He would say to me, this is my choice, what do you have that is relevant to it, and then he would sit back and listen." Finally, a client must attempt to understand the technical aspects of the advice. I say "attempt" because it is not necessary for him to become a technician but only to appreciate the rationale or theoretical basis of what he is being told. Today, so much policy has a technical component, from economics to physics, that clients can hardly avoid picking up some understanding. This understanding is handy not only for promoting the client-analyst relationship but also for converting the analysis and its recommendations into policy. When clients do not attempt to understand, one hears this typical gripe from analysts: "Lawyers have too much to say in the ———— Department over ———— policy." The lawyers get blamed for the client's ignorance because they are the ones who draft the legislation.

What are analysts supposed to do to promote trust? I have already pointed out that the analyst provides information, direction, and protection; and what I have to say now has to do with the style, with the way, in which he does these things. The analyst has to be loyal. For a lasting relationship, one in which he earns credits or IOUs, he cannot expect to go around his client. If he is indifferent to a particular client, he can go look for another one. But once he has a client, he should not play games, leak studies, or try to show up his boss. He must not merely give the appearance of loyalty; he must be loyal or resign. Next, the analyst must be right.

Not all the time, of course, but at least enough of the time to maintain a "good batting average." Being right also means being accurate or, as one analyst said, making sure that "the facts are dependable and the report is in a form and contains arguments that can be defended." The surest way to destroy the confidence of a client is to present him with a report containing many minor surface errors. The client reasons, "If this analyst can't add, then why should I trust the rest of his report?"

Trust is also nourished by the analyst's attempting to be objective. This does not mean that either the analyst or the analysis can be objective in an absolute sense. Both do have their values. What it does mean is that the analyst should attempt to give as straight an answer as he can. One analyst tells us that if his client "is not prepared with straight answers, he will look foolish. Besides, unless he has straight answers, he will not be prepared to judge when it is possible to modify his position." Being objective is also a way out of the dilemma when the analyst does not know the client's position. As many analysts know, there is a great deal of pressure to keep the client happy and tell him what he wants to hear. Although a relationship of confidence can be initiated in this manner, it cannot be maintained by such supine tactics. Sooner or later the analyst will have to tell the client what he does not want to hear. The analyst provides "the information the client needs but doesn't know he needs. We are expected to look more broadly at problems and to give a more balanced, unvested viewpoint." In short, the analyst's obligation is "to keep arguing with the policymakers."

Finally, the analyst must be practical. He has to understand the place of analysis in the process of policymaking. He cannot accumulate facts with little policy purpose. The most essential elements of practicality are a sense of timing, knowing when a policy will move, and knowing when the client will need the information. As a chief analyst puts it, "Unless the analysis reaches the decision maker at the time that he is considering the decision, the analysis cannot be successful. Some analytical staffs are operated as research staffs. These simply pull together random information and ideas. They just don't realize their responsibility to make the linkage between the information and the decision maker."

A fascinating feature of a relationship of trust is that once it starts, it builds. Once the credibility of the analyst is established, the client will ask for more. In difficult technical situations, trust works because there is "a mutual willingness to struggle with the communication problem."

VICTIMIZATION

While trust is important, it is also a rare commodity. Most analysts are too distant from their clients, and most clients are not open. Besides, the political process makes it difficult. Imagine the analyst who was caught between the changeover between the Eisenhower and Kennedy administrations. For the previous director of the budget, he was writing memos that supported no change in unemployment insurance rates. For the new director, he was writing memos supporting increased unemployment insurance rates. A man of dubious ethics, he tried not to lose the confidence of either client.

When both analyst and client are interested solely in expanding their own influence, victimization is a likely result. The client can victimize his analyst by citing his work out of context, by misquoting it, and by cutting or suppressing negative evidence. He can play on the loyalty and feelings of his analyst to get him to rewrite, to fudge in slight ways so that the analysis is consistent with his preconceived preferences. He can exploit the reputation of his analyst, or he can withhold recognition so that the analyst will never have a reputation. He can also fire the analyst. The list of abuses by the client is endless, but so is the analyst's list. He can be so glib and simplistic in his presentations that the client suspends his judgment and sponsors a proposal that gets him in trouble. The analyst can withhold information so that the client will not know what he is getting into. He can assume that he knows more about the subject and what the client wants than the client does. He can embarrass his client by giving his analysis to the client's enemies.

Ironically, while propinquity can encourage trust, distance or remoteness can discourage victimization. The client can shield himself from his troublesome analysts by placing several layers of hierarchy between himself and them. Indeed, one point of such an arrangement is to make it appear that the analysts work for someone else. Remoteness can also serve the analyst. Unaware of his client's personal needs, the analyst is less likely to compromise his work. The resulting straight story can work for both of them, since the analysis will appear less captive and more objective. If the analysis is consistent with his preferences, the client can take advantage of this halo of independence. And it if it is inconsistent with them, he can easily disengage from it.

Communication is essential, but it should not take any form that potentially or actually creates victims. It is one thing for the analyst to write clearly so that the client understands; it is quite another to write with such force that the client is mislead. It is one thing for the client to ask for revisions so that he can give the study to a broader audience; it is quite another to ask the analyst to distort his work in the name of clarity. When there is trust, there need not be victims. While trust is difficult to build and maintain, it is quite simple to know when one does not have it. One analyst puts it this way: "If the secretary ignores me four times in ten, I'll quit." The payoff from communication based on trust is that the analyst does influence his client and the client benefits from that influence.

CONCLUSION

If communication is such an integral part of analytical work, as I claim it is, why have I not treated the subject in an earlier part of the book? And surely the notions of trust and confidence encompass something more than just communication; or is it that communication is something larger than establishing trust? As to the first question, if we see communication as a process and as a central means of linking the analyst to a client, then the logic of the presentation may become apparent. It was necessary to describe the analysts, what they do, the bureaucratic context in which they work, and their clients— the elements of a process of communication—before discussing communication, the cement that links them.

The second question is more troublesome. Why should I connect, almost equate, trust with communication? I do so because far too many policy analysts ignore it. These analysts perceive only one of the functions of communication: *to pass on selective information.* But there are other functions as well. Besides *promoting trust between analyst and client,* communication serves at least three other functions. One of these is *to develop political support and neutralize opposition,* which was illustrated by the use of briefings as a means of building consensus. The second is *to direct the client's preferences,* of which the tactic of writing a speech to commit a client is an appropriate example. Extending the second, we come to the third: *to control the future.* This last function was not given its fair share of attention in this chapter. Yet it is one that many analysts, intentionally and unintentionally, fulfill. The legacy of legislative bills, technical studies, and presidential commission reports does, more often than not, set a groove for our thinking about alternative policies.

In short, we have to appreciate the range of functions inherent in a process of communication. This is not to say that the analyst and client can always take them into account in a single mode of communication. A written report is suitable for passing on complex information in a selective way. Its length, however, may make it inadequate, by itself, for gathering political support. The opposite is probably the case with the briefing and the single-page memorandum.

But being sensitive to the various functions of communication is still not enough. There are hidden agendas to be teased out of each communication. With each there are risks to be assessed and unintended consequences to be dealt with. Finally, it is necessary for the participants to choose multiple modes of communication; no single mode can do the whole job.

8

Predicaments

Sometimes I think that policy analysis creates more problems than it solves. But it is only a fleeting thought, because I want policy analysis to prosper. Not able to climb out of my own skin, I still believe that knowledge and its purveyors can enhance public policy. Yet there are plenty of impediments to that enhancement. Some are problems that can be solved by energy and imagination. Some are dilemmas of policy analysis that cannot be resolved without painful choices. I would like to be able to write a concluding chapter which, with a magic wand of suggestions, would convert problem into prospect, constraint into opportunity; but, as we shall see, some predicaments of policy analysis are not likely to go away.

It is not easy to explain the conditions for success or failure of analytical advice. We have seen that there are different types of analysts, different types of clients and uses of advice, different types of analytical advice and tasks, and different organizational situations in which various ingredients interact. While there may be modal types of analytical processes yet to be identified, it seems clear that there is no single analytical process. Similarly, I suspect that there is no single decision-making or policy process except at some aggregate and abstract level which cannot do theoretical justice to the variety of policies and their politics. For the future, the difficult conceptual task will be to develop empirical models of both analytical and policy processes with theoretical linkages between them. For the moment, let me indicate some of the complexities that might be involved in such an undertaking. At the same time, I will be able to point out several central predicaments of analysis.

Consider that an analytical process is composed of a number of steps or stages. The particular sequence of these steps would probably distinguish different processes; but we will discuss only the most straightforward, simple, and somewhat artificial process which starts from a stimulus—the recognition that there is a problem—and ends with an impact on a segment of the public —the beneficiary. The steps take place within a finite period of time, so that we are not dealing with the use of analysis in future generations. Here then is a description of that process:

AN ANALYTICAL PROCESS OF PROBLEM SOLUTION

Step	Description
1. Selection: stimulus (chapter 3)	Cues such as size or public concern set analytical agenda.
2. Selection: client asks (chapter 3)	Client asks for analysis. Higher probability of use by client than if analyst suggests problem be studied.
3. Definition: congruence (chapter 4)	Client and analyst agree on definition of analytical task. Lack of congruence can result in lower probability of eventual use by client.
4. Definition: technical feasibility (chapter 4)	Task must be within state of the art; otherwise it will be abandoned or, if attempted, easily discredited.
5. Documentation: access (chapter 4)	Access to information and computational resources is required for completion of credible product.
6. Documentation: quality (chapter 4)	Product must be of sufficient quality to be capable of defense; a poor job will likely be discredited and not used.

7. Communication: organizational acceptance (chapter 7)	The client's other advisors accept the product. While organizational consensus is not required, open hostile criticism lowers probability of use.
TYPE A USE: SYMBOLIC	Client uses product to legitimate agency program or for personal advancement. For example, product can be used to show that the agency is "doing something" without really doing it. Also satisfies maintenance needs of analytical shop.
8. Communication: type of client (chapter 6)	Communication will be easier with "intellectual" rather than "executive" client. "Immediate" client more likely to use product than other types.
9. Communication: credibility (chapter 7)	Analyst is so persuasive that client believes the recommendations of the analytical product.
TYPE B USE: UNDERSTANDING	Client's understanding of problem and policy is altered by product.
10. Implementation: attendance	Analyst able to attend crucial meetings to present case or see that it is presented. Nonattendance may result in nonuse.
TYPE C USE: ALLOCATION	Analytical product is used to alter budgetary allocation as a mechanism to initiate recommended policy changes.
11. Implementation: client purview	Client is capable of initiating implementation of analytical recommendations.
12. Implementation: level	Recommendations are congruent with the level at which implementation is to be attempted. Analysis is consistent with actual behavior.
13. Implementation: cooperation	Implementation requires cooperation and political support of client's agency administrators; external political actors (for example, congressmen); external

administrators (for example, state and local government actors); and beneficiaries.

TYPE D USE: IMPACT   Policy change results in an improved, effective impact on beneficiary of policy.

Many more steps could be added to this list of thirteen. But even with this list one can see how easy it is for a policy analysis to be derailed. In a sense, each step is a necessary condition for the next one, and it should be clear that these conditions are often not met and that studies do get shunted aside. Considering the steps, what is remarkable is not that analytical products are not used but that they are used at all.

Understanding the analytical process as a series of dependent steps, however, is not enough. Some work should also be done to establish the conceptual appropriateness of each step. The description of each could easily be converted into a hypothesis and then be tested. For example, while I feel that the higher the quality of the analytical product, the higher the probability of use, it may be that quality has nothing to do with use and that bad studies are just as likely to be used by naive clients as good ones. Even by the hard test of an effective change for the beneficiary, an inadequate study could conceivably create reasonable results. One lesson is clear: much more research should be devoted to analyzing analysis. The analyst is so busy doing his job that he does not have time to understand the chemistry by which he does it. Knowledge about the analytical process is just as important as knowledge about policies if the effectiveness of public policy is to be improved.

Sprinkled throughout the thirteen steps are four different uses of analysis. The most important one—the most consequential use—is impact (D), because payoff from the analysis of public policy comes not from changing the mind of the client but from improving the lives of our nation's citizens.

The irony of the current analytical situation, however, is that beyond the efforts expended on symbolic (A) uses, the bulk of attention is devoted to changing the client's understanding (B) and seeing to it that he changes the allocation (C) of public funds. Besides evaluation efforts, which have a postmortem quality, and some minor (mostly academic) interest in who benefits, bureau-cratic policy analysts all too often heed the incentives of their en-vironment. They do symbolic studies because these will please someone. They feel satisfied when the secretary of the agency changes his mind because of an analytical study. As for success—well, there is no more tangible evidence of success than changing the budget. Moreover, the Type D use, impact, is so distant in time and space from the analyst that he seldom gets feedback on how well he has done. If the policy fails, he is not likely to be blamed. The connection between an analytical effort and future events is just too loose, and analysts have sufficient incentives to set their expectations low. What should be considered an impor-tant *preliminary* use—getting the client to agree—unfortunately becomes an end in itself.

The complexity of the public policy process, of course, encour-ages this situation. There is a limit to what we can expect from a federal policy analyst who is working with local and often idiosyn-cratic conditions. Despite some of these inherent limitations, there are some things that can be done. First, analysts should be encouraged to consider implementation concerns (particularly steps 11–13) when defining the problem and presenting their recommendations. It is not enough to determine the policy, that is, what to do; analysts should also get into the business of how to do it. I realize that our current dearth of knowledge about implemen-tation makes this rather empty advice, but at least it pushes us in an appropriate direction. Second, clients could hold their analysts responsible for what happens in the field or at least judge them by results in practice and not merely by what is on paper. Some clients would have to stay around long enough to see a policy through, and they would also have to alter the rewards and agenda so the analyst would want to extend his investigations. If they will fix their eyes on the right target, so will the analysts. Third, where possible the analysts should get feedback, negative and positive, on the quality of their estimates. More contact with field personnel and beneficiaries can be of help in this respect. If a program ends up costing three times the original estimate, the analyst should bear some of the collective guilt—not to make him more anxious than he is but to encourage him and others to refine the methods and data of analysis.

LIMITATIONS OF KNOWLEDGE

The notion of some analysts that knowledge will carry the day is absurd. Knowledge does not and cannot govern. Even if we knew everything there would still be obstacles that would ensure the failure of knowledge. America would have to be quite different from what it is for knowledge, alone, to prevail. The diversity of our society and institutions sets the conditions for conflicting values to be maintained. Once we realize that problems of public policy are not solved but adjusted by policymakers, then it should be clear that the degree of trust within our society is equally as important as its knowledge. Nor is there any way of stopping our political and economic institutions from adopting convenient ideologies for coordinating their complex affairs. This is not to say that we should not continue to improve our base of knowledge and data, but it does assert the fragility of knowledge as a primary means of governance.

Most analysts complain that their work is limited by the availability of data. They feel that they are often flying blind or making studies out of whole cloth, that is, picking numbers out of the air. For a pressing policy issue, analysts see the data problem as linked to the constraint of time, not money. When a client needs an answer in a hurry, there usually is no time in which to do research or even contract for it, and the analyst has to make do with what is available. Ironically, for less pressing issues there may be sufficient time but insufficient money. Sometimes an analyst will complain about the inadequacy of the methodology, such as the crudeness of cost-benefit methods in accounting for the variance in actual programs; but for the most part a central problem for analysts is not knowing much.

More often than not the data they have tell them what does not work, not what might work. Analysts of the housing supply, for example, understand fairly well the inadequacies of current programs. They know that technological approaches, such as Operation Breakthrough, will not work; but they are not sure what will work to overcome the splintered production-system methods created by myriad unions, builders, and local officials. Similarly, unemployed adults may not learn well in a classroom situation, but it is only an analyst's guess that their learning will improve if they get on-the-job training. The limitation is in policy analysis itself. If one of the analyst's persistent concerns is to suggest untried alternatives, the available experience is likely to be all too limited; consequently, only meager information and knowledge can be developed.

Policy analysis attempts to assess future consequences, even if it is a short-term future. If a nuclear reactor is installed, what happens to the fish downstream? If poor people are given money, will they lose the incentive to work? What are the people's preferences for services? Why are more people living in substandard housing when we thought our housing programs were effective? At any point in time, the analyst will guess, estimate, and produce answers to these questions. And at that point the answers will appear reasonable and policymakers will be pleased with their analysts. Unfortunately, the future makes a mockery of our attempts to use information to cope with uncertainty. Who would have built a multilane national highway system knowing that we would have an energy shortage and would want to keep our cars in the garage?

In the late 1960s a capable university colleague of mine was urging that public policy had to be reconsidered in the emerging context of affluence. Then in the early 1970s this same colleague began urging a further reconsideration because of an emerging scarcity of resources. One can imagine that policy analysis would be quite different depending on whether scarcity or affluence were accepted as a premise for policymaking. Different problems would be selected for attention, and different solutions would be chosen. For the policy analyst to do better, the professional knowledge builder, the university scientist, should do better at anticipating the trends and conditions that affect our society. At best, the policy analyst is a broker, a middleman between scientist and policymaker. He recognizes his dependence, as shown by the analyst who said to me, "When the issue is important we just don't have time to research it thoroughly. We in the federal government are here to put proposals together using the more thorough and thoughtful work done by contractors, universities, and institutes."

His dependence may be misguided, however, because it is based on the dubious assumption that the inhabitants of universities, for example, know more or can know more than the inhabitants of the bureaucracy. Yet there are many problems of public policy where no one knows or can know enough by the time decisions have to be made. Besides, universities are really not in the policy analysis business, since there is a fairly large gap between what scholars do and what policymakers require. Advancing a discipline results in categories, definitions, and problems that are different from those that the policymaker must address. At some point the research work done in a university will have an impact on public policy, but one is not sure when. At the university our incentives, organization, and interests pull us in directions that may be inconsistent with the demands for knowledge for policy analysis. What to do about increasing the utilization of knowledge generated in universities is a serious and complex problem. Unfortunately, all we can do is note that the problem exists and that there are serious deficiencies in our basic knowledge for public policy.

Even if contractors knew how to do what they are asked to do, their product would often be unsatisfactory for policy purposes because of the way in which the contract is administered.[1] According to a number of informed analysts, the problem and the required information are not clearly defined for the contractor by the government. Qualified staff are not always available to monitor the contract with sufficient intensity. The contractor usually has too little time in which to do the work, and he wastes much of his time in writing and selling proposals in what many people feel is a meaningless competitive system. Here is how one analyst summarizes the problem with contractors:

The federal government is in the business of problem solving. When it contracts basic research, though, it is bound to failure. Either the problem which is designed for basic research is too vague, or the federal government moves ahead independently in the problem field while the contractor is working independently. In the process of acting, the federal government is redefining the problem. The contractor, though, is proceeding under the former definition of the problem. The result, when it comes about a year later, is irrelevant and useless.

Another limitation of knowledge is that both organizations and their analysts have poor memories. They forget, ignore, or do not take advantage of what has been learned in the past. When I

---

1. For a vivid illustration of deficient research contract procedures, see Edith Green, "The Educational Entrepreneur: A Portrait," *The Public Interest* 28 (summer 1972): 11–25.

worked for a public utility, it was possible to go into the files and examine studies that had been done twenty years ago for the same service area. There was excellent feedback from the past which helped the utility to cope with a rapidly changing present and future. One suspects that within small governmental bureaus with some longevity, there are similar files. However, the central analysts working for the department secretary often do not know about them and have problems of access. They are ignorant of the files not only because of turnover but also because they are a threat to other parts of the organization. Some bureau in the organization will have the required knowledge but no incentive to share it. When the bureau does cooperate, the analyst, as ferret, can make a contribution by pointing out to the organization what it once knew.

The analysts themselves can be responsible for failing to increase their feedback and knowledge. For example, they seldom if ever analyze their own work. "They have a poor memory," charges one analyst, "because they never seem to get back to the policy and evaluate whether their original analysis was correct. Unless their projected rate of return closely compares with the rate of return on the policy put into effect on the basis of their analysis, it was poor analysis to begin with." In partial defense of analysts, I must point out that they are not encouraged to evaluate their work, and that the analyzed policies are seldom the same as the programs which are accepted and implemented, and that the program itself generally does not last long enough to generate the necessary information or was not designed to provide it in the first place.

Despite limitations in our knowledge, policy analysis is still useful. It can cope with complexity. It can help formulate problems and policies. It can avoid some disasters. We can learn from our mistakes as well as our successes in public policy. While analysts should understand the limitations of their work and be modest about their capacities, there is no reason for them to be paralyzed because of a lack of information. Policymakers cannot wait for certainty, and neither should their analysts.

The consequences of not knowing much, of having uncertainty and ambiguity surround the products of policy analysis, are that any study can be discredited and analysis becomes a resource in the kit of the various adversaries of the policy process. It is relatively easy to discredit a study, and anyone who doubts this assertion need only pick up and read an article or book review from any journal dealing with public policy—say, *Policy Analysis,*[2] *Public Policy, The Public Interest,* the *Journal of Human Resources,* or the *Harvard Educational Review.* Analysts and researchers are shot down for wrong assumptions, for too circumscribed or biased a view of the problem, for bad research design, for faulty and misleading statistics, for lack of causal connection between hypotheses and findings, for simpleminded hypotheses, and for alternatives involving conflicting objectives. Destroy one number and discredit the study. If the analyst does a study showing how a program benefits an individual by increasing his lifetime income, a critic can always come back and say that the proper measure would be the benefit to society. If all else fails, the critic can attack the analyst as a racist, sexist, intellectual, or not to be believed because of the organization that sponsored his work.

In a study that examined whether veterans' hospitals should be expanded or the services contracted out to private hospitals, analysts estimated the cost per bed of various alternatives. The Veterans Administration did not agree with these estimates and questioned the numbers. In this case analysis failed to resolve the policy problem because of the lack of data on the costs of hospitals. A disputed study, however, can still be used by the various participants. Arguments shift as political adversaries, the immediate and peripheral clients, take over from the analysts, who now must spend most of their time defending and documenting their numbers. The analyst is not given the time to improve his work but rather must show why what he did is correct. The adversaries, for their part, assert their preferences with arguments that are, more often than not, independent of the particular study. Thus, a senior official criticized income maintenance efforts on the grounds that the poor do not know how to spend money; they just need help. The process of coalition building begins; and analysts, experts, and their wares are used and abused.

Like any other political resource, such as money, office, status, or reputation, the capability to do policy analysis is not evenly distributed. The executive branch has a much greater analytical capability than Congress, and politicians soon realize this fact. The

2. My experience, as editor of *Policy Analysis,* in reviewing manuscripts and the comments of reviewers has confirmed the general point of how easy it is to discredit, especially if it is appropriate criticism, the work of someone else.

executive branch conjures up the image of 4,000 computers and many analysts, which is enough to picture Congress as deprived and suffering from analytical malnutrition. Thus, former presidential assistant Joseph A. Califano, Jr., like so many before him, urged Congress to buy computers and analysts:

As the Congress thrashes out in frustration at its separate but unequal status among the branches of government, it must realize that its houses are made of glass. Before its members throw too many stones, they might recognize that they hold in their own hands the power to vote themselves the staff and analytical capability they need, to establish a central systems analysis and program evaluation office, to reorganize their committees and thus to assume their constitutional role as the most effective and responsive representative legislature in the history of mankind.[3]

And so Congress did just that: With the Legislative Reference Service, General Accounting Office, Office of Technology Assessment, and the various analytical offices created by budgetary reforms, Congress will not want for policy analysts. Is Congress on its way to becoming another bureaucracy? Increasing staff, by itself, is not likely to make major changes in an institution. It is the analysts who are more likely to change than Congress. They will have to put up with senators who use the Senate floor as a public relations vehicle and as a point of departure to the presidency. They will have to cope with a division of labor in the House, which, as Nelson Polsby points out, is "its great strength" but which may also be inconsistent with analytical perceptions and definitions of policy problems.[4] They will come to appreciate the importance of constituencies, parties, the leadership, and caucus.[5] In short, they will be used as it suits the purposes of the men and women of Congress.

---

3. *Washington Post,* 13 July 1971.

4. For a concise and excellent discussion of the differences between the Senate and the House, see Nelson W. Polsby, "Policy Analysis and Congress," *Public Policy* 18 (fall 1969): 62–66.

5. The effect of constituency on analysis was recently illustrated in the determination of a formula for revenue sharing. Richard P. Nathan and his colleagues describe the behavior of members of the Ways and Means Committee as follows: "Each day's new version [of the formula] was computer tested the same evening so that on the following day committee members could study the impact of the various changes on the governments in their districts. This process went on until . . . a formula acceptable to a majority of the committee was devised." Richard P. Nathan et al., *Monitoring Revenue Sharing* (Washington, D.C.: Brookings Institution, 1975), p. 364.

Because Congress has analysts, we should not expect that public policy will necessarily improve. What the analytical allocation to Congress would do, perhaps, is correct the balance of resources between the branches of government, but it would not significantly change the major features of the policy process. After all, our society and its institutions, for the most part, have not changed. And even with quantum jumps in the availability of unequivocal hard intelligence and knowledge, we can expect policy in the future to be made much as it has been in the past. For now, without an all-powerful intermediary, a court if you will, to judge the equivocal data we do have and make decisions for us, the policy process will continue to be shoved along by the interaction of political actors and their preferences, with policy analysts more often having to go along for the ride than being able to drive.

POLITICAL SENSITIVITY

Far too many of the current group of policy analysts are politically naive. They do not understand the political judgments they accept, and they do not appreciate the opportunities politics offers. In some ways the advisory apparatus would be better off if analysts were completely oblivious to politics. But this is not the case, because naive analysts are all too ready to swallow conventional political wisdom. When they do, this "knowledge" of politics reduces rather than enlarges the spectrum of possibilities. The analyst focuses his client's attention on a restricted number of alternatives or perhaps on the wrong problem. Politics is expressed as what will not fly, not go, not pass—not as what will. It is a negative thing, or, as one analyst described it, a kind of "anticipatory demoralization." In short, political pessimism prevails within the community of analysts.

We should be skeptical about political feasibility judgments. As Robert Harris, an experienced analyst, puts it:

Immediate political feasibility of implementation can be a very bad criteria for choice of policy analysis projects. Major policy shifts seem unpredictable within a time frame amenable to getting good policy analysis done from scratch. . . . It is clear to me at least, that no one I have had contact with is a very good predictor of political feasibility —except for the very short run. Public employment programs have not been carefully considered by policy analysts. Yet they seem to be upon us politically. One reason for their neglect has been past assessment of "political feasibility." Because they were thought "infeasible" several years ago, they have received only casual analysis.[6]

One might conclude that analysts should make no judgments at all about political feasibility. But that would be naive, because analysts do and because there is really no effective way of stopping them. Since many analysts want themselves and their work to be used, they will predict political futures, consciously or subconsciously. The problem, then, shifts to one of improving the accuracy of such predictions. A number of simple things can be done. First, analysts can test prevailing assumptions about political considerations. Second, they can enlarge their group of political informants. Besides talking to an agency's congressional liaison people, they can make friends with lobbyists and congressional staff. Third, the analytical office can hire specialists who are more adept at mapping the political environment than the typical analyst is.

Certainly it is difficult to have a high batting average when it comes to making conjectures about politics. The political situation is highly fluid; today's constraint may become tomorrow's opportunity. Actors, the meaning of events, consequences, criteria, and information shift and change. No wonder some analysts try to ignore politics in an effort to keep their lives simple. Yet we do know that other analysts have a good sense of "what can move." As one of them put it, "the trick is to figure out what makes sense at a particular time." These analysts are able to plan, to anticipate when their client will be open to new suggestions and when political conditions will be right for pushing a policy change. I agree with the analyst who said that "it is really difficult to find people who have this sense of strategy"; but if some can do it, others can learn.

Besides getting analysts to improve and be explicit about their political judgments, we should ask that they be more sensitive to the rationale behind politics. All too often analysts set up politics as an enemy, a kind of poison to which analysis is the antidote. Here, for example, is analyst J. A. Stockfisch who, having concluded that

6. Robert Harris, "The Implementation of Policy Analysis" (Paper prepared for the New York City meeting of the American Society for Public Administration, March 23, 1972), pp. 16–17.

take it as a mixed blessing when Rivlin points out the advantages of
a new tax model:

Advances in computer technology have improved estimates of who
"wins," that is, who benefits from income transfers, and who
"loses"—who is affected by changes in tax rates and tax structures. In
particular, our understanding of who bears the burden of changes in the
federal income tax has been enhanced by the introduction of the so-called
"tax model."[11]

Some may argue that explicitness is a necessary condition for
democracy. One can imagine, however, that widespread disclosure
could reduce the maneuvering room of political actors and unglue
their attempts at coalition building. So the argument about disclosure and explicitness hinges on who will be given the knowledge.
Supposedly, the bureaucratic setting of analysis takes care of this
problem by confining dissemination to the few. Schultze believes
that restricted dissemination is possible when he says, "While it is
often strategically and tactically important for participants in the
bargaining process to conceal their objectives from their adversaries, it hardly behooves them to conceal them from
themselves."[12] But, as I demonstrate in chapter 7, analytical
products cannot be kept secret for long. The analyst's desire for
explicitness inevitably conflicts with political requirements for
obfuscation. While analysts appreciate the importance of the timing of their intelligence—it should be available when policymakers
need it—they do not fully appreciate that timely information may
not be supportive information. When a fragile consensus has been
achieved by policymakers, they may not want to hear countering
evidence.

This is not to argue that analysts should behave much differently
from the way they do now. But it might be helpful if they were to
recognize that analysis is most useful in the early formulation of
policy and in the later execution and evaluation than it is in the
stages in between.[13] Advisors, of course, operate at every stage of a
cradle-to-grave policy process—consider a congressional staff, for

---

11. *Ibid.*, p. 35.
12. Schultze, *Politics and Economics of Public Spending*, p. 66.
13. For example, see Rolla Edward Park, "The Role of Analysis in the
Formation of Cable Television Regulatory Policy," *Policy Sciences* 5 (1974): 71–81,
in which policy analysis was found useful because it provided a "common
framework" for discussion but differences were adjusted by political compromise.

example, during a legitimation stage—but analysts have a comparative advantage when they concentrate their efforts at the extremities (with a handle, so to speak, on cradle and casket).

The analyst who understands politics uses his knowledge instrumentally, mostly for enhancing acceptance of himself, or of his work, or of his client. Yet there can be unintended consequences in the exercise of such political sensitivity. For example, an analyst who wants to be liked by his client and colleagues may, without knowing it, provide advice that can damage both his client and himself. By pursuing acceptance, he may also be abandoning judgment. Working in groups, as many analysts do, he may succumb to group pressures and become and create another "victim of groupthink." According to the groupthink hypothesis," Irving Janis explains, "members of any small cohesive group tend to maintain esprit de corps by unconsciously developing a number of shared illusions and related norms that interfere with critical thinking and reality testing."[14] Certainly the analyst should become sensitive to the client's needs and perspectives. Certainly he should learn to work in the bureaucratic context. But he should not be politically sensitive at the price of ceasing to be an analyst.

Only a handful of analysts concern themselves with broader questions of the interaction between politics and analysis. In this handful, there are analysts who believe that there is little demand for rigorous analysis (for example, cost-effectiveness analysis) and that the political system will have to be restructured before analysis can be used. These analysts are quick to point out that the FBI during the 1950s spent more resources on recovering cars than on enforcing civil rights because it was good politics to do so, or that some congressman was given a program in his district as a payoff. To them, the lack of the use of analysis in policymaking is a problem of incentives, which can usually be traced to a quiescent public that accepts our political institutions as they are. As one analyst put it, "When the secretary stands up publicly and gives out that gobbledygook, why doesn't the press print that in reality, in response to a direct question, the secretary did not answer the question? Or why doesn't the Senate ask for more specifics? Instead, they and the public are satisfied with decisions based on mush."

14. Irving L. Janis, *Victims of Groupthink: A Psychological Study of Foreign-Policy Decisions and Fiascoes* (Boston: Houghton Mifflin Co., 1972), pp. 35–36.

The idea is to design incentives so that policymakers and people will "want to know" and therefore will want analysis. Right now these analysts are in the talking stage, but, who knows, perhaps they will do something. The design of structures of governance, of course, have preoccupied political philosophers for centuries. These analysts will not have an easy time of it, because they believe that it is possible to have a normative view of the role of government as a jump-off point. Yet it is not likely that there will ever be a consensus on what government should do, and this deficiency alone will continue to subject analytical means to the vagaries of political ends.

A few analysts have also started to enlarge their conception of analysis. They are becoming implementation minded. What good does it do to get a bill through Congress if everybody —administrators and the public to be served—drags his feet or actually interferes with the accomplishment of a public policy? As one aspect of this concern, these analysts want to figure out how to get off the hook of an inadequate program. Governmental programs, once started, favor some and hurt others; but in most cases people adjust their lives and expectations to them. It is not easy to terminate a program once people have adjusted to it, and in some cases it may be necessary to compensate people for their loss due to termination. So how to get rid of a bad program is an important problem which joins political and analytical issues. The handful of analysts who are concerned about this problem are demonstrating a political sensitivity that should be encouraged in other policy analysts as well.

EFFECTIVE ETHICS

To be politically sensitive does not mean to be insensitive to ethics or morality. Mendacious analysts who write contradicting opinions to different clients and distort their work to please a client should be fired and not encouraged by bureaucratic norms. Those who are dishonest, distort their work, and deliberately lie should have no place in the analytic fraternity. After their liberal education and professional training, analysts generally start off their careers with a respect for data, norms of openness, objectivity, and full disclosure and with a sense of loyalty to the client. Here is an analyst who still adheres to these standards:

Mine is an operations research background. This trains me to be neutral. When I go home at night, I am an advocate too; but while I am doing government work, it is important to be a neutral professional civil servant. The taxpayers pay my salary to serve the president which they select. The administration would do better work if it understands the objectives, alternatives, and consequences of the problems it identifies.

When working for her political client, she believes that it is her duty to collect and organize the information in such a way that "within his philosophy he can make decisions. If the information does not support his decision, I will give him the information unchanged. First, because I will not fake a study, and second because I cannot suppress research once it is completed."

The "Guidelines for the Practice of Operations Research" state similar standards of behavior:

> The client is entitled to receive timely, relevant, competent analyses from the analysts he retains. The client requires analyses that will provide him with expert quantitative illumination of the consequences of the alternative courses of action that are open to him.[15]

Moreover, the analyst should not deliberately distort his work:

> the debating practice of leaving out essential and known parts of the truth, or quoting accurately but out of context, or making allegations without support, ought to be avoided by an analyst when he is presenting himself in his professional role. Nor should he use improper methods simply because they sustain a line of argument.[16]

But the Operations Research Society, unlike the analyst quoted earlier, understands that an analyst often cannot avoid becoming an advocate, if for no other reason than "that he is recommending a course of action. He is trying to convince others to adopt the course of action that he believes is right."[17] In addition, "when he then represents his client as an expert in the adversary procedure he should be expected to act as a responsible advocate and present information in as forcible a manner as possible."[18] But how does an analyst determine whether he is a responsible or irresponsible advocate?

There is no simple answer to this question, and guidelines, standards, and norms of ethical professional behavior are not

---

15. Operations Research Society of America, "Guidelines for the Practice of Operations Research," *Operations Research* 19 (September 1971): 1143.
16. *Ibid.*, p. 1135.   17. *Ibid.*, p. 1133.   18. *Ibid.*, p. 1135.

always helpful. The roots of the problem lie in the basic incompatibility between the roles of analyst and advocate. The more the analyst pushes the client's preferences, and the more he tries to be persuasive and gain acceptance, the more he will encounter ethical choices. The more active he is politically, the more he will be in conflict with his analytical standards of behavior. He will be tempted to act like his political counterpart, his client, who, in practicing the art of the possible, is quite prepared to act expediently. Policymakers, having their own standards of behavior which make possible log rolling and bargaining, have been known to obfuscate, to lie by omission, and to get what they want by whatever tactic will work. Thus, with much realism and a little bit of cynicism, Hannah Arendt tells us that "truthfulness has never been counted among the political virtues, and lies have always been regarded as justifiable tools in political dealings."[19]

The politician-type analyst has few ethical problems, because he has, for the most part, given up being analyst.[20] It is the technician and entrepreneur who have the problems. Often the analyst is not aware that he confronts an ethical choice, because he is not openly asked to distort his work. Change a few words, put this table in the back, leave this chart out—it all sounds like reasonable supervision. When he is asked to explain his analysis, how can he help but try to justify it? The more the analyst has to support a policy, whether he believes in its objectives or not, the more he will have to struggle with himself to determine where to draw the line.

The bureaucratic analyst does not have the option of giving the money back to the client when he wants to disagree with him in public as the Guidelines suggest.[21] He works and has to live in the bureaucracy. What should he do if he knows that his client intends to misuse his work? He can keep quiet and be loyal to his client but disloyal to himself and to the public trust. He can go to the client and threaten disclosure, in which case he will be viewed as disloyal and will have no future in the agency. He can quit and look for another job in which to fight the good battle; but if the policy in contention is central to the political administration and he is a fairly

19. Hannah Arendt, "Lying in Politics: Reflections on the Pentagon Papers," *New York Review of Books,* 18 November 1971, p. 30.

20. From a normative point of view, the politician-type analyst is one whom we could live without. He should be replaced by the entrepreneur.

21. Operations Research Society of America, "Guidelines," p. 1134.

senior person, there may not be a job open to him in the bureau-cracy. The last places of retreat are the think tanks and universities.

Analysts usually do not have to leave the bureaucracy. For one thing, the competition of analysts and advice always makes it possible for the analyst to argue with the client that the latter will be shot down by others if he pursues a certain course. Second, many policy issues are trivial; they are simply not worth taking a stand on. Policy issues can also be clouded by such ambiguity and lack of knowledge that any particular direction can be questioned or supported. Finally, the analyst may be at such a low and distant position from the client that he may not even be aware of how his work is being used. Such a situation does not excuse the client, but it makes the behavior of the analyst understandable.

Effective ethics must rely on the individual analyst's integrity. Each analyst should act as if he is his client's sole source of advice or information and, as such, should assume responsibility for presenting as complete and straight a story as possible. He is the only one who can know which technical standards can be relaxed. Whatever he has learned in school, however, can soon be eroded by bureaucratic forces. While there are some professional peer group pressures to maintain quality, they do get diffused when the individual leaves his profession, so to speak, and becomes a policy analyst. There are still no effective professional organizations of policy analysts to police analytical behavior and conduct. Nor, to my knowledge, have any of the schools that educate policy analysts set forth statements of appropriate behavior. Although not usually viewed as an ethical problem, the analyst's choice of client is crucial. One would hope that those clients who want a straight story will attract people who will give it to them. Those who want something else can get it from someone other than a policy analyst. For the moment, it seems that it is up to the analyst to make the ethical choices and to make them wisely.

THE VALUE OF PERSISTENCE

When asked about political considerations in his work, one analyst replied, "I may have value system differences with my superiors, but I am a professional planner. I never delude myself into thinking that I have all the relevant facts. I try to understand the political needs of my superiors. There are no reasons why political considerations which my superior sees should not override matters of efficiency when he desires it. If I fundamentally believe that the agency is not meeting the mission that I believe it should, then I will resign." By all means do resign—but don't leave the bureaucracy. As many analysts know, the bureaucracy is not a monolith. It offers many places in which to work and usually there will be people in these places who will agree with your values and preferences. Of course, the disenchanted analyst can go to Brookings or to a university and be an outside stimulus for encouraging policy changes. But regardless of the effectiveness of such outside critics, the bureaucracy still needs a cadre of insiders who will continue to make problems visible, to remember discarded ideas, and to push these ideas at the appropriate time. Persistence does pay.

With the exception of policies generated by crisis and almost instant popular support, most policies develop slowly, incrementally, by accretion and from experience. This lethargic pace of the policy process provides many opportunities for gentle intervention over the course of time. Even the fire-fighting analyst, the creator of instant analysis, can make an impact if he stays around long enough and does not forget who he is. I am not sure whether the analyst's task is to push a big rock up the hill of bureaucracy or to prevent the rock from falling down on people's heads, but I am certain in any case that he should evaluate his efforts from the long-term perspective of a career in the public service.

Over the long term the analyst can survive many changes in his political environment and still keep an issue moving. For experienced analysts, "moving" means keeping the policy problem or idea alive. The movement doesn't even have to be in the right direction. One analyst I interviewed, for example, was helping to keep pension reform moving. He did not like its present direction but expected to change that direction in future years. Such an expectation is not a psychological defense mechanism but is based on past experience. Through the years the currency of a policy idea varies, perhaps like a sine wave, but at some point there will be enough people who respond to the idea in essentially the same way. One suspects that there is a kind of policy watershed at which academic literature, congressional testimony, the administration, and group spokesmen converge. A latent, almost discarded, idea then becomes respectable, and at that point the analyst slips it into the policy mill.

The analyst has to stay in the bureaucracy to resurrect the idea—not just to suggest it as outsiders can do, but to make sure that the rest of the bureaucracy and other policy officials pay serious attention to it. Merely staying in the bureaucracy, however, is not sufficient. The analyst must also be in a position to say something and be listened to. Let me point out two extremes to show what I mean. First, there is the yes-man who, after many years in the bureaucracy, has traded in his reputation for having something to say for personal acceptance.[22] He has tried to please his superiors too often. He is no longer a repository of the institution's memory, because he has forgotten that policy analysis is "nine-tenths a good filing system." He is truly obsolescent, because all he can do is mirror his current client's policy ideas. When a client seeks some departure from present policy, he will not ask the yes-man, who now has a reputation for having nothing to say.

The second extreme is the "hobbyhorse rider." He is quite persistent, so much so that he has developed a reputation for being a zealot. He has been so stubborn in pushing his policy idea that he has forgotten to calculate "how far he can go" with his client. His policy itself may have merit, but he is the kind of an analyst who will win the battle but lose the war. One senior analyst for the Department of Army, for example, pushed the department to procure a new rifle. Convinced that he was right and with a somewhat abrasive personality in any case, he alienated a number of senior army personnel. In a system that usually develops a consensus before going to the chief for a decision, he broke the

22. Perhaps telling a client what he wants to hear is a tactic that works, but sooner or later it can have unfavorable consequences, not only for the analyst but for society as well. As Clarence Philbrook put it, "Of course the man least demonstrably ineffectual is he who advises others to do what he knows they will do without his advice. . . . Society tends as a result to lose the benefit of that disinterested, fundamental, continuous criticism." Clarence Philbrook, " 'Realism' in Policy Espousal," *American Economic Review* 43 (December 1953): 847. On this same subject, a reviewer of my draft manuscript for this book had this to say, "I meant to note cases of successful analysts who try to predict what their clients want them to say and who suppress countervailing analytical evidence. These all tend to be 'politicians,' by your definitions. I have known several, but would rather not name them. I have also known environments in which it is an impediment to success to be unwilling to do this; but I'd rather not name those either."

rules by acting as an informer and troublemaker. The army finally did purchase some of these rifles, but the analyst and the people who worked with him were discredited.

Both the yes-man and the hobbyhorse rider have lost their reputations for objectivity and balance. Clients will be indifferent to what they have to say, no matter how correct or appropriate it is. Now the analyst who wants to maintain a reputation so that he will be listened to is in a dilemma. If he persists, says it too often and pushes too much, he will be labeled a zealot, a hobbyhorse rider. If he persists only a little and then caves in, he will be labeled a yes-man. Persistence does pay, but evidently it is the quality of the persistence that counts. Unfortunately, the quality that is desired is hard to capture in words, but I do know policy analysts who have acquired it. There is the Treasury analyst I interviewed who wanted the bonds of governmental units, such as municipalities, to be taxed and was making progress in that direction, if not for municipalities then perhaps for public hospital corporations. There is the analyst at Interior who had been trying for a number of years to get the government out of the business of paying for helium it did not need and finally saw success on the horizon when the president endorsed the policy change. Staying in the bureaucracy and learning from it can enhance the value of persistence.

LOCATION, RECRUITMENT, AND TURNOVER

Suppose one has a limited number of analysts and wants to know where to put them. Most analysts would advise locating them in the secretary's office. The basis for their advice is simple: the higher the analyst is placed in the federal government, the more likely he is to work on broader problems and the less likely he is to suboptimize. No one wants to work on some nitpicking, narrow, and perhaps misconceived problem in the bowels of the bureaucracy. Of course, the logic of this position means that all the analysts should transfer over to the White House or Congress.

Analysts working at the top, however, also have their problems. They will be disenchanted when they find that all power does not reside at the top. More significantly, they will not know much about the operating programs of the agencies. As outsiders they will have a hard time learning from the people at the bottom. If the central analyst asks people at the bottom about their problems, they say "We have no problems." If he offers to help, they say "We can solve our problems ourselves." If he applies bureaucratic force, they say "We'll work with the analytical staff if we have to." It takes years for the central analyst to develop friends at the bottom so that he can do his job. Thus, the organizational dilemma is: at the top one works on the right problems but with the wrong information, and at the bottom one works with the right information but on the wrong problems.

Only if there are a few analysts does a choice have to be made. But how can the government get more analysts? It can get analysts, but mostly inexperienced ones, from graduate schools or departments of public policy, economics, planning, and business, for example. Or it can try to convert old bureaucrats into new analysts. My own experience with trying such an on-the-job conversion is that it fails,[23] some type of formal training or education is essential. Here we run into the problem of agencies not wanting to release good people to go back to school for long periods. Resorting to two- to six-week exposure courses, usually run by the Civil Service Commission, just cannot do the job. It takes at least a year to begin to inculcate the necessary technical skills to make a policy analyst. Of course, many agencies do send their people back to school for graduate work, but we can do more. For example, we could provide adequate incentives to agencies and compensation to both schools and individuals, so that policy specialists from agencies with similar interests could go back to school together.

Students of personnel administration have often worried about the government's problem of attracting people of high caliber. What has always amazed me is that government does indeed have high-caliber people, and that they do interesting work. Unlike some analysts who believe the civil service system stultifies effective recruitment of experts, I would not abolish civil service just to

23. Once I had the responsibility of training a group of accounting and budgetary personnel to take over and run a sophisticated computational model. None of them had had any exposure to models, computers, input sheets, statistics, and the like. After a considerable period of instruction and the development of detailed step-by-step manuals, they were not able to run the model. Some of them did not try to learn because they were retiring soon. Others were afraid to admit that they did not understand, and a few deliberately tried to kill the project. Evidently years of writing justifications for budgets had eroded their number sense and whatever latent analytical skill they might have possessed.

increase the supply of "really skilled analysts," because the problem is not just one of attracting more good people but keeping them. Even before a new administration or secretary comes in, the office is paralyzed while the analysts anticipate a change and start looking for some other place to go. Perhaps they will go to a think tank, or to a university, or to a city or state. Some of the turnover is within the bureaucracy, but much of it is not.

The unfortunate aspect of this turnover is that the analyst leaves before he has had time to become a skillful bureaucrat; he doesn't stay around long enough to learn how to see something through. In this book, we have discussed some of the folkways of the bureaucrat, both good and bad; but while we can teach students analytical skills, we can only expose them to the bureaucracy. One has to live for some time in a bureaucracy to develop the skills and knowledge essential for effective policy analysis. When an analyst leaves the bureaucracy he takes his knowledge of a policy problem with him but loses much of his investment in knowledge of the bureaucratic context. Insight into the operating characteristics of a specific bureaucracy is only gathered over time. It takes time to develop friends and contacts, to know where the information is, to refine one's sense of what is possible.

Bureaucratic policy analysts who have patience, who have ideas, who are willing to push them and to learn when to push them do make a significant contribution to public policy. It is the analysts who expect immediate gratification—who think that policy is made overnight—who get frustrated and soon leave. "Bureaucracy is driving me crazy," a prospect for leaving told me. "I think I would rather work in a small organization where I can see the results of my work. I have real doubt that the people in this agency are really concerned about ridding the country of poverty—no one has a depth of gut commitment, no burning sense of helping the poor."

I do not question this analyst's commitment to the poor, but is there not another kind of commitment, a commitment to stay? Clientele groups cannot rely on a fleeing analyst. They must look to those with staying power, with *Sitzfleisch*, who will provide continuity as well as concern. Launor F. Carter, reflecting on his experience as chief scientist of the United States Air Force, found that survey studies, for example, were not being effectively used because of a lack of continuity:

the people who were responsible for conducting the survey are no longer at the Headquarters bringing their results to the attention of responsible officials. Most of the problems still exist and several other ad hoc groups have been working on the matter, but fundamentally there is no group with sufficient prestige and high-level support to integrate these studies and implement their action implications.[24]

Why is it that a study sits on a shelf and gathers dust? One answer is that there is no one around who remembers it. How can something be used if no one knows it exists? Instead of worrying about where to locate analysts—on top, in the middle, or at the bottom—or in designing organizational solutions, such as setting up a governmental corporation to do evaluation and analysis, we would get much further in using our intelligence resources if we could just keep analysts in the bureaucracy.

THE INNOVATIVE ANALYST

If the use of policy analysis is not in the interest of any of the participants involved in policymaking, then we might as well forget about the analyst as an innovator. Analysis cannot be expected to be an innovative force by itself. Somebody has to want it. That somebody can be a temporary appointed official who has just joined an agency and is after a quick record. Or it could be a client in the White House who is cut off from sources of information. Perhaps it will be possible to develop a cadre of clients within the bureaucracy who can provide some measure of stability in the demand for analysis. Certainly new situations, such as our energy problem, create new demands for analysis. And surely the disenchantment with some of our governmental programs, the increasing use of technology, and the complexity and interdependence of and between public policies should encourage some policymakers to seek out analysts for explanation if not always for direction.

So policy analysis needs a hospitable home and an appreciative client, knowledge about policy and process, and analysts who will persevere with political sensitivity and a strong sense of ethics. What is also missing from this shopping list is the analyst's motivation to be an innovator and the bureaucratic context to encourage such innovation. To be an innovator, by definition the analyst must break out of the prevailing bureaucratic consensus. Not having a boat of his own, he becomes a boat rocker.

The capability for innovation is a central ingredient of organizational adaptation. Although other intelligence systems, such as cost accounting, are also useful for adaptation to changing circumstances, policy analysis with its focus on the future and its sometimes stumbling attempts to bound uncertainty could be indispensable. But the analyst's bureaucratic desire for influence and relevance threatens to destroy his capacity for innovation. He cannot look too far ahead lest he find himself working on problems that lack client interest. Since clients have other sources of advice, the analyst working on some long-range concern can soon lose his position in a reorganization. The analyst concentrating on issues with short-range payoff remains and flourishes. As one analyst described the situation, "career bureaucrats have a well-developed view of punishments and rewards."

The analyst who tries to be innovative takes other risks as well. Innovation threatens people. When existing programs do not measure up to expectations and the analyst searches for new alternatives, he must focus on embarrassing and fundamental questions which are threatening to the defenders of present policies. Consider the manager who has the requisite legislative authority and political support for his health program. He has been in business a long time. Then along comes our intrepid analyst who asks: Why are you here? Why this program? Why are you training expensive doctors when assistants are cheaper? Regardless of the organizational level at which the analyst poses his questions, he is viewed as a threat. Of course, an experienced analyst knows when and when not to play gadfly. But all analysts, despite their skill, are threats. The higher up his client is in the organizational hierarchy, the more likely it is that the analyst will be perceived as a threat. Even if he works for a branch chief, he will be a threat to someone. And that someone will attack him and his work.

Therefore, the policy analyst who departs from the bureaucratic consensus is bound to run the risk of being attacked, discredited, ignored, or even fired. In addition, the bureaucratic situation encourages analytical work within the consensus of ongoing programs and approved policies. But despite the effect of the bureaucracy, analysts have been innovative. Improving maternal and child health care, welfare reform, creation of deep water ports, the avoidance of major federal financing of local schools, the determination of the price consequences of deregulating natural gas, and the demonstration that the costs of storing helium were greater than its value are just a few examples of their contributions to public policy.

By their work analysts demonstrate that something can be done. All too often the intractable problems of public policy encourage a can't-be-done atmosphere which is preserved by organizational mythology. By questioning cherished assumptions, by examining nonfeasible alternatives, or by simple demonstrations, analysts can show that indeed something can be done. Of course they run the risk of coming up with something so simpleminded that it will be worse than doing nothing, or of producing something so complex and open to such varied interpretations that nothing is done. All in all, however, it is better for the analyst to act as a counterweight to the bureaucracy's general tendency to wait and see.

Policy analysis should not be used as a crutch for avoidance or as a force for change for its own sake. Yet policy analyses, like experiments and demonstrations, are often used to postpone action and avoid departing from established procedures. Studying something is preferable to doing it. It costs less and makes less political trouble. When policymakers do not want to make a decision, a policy issue is likely to be studied to death. But when they do want to make what appears to be an unfortunate decision or pursue a new and untested policy, the analyst may have to say no. While there are organizational and personal incentives for him to be on the side of change, he is also trained to be a professional skeptic —to point out disadvantages and pitfalls—and as such he can and should dampen aspirations. Obviously, policy areas of great uncertainty call for stingy resource commitments, marginal changes, and a great deal of study. But that we should proceed by contingency and incrementally in some areas does not mean that we should do so in all.

Policy analysis should aim at providing information that can help make an agency politically adaptive and socially responsive. If policies are the goals, objectives, missions, and motivations that steer the agency, then analysis should evaluate and sift alternative means and ends in the elusive pursuit of policy recommendations. By living with but overcoming the firehouse environment of day-to-day advice, policy analysis can conceivably find knowledge and opportunities for coping with an uncertain future. Policy analysis should be concerned not with projecting the status quo but with tracing out the consequences of innovative ideas—stopping some of them while promoting others. All this is not to suggest that policy analysis serve as a substitute for the head of an agency doing his own thinking. Complementing the agency's decision-making process, policy analysis can be one way of preventing bureaucratic rigor mortis.

How innovative can a bureaucratic policy analyst be? He is more likely to garner praise when his recommendations are compatible with the goals of the members of the bureaucracy, not when they conflict with those goals. Can the analyst over the years resist succumbing to the rhythm and rewards of the bureaucracy? Can he be different from other bureaucrats? The answers do not depend on brave advisors continuing to have their heads cut off, but rather on recognizing that policy analysis need not stay wedded to the current situation. We may have to recognize that the basic knowledge and research about public policy has to be developed outside the bureaucracy—in the universities and private research organizations. Or it may be desirable to move the bureaucratic policy analyst closer to the posture of a scientific problem solver who, because of his expertise, will be listened to.

The training of a greater number of more skillful and capable intellects for the public service, however, would be an incomplete way of making this move. The bureaucratic context of analysis would also have to be changed. In the eventual conflict between bureaucratic authority and expertise, analysts would have to be given greater resources, such as some control over budgets and manpower ceilings, to counter the forces deriving from constituency and jurisdiction. At present their meager resources are derived from their clients, who are not always as constant in their support as they might be. But giving considerable resources to analysts may also conflict with democracy, and it is not clear that we want to be ruled by experts. Changing the bureaucracy, therefore, may mean changing the political system—no easy or necessarily desirable objective, but certainly a worthy subject of study for present and future generations.

Appendix:
Methodology

After deciding to do an exploratory study of policy analysts, I developed a list of questions that focused on the analyst and his work. I pretested this initial list with analysts in the local area, such as those who worked for the University of California administration, and then made some modifications, settling on the following questionnaire:

POLICY ANALYST QUESTIONNAIRE

The analyst
1. How do you see yourself? As a policy analyst, economist, systems analyst?
2. How do you describe your work to others?
3. How did you get into the policy analysis business?
4. What do you like about the business?

Analysis in general
5. What are some of the major problems facing the use of policy analysis in government?

Selection of problems
6. From your own experience, how did you know which problem to work on? (How did you decide on your own allocation of effort?)

7. What criteria are usually used in the selection of problems for analysis?

Problem definition

8. Who defines the problem for analysis, or how do such problems get defined?
9. Should the analyst alter the definition of the problem?
10. How do you go about setting up a problem for analysis?

Internal analysis and variables

11. What are the key steps in analysis?
12. The creation of new alternatives is an important part of analysis. Where do new alternatives come from?
13. Did you ever come up with a new alternative? What happened?
14. There is a wide variety of quantitative tools and models which could be used in analysis. How do you know which ones to use?
15. As an analyst, did you take political considerations into account? How did it affect the analysis and the outcome?
16. How do other analysts integrate these "softer," nonquantifiable variables into their studies?
17. How do you approach the problem of measuring costs and benefits?
18. As you see it, what are the chief technical problems in doing analysis?

The use of analysis

19. After you have identified alternatives, what criteria do you use in selecting and recommending a particular course of action?
20. Is there is problem in identifying suitable criteria?
21. What happens to an analysis after it is completed?
22. Do you ever follow up what happens to your analysis?
23. How do you define success in analysis?
24. Did any of your studies influence public policy?

Analysts and clients

25. Who are the clients for analysis?
26. What has your role been with respect to your clients?
27. What should the role of the analyst be with respect to his client?

28. Do you have problems in communicating the results of your work to your clients? Which ones?
29. Should an analyst "sell" the results of his study?
30. In your experience, do clients misuse studies such as form window dressing for their own preconceived notions of what ought to be done?
31. Could you describe what you consider the best examples of your work?
32. Do you have any examples of your work which I could have and which you believe are good examples of analysis?
33. Who else should I talk to about these matters?

Having decided what I wanted to find out, the next problem was to determine from whom I could find it out. At the time of my research, many analysts did not see themselves as *policy* analysts, so there was a problem of identification which made drawing a random sample almost impossible. I decided to opt for a more selective approach and made tentative lists of respected analysts with whom I had worked in the past and could contact in order to get other names. Thus, the first selection of analysts to be interviewed in 1970 consisted mainly of those whom I knew and who had reputations for doing analytical work of high quality. In 1971, when we were going to make a second pass through to round out the number of interviews, I decided to try to be somewhat more systematic. To this end I requested a list of senior civil servants from the Civil Service Commission and tried to make a random selection from it. While this list was helpful in spreading our coverage of analysts throughout the federal government in Washington, often it also proved to be misleading, as the senior civil servants bore titles that did not always jibe with what they actually did. But in these cases personnel in the wrong office usually pointed out the appropriate policy analysis office. In addition, as part of their advice about whom to interview, personnel in the Office of Management and Budget suggested a list of analysts from which a number of names were selected (see pp. 173–175). In short, the sample was strategically chosen to get at the senior, central, and highly educated policy analysts of the time.

The interviews usually lasted for over an hour, but some ran as short as a half-hour and others as long as a full morning or afternoon. In those situations in which we were trying to establish

some of the details of a case history, such as in the transportation
revenue sharing example, a number of follow-on interviews were
held. The style of the interview was generally nondirective, and
questions were often modified to fit the specific interview. The
interviewer's usual procedure was to take detailed notes and then,
immediately after the interview, to go to a quiet place and
transcribe his notes to tape. The tapes were then sent to Berkeley
for typing and checking. Through this process, 116 usable
interviews were obtained from policy analysts.

While analyzing my interviews I discovered that I still lacked
some of the information I needed on the background of the analyst,
so I followed up with a mailed questionnaire to see if I could fill in
some of the holes in the data. This effort was not entirely successful
and precluded to some extent a more quantitative analysis of the
interviews. In any event, I began to see from my reading of the
typed interviews that analysts varied considerably, both in their
views and in their reported behavior. They seemed to differ mostly
according to whether their interests fell along mainly technical and
analytical lines or whether they were concerned instead with
bureaucratic advancement and acceptance of themselves and their
ideas. Some analysts seemed to be more concerned about their
bureaucratic environment than others did. I then suggested to a
research assistant that we check out this insight by classifying the
interviews on the basis of whether the analyst concentrated on
bureaucratic skills and concerns, or on technical skills or concerns,
or on some combination of these. After going through the
interviews, the research assistant classified the analysts into each of
three categories—technicians, politicians, and entrepreneurs. I
then classified the interviews independently and checked my
classification against that of the research assistant. There were very
few cases of disagreement, and these were easily adjusted. Having
developed the classification system, I then analyzed the interviews
to see how the types differed, particularly in their motivations,
beliefs, resources, and how they did their job. Most of the results
of this analysis were reported in chapter 1 and occasionally
throughout the book.

In addition, I tried to explore some of the background variables
of the three analytical types. I came up with two tables which tell
us a little bit more about the sample of policy analysts. First, as
table 1 shows, not all Ph.D's are technicians and, as one might

APPENDIX TABLE 1: Degree and Analytical Type

| | Degree | | | | | |
| | Ph.D. | | Other | | Total | |
Analytical Type	No.	%	No.	%	No.	%
Technician	21	54	27	35	48	41
Politician	4	10	37	48	41	35
Entrepreneur	14	36	13	17	27	23
Total	39	100	77	100	116	99

suspect, very few of them are politicians. Over one-third of the Ph.D.'s, however, are entrepreneurs. Those with other degrees contribute the most to the ranks of the politicians.

Second, as table 2 shows, length of government service seems to have affected the mix of analytical types. In the case of analysts who have been in government for up to ten years, the percentages of each type are stable, but once the ten-year mark is passed there is a shift. The proportion of technicians decreases from 54 percent to 21 percent, while the percentage of politicians almost doubles and that of entrepreneurs also increases. It would be reasonable to conclude that an analyst who stays in the bureaucracy and survives for over ten years is bound to become socialized and develop some political skills. Some keep their analytical skills and become entrepreneurs, while others lose their analytical skills and join the ranks of the politicians. Another explanation is that the shift is an artifact of the particular group of analysts we chose to interview and of the establishment of PPBS throughout the federal government

APPENDIX TABLE 2: Years of Government Service and Analytical Type

| | Years of Government Service | | | | | |
| | 0 - 5 | | 6 - 10 | | 10+ | |
Analytical Type	No.	%	No.	%	No.	%
Technician	25	53	14	54	9	21
Politician	12	26	7	27	22	51
Entrepreneur	10	21	5	19	12	28
Total	47	100	26	100	43	100

in 1965. Perhaps the policy analysts who went into the public service before PPBS were more political than technical when they were recruited. In any case, whether one accepts the recruitment or socialization explanation, most analysts with over ten years of governmental experience have political skills.

Reflecting on my own experience and that of others who have investigated the use and practices of analytical techniques, I think two avenues of research should be explored. The first is a systematic testing of hypotheses about the relationships between analytical types and specific aspects of analytical problem solving (for example, problem selection, problem definition, and client-analyst interactions). The second is a case history approach—an analysis of analysis—in which a participant observer can work as part of an analytical team and thus be able to reflect on the origins and outcomes of a particular study.

Index